ARMED CANDY

Armed Candy is a real-life story of sex, drugs, crime and murder told in a real city in real time. It has only been possible to write it due to the courage of beautiful Kay, who lived it all and survived. Almost all the names have been changed – pubs, areas and people – for an important reason. This book is not about finger pointing or blame. It is about understanding and survival; the survival of one important person – Kay.

Reg McKay

ARMED CANDY

A True-life Story of Organised Crime

REG McKAY

MAINSTREAM
PUBLISHING

EDINBURGH AND LONDON

This book is dedicated with love to my big Paul –
you know who you are. Always.
Kay
March 2002

To all the working girls – walk tall.
Reg McKay
March 2002

First published in Great Britain in 2002 by
MAINSTREAM PUBLISHING COMPANY (EDINBURGH) LTD
7 Albany Street
Edinburgh EH1 3UG

ISBN 1 84018 571 6

Reprinted, 2005

A catalogue record for this book is available from the British Library

Typeset in Trixie and Van Dijck
Printed and bound in Great Britain by
Antony Rowe Ltd, Chippenham, Wiltshire

Contents

THE END

'*I loved him yet wanted him dead.*'

'*Must have been . . .*'

'*Hard? Still is, worse each day.*'

'*And he was so young.*'

'*The police thought it was just another street shooting. Another young boy wasted in some petty squabble. If they only knew who was behind it all . . .*'

'*But why was he killed?*'

'*They were scared of him. Terrified he'd take over.*'

'*Was it a one off?*'

'*No way — just the start. Disappearances, suicides, people gunned down and worse. Craziness. All unsolved, all unrelated. As if.*'

'*Do you know who killed them?*'

'*Yes, and why and who gave the orders.*'

'*Did you tell the police anything?*'

'*Not a cheep. Do that and you lose self-respect, you lose everything. Besides, they think the women are just arm candy, nooky machines.*'

'*What are they then?*'

'*Some of us are more. I am . . . I was much more.*'

'*Will you tell me who killed them?*'

'*Everything, so you can tell people. As many people as possible. I'm out of it now but it needs to be stopped.*'

'*They'll kill you when they suss you've been talking.*'

'*They don't scare me anymore.*'

'*And you. Will you tell me what you've done? All of it? Truthfully?*'

ARMED CANDY

'*Even when I don't like it or don't understand. I've needed to speak for a long time, too long.*'

'*Okay, where will we start?*'

'*At the beginning of the end I suppose . . .*'

Hot for Winter (1998) - Part One

Red-varnished, manicured fingers gently tug a taut pencil skirt up at the knee as a slim leg slowly lifts and crosses, revealing a slither of silk stocking. A small, squat woman with tightly permed hair waddles quickly over to the empty leather armchair in her shapeless floral frock, flops down, folds her podgy hands across her belly and begins to answer questions. Yes, they'd been married for twenty-three years. Yes, she preferred him as her. She was proud of how good he looked. Of course she knew all about the young men he brought home. Definitely, they were a bit rough but handsome and so virile. They'd often have tea together with the best china, biscuits and all. No, she didn't think it was wrong. She sometimes watched if they let her. Beside her, her husband adjusted his skirt again, preened and giggled. Yes, she'd been a Methodist Sunday school teacher all her adult life. Voices protested and gasped while the questioner raised her eyebrows in her trademark expression of mock shock.

Nobody in the house was watching daytime TV. They'd more to concern them than another stale portion of histrionic confessions. In the kitchen a lean-bodied woman with a handsome, life-beaten face made yet more tea, pushing short blonde hair off her face, anxiously rubbing her scalp where the roots turned mousy. Two men sat open-legged at opposite ends of a battered sofa, ignoring each other. The heavily built middle-aged one slurped lager from a can. The pasty-faced younger one teased at some tobacco, rolling a joint on the glossy cover of a car magazine. Both gave all their attention to their simple, everyday actions. A tall, good-looking young man paced in front of the window, peering out at the street as if wishing he was already there. Broad-shouldered and dark-haired, he seemed over-large for the room, locked in and too vital for its limited floor space.

The twittering of the television and clatter of spoons in mugs were the only sounds in the flat till the lager drinker spoke out in a voice ravaged by too many cheap cigarettes.

'Paul, sit at peace, man. Yer giving me the heebie-jeebies.' He was ignored. 'Come oan, Paul, yer safer waiting in here. Besides, it's bloody brass monkeys oot there.' The restless young guy turned and shrugged, grimacing and mocking in one look as he headed for the door. 'Suit yersel then. Ye always fuckin' do.' With his fist gripping the handle, Paul turned and sucked tut-tut through his teeth, shaking his head at the company who looked back po-faced, emotionless, slack-jawed.

As Paul strode down the stairs, the woman abandoned the teapot and the kitchen, picked up the phone and dialled.

'He's gone. Naw, that's whit Ah'm sayin'. He's no waiting in here for the taxi. He's oan the street. Aye, that's right. Right. Good.' She rattled the phone back in its cradle before bawling, 'Hey, you! Get the hell away frae that windae. What are ye, fucking kamikaze?' The older man with the lager jumped and slunk back, slouching down in his seat by the electric-barred fire. Snatching up the remote control, the woman zoomed the TV volume to maximum before heading back to the kitchen. Out in the close you could hear him – the cross-dressing, bisexual accounts clerk from Hull – revealing he and his frump wife would have three-in-a-bed sex sessions whenever opportunity allowed. The two men sat dully staring at the screen. The woman fretted in the kitchen, wiping imaginary crumbs from the beige Formica surfaces for the umpteenth time that day.

It was a grey winter afternoon and the streets of Glasgow were shrouded in a frosty haze, threaded through with bitter, damp cold. Paul stamped his feet on the pavement and looked about him. This was his scheme, his area. What had he to be scared of? Besides, he was Simmy, Paul Sim, and he wasn't frightened of anything or anyone. From a primary school nearby, young children were straggling homewards, wrapped stiff in scarves, gloves and thick coats. Here and there shop-bought ski hats with bobbles displayed a leaning towards the Green rather than the Orange, designer labels rather than the Green. Paul smiled as he watched the youngsters bursting with energy in spite of the weather and the mummification. It took him back to that time when he would run and run in spite of it all. They starved him, beat him, locked him up but he just kept going. Buzz-Bob. Buzz-Bob. Buzz-Bob. He wondered if these little toerags felt as he had at their age – free and forgetful of what was waiting for them back there, eventually. Drunk, vengeful, angry, violent adults – he knew them all. Most of these kids wouldn't be spared that – this was one of the worst schemes in Glasgow after all.

'Fuck it,' he thought, 'the weans are havin' a great time.' And he smiled as he turned again to watch them.

A little fat boy in a puffed-out maroon ski-suit was lumbering after a group of girls who were forced to run slowly to glean some scream-worthy excitement from the sport. Three lassies were playing Chinese ropes at the side of the road. The gangly one in the middle hiked up her short skirt, bending, stretching, twisting and leaping the multi-coloured rubber bands as cars sped past yards away. In a flourish the girls half-chanted, half-sang, their breath streaming misty grey in the cold air,

New York
London
Paris
Rome
Wherever ye go
No place like home

Before upping the tempo and ending in a flurry,

> *It's hot*
> *It's hot*
> *It's bloody, bloody hot*
> *It's hot, hot, hot, hot, hot, hot, HOT.*

The lanky girl's legs moved in a blurred fury before stamping to a finale astride the rubber ropes, hands on her hips.

'She'll have good shagging thighs when she grows up,' thought Paul, smiling to himself. It was the kind of observation he would've shared out loud with his woman and she would've punched him on the shoulder while giggling and squeezing her thighs together. Christ, he missed her. Felt lost without her.

BANG. Paul instinctively stooped and swivelled, reaching one big hand inside his jacket. His eyes scanned the street, missing nothing, till they came to rest on one scantily clad scallywag making a pistol of his fist. Paul followed the kid's aim and, sure enough, found the culprit. A skinny little kid wearing cheap canvas sandshoes, oversize denims and a manky-looking shirt was holding the latest in kidology – a pug-nosed pistol firing special caps that exploded like a bullet heading your way. BANG, the kid shot at a playmate as if to demonstrate his agreement with Paul's thoughts.

'Yer fuckin' deid,' the boy protested. 'Lie doon when yer shot or Ah'll gie ye a fucking doing.' BANG. Paul almost jumped, even when he knew the gun was a fake.

'Gun cost a fuckin' fortune,' he muttered, looking at the child's pale, unwashed face and thin clothes. 'Aye, like he paid for it.'

Grass verges split the road like a dual carriageway so he had to watch both sides in case the taxi driver was lost. Broad, tree-lined avenues edged with grass were the only promise the planners had kept in building the scheme as the model estate for the twentieth century. Paul had always liked the streets – it was the shitty houses and desperate people he hated. On the other side of the road a saloon car pulled in.

'Wanker taxi driver doesn't even know the area,' Paul cursed.

'Yo, Simmy!' A familiar face shouted out of the open driver's window. Paul grinned and swaggered across the street – walking tall, chin out, confident. As he reached the grass shoulder he leaned over to talk with his friend. Paul always looked people straight in the eye – stared them down. He didn't like what he saw. Frowning, he growled and reached inside his jacket,

BANG. BANG. BANG. BANG.

Behind him, near the school, the scruffy waif spun and pointed his cap gun in all directions. Finding no ambush he turned again and ran at the red-faced maroon Michelin man still teasing the girls, kneed him to the ground and blasted him three times in the head from point-blank range. BANG. BANG. BANG. The victim sat on the road, snotter flowing down his chin as he wailed for his mammy.

People turned to see what the noise was as the car burned rubber and sped away. They knew the motor and its driver well but would tell the police nothing – those were the rules. Only then did they notice the heap spread out on the grass. Three bullets had hit Paul. He'd hang onto life for four hours but, even as he lay on the sodden ground, Paul Sim was dying.

Street Party (1998)

Kay faced a dangerous decision. Left for home and safety. Right for trouble and danger. She never went to that scheme – not since he'd threatened to shoot her. The car engine ticked over as an impatient queue grew behind her. A hackney cab taxi blasted its horn and the driver gesticulated, mouthing 'Fucking useless women drivers – get oan wi it for Christ's sake.' Normally she'd give him the V sign and offer to give him a slap. Normally she wouldn't hesitate at a crossroads. Normally she wouldn't think of going right.

She turned to her young niece in the passenger seat and apologised, 'Sorry – I just have to.' Spinning the car round to the right, she slipped into the fast-flowing traffic and off towards certain trouble.

The teenage girl protested, 'Kay! Where are we going for fuck's sake? Ye'd better turn back, man.' Kay drove on silently ignoring her pleas. 'Ye crazy cunt. We're right in the shit now.' The teenager slid down in her seat till the top of her head was below the door level, pulling the collar of her anorak up over her ears, her mouth, her nose. With no explanation and nothing to say, Kay drove on, leaning over the steering wheel, tight-lipped and grim-faced.

Police cars blocked off the street and blue uniforms were out in force. Down the middle of the road, a stretch of grass was taped off around a long crimson stain, stark and beautiful against the frosted green backcloth. A copper blocked Kay's entry to the street with a raised hand.

'Is it Shuggie?' she shouted to him.

'Shuggie who, hen?' he asked, swaggering over to speak with her.

'Shuggie Patterson, a pal of mine – that's his house just there.'

'Naw, it's somebody else, doll. Don't you go bothering yer gorgeous little heid about nothing.'

'Thank God for that,' she replied with obvious relief.

'Is he a good friend of yours, like?' The young policeman was now leaning in the car window, his face inches from hers. She could smell last night's curry and stale lager on his breath through a thin veil of mint chewing gum his jaw constantly worked on.

'No, just a pal, you know.'

'Just good friends, eh?' he said with a wink. He was a young guy, good looking in a clear-eyed fresh-faced sort of way and full of himself. Not Kay's type at all.

'No. No like that,' she grinned. 'Just a pal.'

'Silly man. Silly man. What, is he queer?'

'Ye'd better ask his wife,' she replied, arching her eyebrows and playing along with his predictable little game.

'No my style – complications. Free an' easy, that's me. How's about yersel, doll?' Before the policeman allowed her to drive away he pestered her for her name and phone number. She obliged, writing it down in his notebook in bold capital letters. As they drove away, her niece piped up,

'That's no your phone number!'

'No, and I'm no called Freda either.' The niece pulled her face back into its customary scowl, crossed her arms and stared out of the side window at streets that bored her like everything else did. All the way home to Arden, on the city's southern border, the two women sat in silence. The niece was furious and had decided to tell her mother of Kay's recklessness as soon as she got home.

'If the wee cow wants to risk her life that's up to her,' the teenager thought. 'But no way should she've dragged me in there with her, man. No wi him still running around. No fucking way the mental cunt should've done that. My ma will treat her to a right doing.' Kay cried slow, silent tears, hoping the girl wouldn't notice.

Parking the car outside the block, Kay spotted her older sister, Amabel, leaning out of her flat window shouting and waving her arms. Before she heard the words she knew what they were. As she pushed the car door open Amabel's screams became audible.

'They've goat him. He's fuckin' deid. Stone fuckin' deid. YA BEAUTY.'

Kay beamed a smile, punched the air and howled, 'Yes. Yesss. YESSSS.' Her niece skipped round the car stooping and hugging her aunt awkwardly where she sat. By the time Kay had stepped out of the vehicle a swarm of people were on the road, the pavement, up closes, leaning over their verandas. They were embracing, kissing each other, singing and dancing. Her sister emerged laughing, shimmying, lifting her skirt, flashing her knickers. Some of the faces emerged. Serious gangsters who'd been lying low for weeks, now outside celebrating like a war had just ended and they were the victors. Kay found herself being hugged right, left and centre. Her small frame was hoisted and swung round with the ease of adults playing rough games with a toddler. Her sister grabbed her in an embrace and they were kissing and dancing down the street arm-in-arm.

'I'M FREE,' Kay hollered as a toothless old man slobbered on her cheek. 'He's gone. Out of it. FINISHED.'

The party moved inside and raged on for weeks. Throughout it all, Kay was the centre of attention. In private moments she felt stymied between joy and grief. After all they'd just killed Paul, her lover, her partner, her man, her Paul.

No Room (1968)

The stone stairs were freshly primed in terracotta red with neat, white borders. The ceramic wall tiles sparkled crystal and crisp even in the limp, jaundiced light of the yellow bulbs. This stairwell spelled class. This was a tenement as tenements were meant to be – not a slum but lasting quality, deserving respect. Not everyone accepted the responsibilities that came with living in such a place.

They heard the blare of rock music as soon as they opened the front door of their flat.

'She's at it again,' she said, looking at him with the tight-lipped grimace that reminded him more and more of her sour-faced mother. He raised his eyebrows in telegraphed sympathy just to keep the peace. Young, hardworking, thrifty and staidly wrapped in tweed outfits and gabardine coats – the couple were typical of the tenement's residents. Flower power, love-ins and personal freedom meant nothing to them. His hair would stay short and greased and hers a lacquer-heavy rock 'n' roll beehive till they collected their pensions. They would take cautious, deliberate steps through life the way their parents had. Not like their downstairs neighbour, Abigail Petrie, with her short skirts and sassy walk and joss sticks and boyfriends and music.

As they stepped down the stairs the clip-clop, clip-clop of their sensibly heeled shoes drowned slowly as the music wrapped around them in an obscene crescendo. By the storm doors she deployed what she considered her subtly disapproving glance and he thought of as her glass-shattering glower. On the ground floor with the breeze from outside, they could talk once again.

'What in crivens sake is she up to now?' she started with a question she would answer herself.

'Goodness knows, dear,' he responded in role.

'Party, party, party every night. She's a blooming disgrace, so she is.'

'Yes, dear.'

'He'll be away on his travels again, no doubt.'

'I'm sure you're right, dear.'

'She'll be up to no good when his back's turned.'

'I'm SURE you're right, dear.' As she stepped out on to the pavement he peeked over his shoulder and back up the close in the direction of the music, the memory of other nights still sweet and sticky and carefree. He smiled.

'No wonder they took her weans off her. This very afternoon as well. Not that that seems to have stopped her.'

'No, dear, I'm sure you're right.' His smile turned stale as he thought of the girls – lovely young things, tiny, cute and full of energy. Lovely. Taken away now, God knows where.

'She'll get her comeuppance one of these days, you mark my words she will.'

'I'm sure you're right, dear,' he said as they marched briskly side by side towards the bus stop and her parents' house for their regular Thursday evenings of damp, de-crusted Spam sandwiches, seven-card whist and maybe one small bottle of her old man's bitter-tasting export, if he was lucky. At the street corner he hovered just for an instant and looked up at the window with the lights shining through the loosely drawn purple curtains and wished he were trapped inside with her.

Behind the purple curtains Abigail was having a good time, unlike the rest of her day. Abigail – she hated her name – just her luck to have a spiteful mother with Victorian pretensions. The old witch had hated every second of her pregnancy and never missed an opportunity to tell her only daughter about her views on sex and relationships.

'It's disgusting. Men are disgusting. You're a one-off, Abigail, and you're disgusting,' her ma had riled through every day of her childhood. 'But your soft father adores you, Abigail.' As ever, the emphasis was on a long-winded gale fizzling into a sarcastic nasal whine.

Her father did cherish her. Even that very afternoon when they'd come to take the girls from her she'd had to give in to that gentle, kindly man.

'Just for a while, pet. Just a wee while till you get sorted out,' he'd reasoned. 'When you and Jacob get settled a bit more. You know, settled down. They'll only be up the road after all.' While her father had soft-soaped, her poker-faced mother packed the girls' clothes with abrupt, impatient movements. Her father was trying to ease the pain but her mother would use this as another opportunity to hurt Abigail. She'd felt like stamping her foot and telling her parents to take a hike but knew she'd be better off without the two girls. She was too young to be tied down and her husband, Jacob, was hardly ever there. She suspected he was trawling the gay bars but, in truth, didn't know where he was. Not that she minded, but she did resent having to take care of everything. Well, she'd a life to live, fun to have and it was hard to feel free with two young girls trailing after you. No, she'd let them go willingly but she wouldn't let on to her mother.

'Come on, pet, you'll be able to see them all the time. We'll take care of them, you know that.' Her father was still fretting.

'I know, Dad, I just feel like a failure.'

'HAAAH.' It was the first noise her mother had uttered since she'd entered the flat and loud enough to set Kay and Amabel crying. Amabel, her oldest at five years, was named in secret revenge for her own name. Kay, her two-year-old baby, she'd just named after some blousy, wet-lipped pop singer – here today, gone tomorrow and who could care less.

'We are short of space here. Could really use a bigger flat.' Abigail's voice quavered. 'It'll be a better life with you out of the city. In the big house in the village.' Abigail's parents were well-to-do, with their own business and a large home in a sheltered idyll of quaint cottages, green fields and old-world charm a few miles south-east of Glasgow. The girls' lives would surely be full of privilege and opportunity, as hers had once been.

'Okay, Dad, I'll let them go with you.' She was relenting graciously, the tears welling up in her father's eyes and the trigger for her final act of grace. At first she simpered then she howled.

'Don't give us that act, you.' Her mother had finally rediscovered the power of speech. Abigail coiled into her armchair, pushing her face deep into her folded arms, and wept louder.

'Leave her alone, for goodness sake.' Her father rose to her defence as ever. After another ten minutes of fussing, her mother was sent to the car with the girls while her father slipped back into the flat to give Abigail a cuddle and a handful of banknotes.

'Just take care, Abby, and don't worry your head. Everything's going to be okay. We'll take good care of them.'

We don't know for sure exactly what Abigail Petrie did next. She may have sat there, as her father left her, weeping and grieving for her children all night till exhaustion quietened her ache. She may have, but it's not likely. Her parents, Fred and Meg Petrie, had come for their granddaughters because of their mother's lifestyle and neglect. But Abigail wasn't slothful, quite the reverse. She took great care, investing considerable thought and energy into everything that was important to her. It was just her children had no place in her priorities – not then, not now, not ever.

From what we do know of Abigail Petrie, however, we can surmise what she did that day. It's likely that she remained still for maybe five minutes or so, until certain that her father wasn't going to come back in for some forgotten knick-knack or teddy bear or whatever it was that kids need. She probably stood by her purple curtains and peeked through the edge, checking that the car had left the street. Reassured she was on her own she'd count the money in her fist, calculating the pleasure it could bring and the number of days or weeks she would phone in sick to her work at the fancy hairdressing salon in the city centre. Abigail would've poured a drink, put a record on the stereo and sat rolling a fat joint while she made her plans for the evening.

Would it be a pub or a disco in the city centre or a little party closer to home? The essential ingredients were alcohol, drugs and sex – lots of sex. She could pass the signal to one of her men friends. Many of them lived in the street and had wives who hated her, feared her, and made life as difficult as they could for her. Abigail wouldn't look twice at most of these men if she were out on the town on the pull. She knew her strengths – tiny with a neat waist, full breasts and a backside that looked just right in anything tight or short. She had piercing eyes she made up to their full effect and an infallible come-to-bed look. Abigail played to her assets. She could pick up anyone when she put her mind to it, but that alone wasn't enough. She enjoyed a little spice with her seductions.

Maybe she invited her next-door neighbour – the young Christian woman with the puritanical, policeman, pain-in-the-ass husband – to come round for coffee, chat and unannounced extras. The husband was always griping about the noise from Abigail's house just because they were having a wee party. He'd taken to phoning the factor and carping on about Abigail forgetting her turn to wash the stairs, leaving a pram out on the landing or whatever. Lately, religious tracts had been pushed through her door as if to remind her he was still on her case.

'What that man needs is a good shag,' she would have proclaimed. 'But then that's a contradiction for a Wee Free policeman with violent tendencies.' And she'd howl with laughter, feeling all superior and spiteful as hell.

Perhaps Abigail did sit and weep for her children all night or, then again, maybe she partied with her neighbours' husbands, or seduced the young Christian woman from next door, or shared her with her girlfriends, or went out to a club and got stoned and laid. That's what Kay's mother did best – she wasn't the fretting kind.

Farewell The Hanging Tree (1978)

Kay thought about The Hanging Tree as she leaned against the wall of her grandparents' house, prising chuckies out of the cement with her fingernails, waiting for her grandfather to drive her away from the village for the last time. She was staving off boredom and impatience, counting what she wouldn't miss about the quaint hamlet. The Hanging Tree came high up the list.

Even in broad daylight, on a sunny day, with her grandfather clutching her hand, that tree sent the shivers running through her if she got too close. Alone, it took all her nerve to run under the sweeping green branches reaching down for her and only her. At night in bed, she heard the swishing of the tree calling out to her to come across the village and feel the coarse bark of its trunk while the man dangled by his neck from a bough with a slow, steady creak. The Hanging Tree terrified her but she always ended up there somehow.

It wasn't the only part of the village Kay didn't like. Worst of all were the other children. She was smaller than anyone else her age and many younger than her, but she couldn't understand why that meant no one liked her. Amabel, her older sister, hadn't helped but instead joined in. When they started shouting, 'BAW JAWS, BAW JAWS, TURD BREATH, TURD FACE' and chasing Kay through the playground, Amabel had been right there, laughing and joking with the group. When they caught Kay and tossed her in the air higher and higher till they stepped back and she landed with a crunching thud on her back on the tarmac, Amabel stood over her, grinning and pointing. Day one at school: that's how it started and how it stayed.

It was different when she played the violin. One day, when left alone and bored with the exercises, Kay started mucking about, pretending she was playing the tune in her head. Unnoticed, the teacher slipped back into the room and stood silently behind her listening till finally she asked, 'Who taught you that, Kay?' The five-year-old Kay jumped, thinking she was in serious trouble for not doing her exercises.

'No one, miss.' Kay hung her head and waited for the onslaught.

'It was beautiful.'

'Miss?'

'Almost perfect and not an easy piece. Play some more for me.' Kay looked up at the woman, trying to fathom if she was laying a booby-trap like her grandmother did all the time.

'Please, Kay.' If she refused to play she'd definitely be in the bad books. If she played she might be in trouble. She took the safer option, wedging the instrument under her chin and lifting her bow. She played by ear, not knowing where she'd picked up the melodies. It was the first thing that was really hers and hers alone.

'A rare talent,' repeated the headmaster to her grandparents. 'Gifted and only seven years old.' Her grandfather sat in his armchair and beamed. 'We should encourage the gift, foster it along.' Her grandmother perched on the edge of her chair, knees clamped together, ankles tucked in, face set in a stiff caricature of beatific respect. 'There's a special school in Edinburgh for such musical prodigies. I'd like you to think about Kay going there.' In the corner Amabel sniggered till silenced by a freezing scowl from her grandmother. Amabel struggled to pronounce prodigies so next day the other kids cat-called Kay by shouting,

'SPECIAL SCHOOL

SPECIAL SCHOOL

DAFTIES GO TO SPECIAL SCHOOL.'

Kay heard no more about the school in Edinburgh till months

later when her music teacher sighed, 'It's such a shame your grandmother doesn't want you to go to Edinburgh. Still, I suppose she wants you with her. Understandable. Now, let's try another tune.'

Her grandmother took more than music from Kay. One time, for no reason, she sat Kay down on a kitchen chair, wrapped a towel around her shoulders and cut off her shoulder-length hair with broad-bladed household scissors. The chopping hurt less than the grip the woman had on her locks, pulling and tugging the hair from her scalp.

'Sit at peace, you. They'll not ogle you now. Not having it, you hear,' Meg Petrie ranted as the thick, dark-brown tresses fell to the ground. Later, Kay looked at her podgy cheeks and ragged shorn hair in the bathroom mirror – the spitting image of an orphan beggar boy in a picture storybook she'd read.

Next day at school was a day of anticipated torment. When the final bell rang they were waiting for her at the gate as promised. She slipped over the metal railings at the side of the building and ran, anywhere, just away. When she staggered into a field on the outskirts of the village they caught her and held her by the arms.

'Kay's turned into a boy. Kay's turned into a boy,' chanted a group of girls.

'Can you play at football now, Kay?' laughed a small boy.

'Or maybe you're good at fighting, eh? Do you want to box, eh? Do you, eh?'

'No sitting down to pee now, Baw Jaws.' It was a girl's voice.

'Show us how you piss, Kay. Go oan.' It was a boy's call followed by sniggers and giggling.

'Well, she can't with you holding her hands, can she?'

'Let her free then.'

'Naw, she'll run off again.' The group circled around her.

'We'll have to give her a hand, then.' An older girl, a tall blonde all the boys fancied, stepped forward and stood in front of Kay.

'Go oan,' someone encouraged.

'Aye.'

'Dare ye.'

'Ye're chicken. Bet ye're too feart.'

'Right, but naebody tells, okay?' Blondie was pointing about her, especially at the boys.

'Right,' the group hollered and giggled. Kay froze as the blonde girl leaned forward, ceremoniously unfastening the buttons at her waist. For long seconds nothing happened. The skirt felt loose but stayed in place. Blondie giggled, reached out and yanked Kay's grey school skirt and navy-blue bloomers down to her knees.

'Haaaa, think ye're missing something there, Turd Breath.'

'How can ye pee standing up, man?'

'SHOW US. SHOW US. SHOW US . . .' the group chanted.

'Ah'll show ye.' A boy pushed forward and stood in front of Kay, who was sobbing and clawing uselessly against the hands gripping her arms. Penis shielded in his hand, the boy leaned back, pushed out his pelvis and shot his urine in a perfect, high curve to splatter over Kay's stomach and legs. Girls' voices yelped with glee. Some hid their faces and looked away, only to turn and ogle her again. Boys jumped up and down, pushing and wrestling each other. Children clasped themselves between the legs, hopping from foot to foot.

'It's the lassies' turn now,' a boy bellowed above the rumpus. 'Fair's fair.' The squawks of horror from the girls were matched by the boys' cries of excitement. 'She's next. Get her.' The boys chased after the tall blonde. All the girls scampered across the field with the boys in pursuit, abandoning Kay weeping where she stood.

As she stooped to pull up her sodden underwear and skirt, her stomach churned. Her grandmother would give her hell. Should she tell how it had happened? Would the woman believe her? Would she even listen? She hadn't bothered herself the day they'd teased her in the school playground about not living with her mother. It had never occurred to Kay before. She thought everyone lived with grandparents. When her baby sister, Agnes, was brought to their house straight from hospital, she thought that was what happened. Your mother had the baby and then it was taken off to live with her grandparents.

'Your mammy's an alky. A bevvy merchant,' the kids had scoffed.

'Lives in a Glasgow slum.'

'She's mad and locked in a loony bin.'

'Yer mammy disnae love you.'

It was the last jibe that hurt most. Kay didn't see her mother much but always knew when she'd visited because of the aroma of warm, flowery perfume wafting through the house. Surely somebody who smelled so luscious had to be a good person?

Meg Petrie ignored her granddaughter's protestations that other children had urinated on her, 'You're a filthy little besom.'

'But they . . .'

'And a liar. Just like your mother.'

'Granny, honest, it was . . .'

'You're just a little lying lassie, Kay Petrie.' It was that growling man's voice and it was the signal.

'But . . .'

'Get up those stairs and into the bath now. You stink.'

Her grandmother was speaking in that voice reserved just for her and the special words would follow – the words nobody else ever heard from her grandmother. Kay knew they were special words because her granny only ever snarled them when they were alone in the house and she was being punished in that way reserved for her. Spilling some water, being five minutes late, hesitating a second – those kinds of things could be enough. Not that she was punished for those misdemeanours all the time, just some of the time and always the same way. Sometimes Kay couldn't comprehend any reason at all.

'Granny, I wasn't being bad. I didn't mean to be bad.'

'Come here, you,' growled the old woman. Kay took off, running through the house in a whimpering panic, knowing what was going to happen.

'Run. Go on, you'll not get far.' If Kay left the house she'd unleash the woman's full fury so she skipped from room to room with her grandmother walking casually but steadily behind her. In every room she scarpered about, searching for a hiding place that didn't exist till eventually she fled up the stairs and into her bedroom. Then and only then did her grandmother lock the door behind them.

As usual, Meg Petrie had picked up the stiff, leather riding crop from the coat stand near the front door and held it in front of her. 'You can never escape from me, Kay. Never, ever in your whole life.' Grabbing the girl by the upper arm she whipped a stinging lash across her calves. Kay hopped and mewled tearlessly as she was gripped by the wrist and dragged round behind the bed to the side farthest from the door. 'Stay put,' Meg growled, stepping away to close the curtains, kicking her slippers off as she walked.

With shaking, clumsy hands, the woman slowly removed her granddaughter's clothes item by item. When finally she stooped to pull Kay's knickers down, the young girl dutifully stepped out of them and, knowing the drill, stood statue still, fidgeting arms held stiff at her sides, legs parted.

'Look away, you,' her granny snarled and Kay twisted her neck, staring at the flowers on the drawn curtains. Kneeling on the floor the woman explored the girl – running her hands down her back, lifting her arms, kneading her buttocks, tweaking her flat chest, sliding fingers into her mouth, sniffing at her hair – all the while threatening her not to look. Clasping one palm over the girl's face, the other hand worked its way up the inside of her thighs. Edging a finger into the puckered opening of her granddaughter's sex, rubbing softly, lightly, up and down. In spite of her stinging calves, her grandmother's touch felt lulling, peaceful and humiliating. This was what Kay hated most.

'Hold still now. Stiff as a board or you'll get worse,' barked the woman, rising to her feet. Kay straddled her pile of discarded clothes, her eyes burning with her fixed stare at those curtains. Too often before her little body had jerked in fearful panic and she'd caught glimpses of what her grandmother was doing, only to be belted with the riding crop – postponing not cancelling what was to come. Kay knew exactly what her grandmother was doing – she was getting ready.

'Don't watch me, cunt features,' she snapped. The special words had arrived and it was time. If Kay's eyes wavered she'd bark, 'You want to watch me. I know you want to see . . . little tease . . . sister shagger . . . selfish, wanking fanny licker.' Kay kept looking away. On her blind side was a hairy, angry beast. Ugly, vicious and stinking like sweaty feet and farmyard and toilets and something else. Stinking of granny. 'Watch-me-you-cunt. You-want-a-taste? What-you-do-with-your-sister? This-a-real-woman's . . .' Her granny's voiced jarred, her panting getting quicker and higher. The soles of Kay's feet felt the floorboards quiver with the woman's exertions, faster and faster till abruptly she stopped and grabbed the young girl.

Plumping her backside on the bed, Meg Petrie pulled her skinned rabbit of a granddaughter in close, high between her thighs. Whispered breath brushed her neck. A heavy breast squashed her arm. Razor hair and the damp heat pushed against the soft skin of the girl's waist as she was rocked to a jig-a-jig beat, rattling her teeth in her jaw. Meg Petrie stroked her granddaughter and frigged herself. Once, twice, three times, four, five . . . the grandmother's wheezy panting and a rhythmic, muted squelching – six, seven, eight, on and on. Then it happened.

'You dirty little fucking whore,' and with the words came the blows from the riding crop. WHACK. 'Just like your mother.'

WHACK. 'Filthy cunt.' WHACK. 'Asking for this, aren't you?' WHACK. 'It's all your fault.' WHACK. Shying away with the shock of the pain, Kay was whisked back over her grandmother's leg, held down by an elbow jammed against her back and a hand clasped over her buttocks, fingers pushed into her. Through tears, Kay looked down at the slither of empty tights snaking from the woman's ankle. WHACK across the feet. 'You want this.' Meg Petrie pulled her granddaughter in closer, riding herself against the girl's skinny hip. WHACK on the thighs. 'Sister shagger.' WHACK across the calves. 'Cunt teaser.' WHACK across the ankles. 'Fish breath.' WHACK. 'Tongue me . . .' WHACK. 'You asked for this.' WHACK.

It ended, as always, with no words, just a long moan shivering out of her grandmother slumped over sweating, chest heaving, breathing slower and slower. With a cough, she stood up, spilling Kay from her lap to the floor where she lay, her face pressed into the carpet, listening to the rustle of the woman dressing. By the bedroom door Meg Petrie paused and without turning around said, 'Remember, it was all your fault. It's always your fault.' Kay never forgot.

Block it out. Block it out. Block it out. But that would never be necessary again now that she was twelve years old and going to live with her mother, Abigail, in the city, in Glasgow. When her sister Amabel had suddenly moved there six months before, Kay hadn't minded. One less person in the village to haunt her was all. And when her grandfather insisted on taking Kay to visit every weekend, Glasgow seemed an exciting place. Her mother was so glamorous people turned to watch as she walked down the street. When Kay asked to move to her mother's she could see her grandfather was hurt. One day he took her for a walk and explained that in Glasgow there would be no stables and no horse, no violin, no holidays abroad, no trips to the seaside, no weekends in the mountains, the list went on and on. She thought then of telling him everything that she would be pleased to escape, but the sadness in his eyes made her stop. Instead she told him she'd miss him. He walked away by himself then and blew his nose a lot. When he joined her again his eyes were red and puffy and he said, 'Whatever you think's best, darling.'

Nobody ever mentioned Kay's father. Her mother had boyfriends and the latest one, Hans, was a huge man with shoulder-length red hair, a rusty-coloured beard and a funny, rumbling laugh. He spoke in a strange way and Amabel told her he was a South African hippy. But that puzzled Kay, who thought it was hippo not hippy, and weren't Africans black, even blacker than Mr Patel from the shop?

Hans and Abigail. Abigail and Hans. Even their names sounded different from the Mc this and Mac that in the village. Hateful names she was leaving behind, forever.

'Ready, Kay?' Her grandfather emerged from the house with the last bag of her clothes. 'All aboard that's going then.' She clambered into the car, perching on the front seat beside her grandfather at the wheel. Her grandmother stood in the doorway and gave a stiff farewell wave that Kay returned – but only for her grandfather's sake. As the big estate car rolled slowly through the narrow, country streets Kay sat quietly watching the village go by, saying a last farewell to wretchedness. It would soon be long forgotten forever. Her mother had come to save her.

'See,' she thought as they passed the school playground. 'My mother's not an alky or a loony. She's beautiful and wants me, so she does.' Farther along they passed under the thick green boughs of The Hanging Tree. This would be the last time she saw it and for the first time she didn't feel scared. She was going to live with Abigail, her mother, in Glasgow. The Hanging Tree couldn't reach her there. Could it?

The 660 Club (1981)

Kay stared into the stream of yellow beams, harsh at the centre, shattering into crystal snowflakes against the dark edges of the night, and resisted the urge to pee. Maybe it was the vodka or maybe it was the cold or maybe it was the misery wrenching her insides. She stuck her thumb out again as another car whizzed past and away down the motorway. A long-distance bus roared by, its brightly lit rear declaring, 'HEATED SEATS, TOILETS, BAR, MUSIC'.

The list of luxuries mocked her loneliness. She stood with stooped shoulders staring at the road, lost in fears, sick with dread, knowing she didn't deserve to live.

'Where you headed, darlin'?' She looked up to see a smiling face craning down at her from the cab of a lorry.

'England.'

'England? Sure you're gonna have a problem hitchin' on the Edinburgh road, so you are.'

Kay shrugged and replied, 'Anywhere.'

'Now there's my destination.'

Her short legs struggled to reach the first metal step she could barely see in the pitch dark. The driver edged over on to the passenger seat, leaning down, offering her his hand.

'Allez oops. Sure you're as light as a feather.' For a minute they sat there squeezed together on the bench seat. 'God, you're all twitchy, so you are.' Back in the driving seat, the man fed the huge circle of a steering wheel through his hands while looking somewhere out to the side of the wagon. As he worked the lorry into the flow of the traffic he yapped on,

'Been standin' there long? Yer frozen tae the bone by the looks of it.'

'A while,' replied Kay, who had no idea how long she'd been at the roadside.

'Now, a while is my kinda clock, so it is. I'll be there in a while. It's a wee while past midnight. *I'll while away the hours wi yese, my Mageee* . . .' Kay stared at the fields hurtling through the tunnel of the headlights back into black and gone forever.

'Where we going?' she asked.

'Edinburgh, if yese survive the trek. Some grub in the back there if yese want.' The driver gibbered incessantly in a torrent of ghost words floating around the young girl in an accent she couldn't place. She sat hypnotised by the road and the memories of the night, of what she'd done. 'Had a spot of bother, ma wee pet?' His sudden question slugged at her reveries.

'Aye.'

'Ah'm a great believer in the healin' power o talk me. Never stop blethering masel an never a day sick in my life.' He waited a moment and then, 'Ye need tae tell somebody, eh? Might as well be a daftie like me.' She looked across at him and he smiled the way her grandfather's face always lit up. A smile you could trust.

'I'd like to kill her.'

'Woah, slow down, young un. Start at the beginning. Ye'll find it's the best place, sure.' He turned his attention away from the windscreen and looked at her. 'Yer mammy, right?'

'Right, my mammy.'

'Is she no nice?' The question jolted Kay back to when she'd gone to live with Abigail three years before in times of hope and grace.

'She's beautiful. Long auburn hair parted in the centre and these green eyes that pierce right through you. And she wears dead good gear – smart, classy. She'd give you anything. Everybody likes her.' That's how she was that first week when Kay was twelve and gone to live with her. They'd walk down the street together and Kay was proud just to be there. In a shop, she'd watch Abigail at the counter, all chatty and confident, and want to stop people and tell them that was her mother.

'She sounds gorgeous, yer mammy.'

'Gorgeous, aye, everybody thinks so.' Perched high above the road, the heat of the cab and the driver's easy, intimate manner seemed unreal, cut off from life. Tight-lipped Kay, who never spoke about herself or her family, started talking and talking about the last three years of her life.

Kay had been living with her mother for a few weeks when one night she roused as she was carried through the flat in her mother's arms.

'You'll have to sleep in the wee room tonight, precious. Your mum's got friends staying over,' Abigail whispered in her ear. It was no more than a big cupboard really, and her bed was the hard floor with an itchy, grey army blanket over her. But Kay didn't mind – anything for Abigail, for her mammy. Waking the next morning, she ran through the flat heading towards her mother and Hans' room. The lounge door creaked open and she spun round, smiling and open, expecting a familiar face, when an unknown woman with wild snake hair padded into the hall with not a stitch of clothes on. The sight of her drooping breasts and vast mound of pubic hair – all rusty-brown and greasy – terrified Kay. From behind the naked woman a man's voice croaked, 'Get us a drink, hen. Ma throat thinks it's cut.'

Kay fled back to the cupboard, squeezing in beside the still-sleeping Amabel. Over her sister's wheezy breathing she strained to catch the noises from the flat, trying hard not to imagine the man with blood pouring from his gaping wound. From somewhere came a noise of people fighting. Two people pushing against each other. A man and a woman but it couldn't be Hans and her mother. They never fought, not like her gran and granddad. When her granny had thrashed her, leaving welts across her calves, her grandfather would fuss, telling her she should never hit children. Her gran sneered at him and if he kept complaining she fetched the riding crop and lashed him across the arms and back till he gave way. Kay lay on the floor praying there wasn't a riding crop in the flat.

'Sounds like a right trendy, yer ma,' the driver butted in. 'No like my dear mammy. No siree, she's all black skirts, rosary beads and the church. A good oul soul but a bit holy, ye know. Like she believes in all that mumbo jumbo.' Kay had heard that phrase before.

'MUUMBOO JUMBBOOOO.' That's what her mother had said to that young woman, a neighbour from that other house when Kay had been too young to remember. A good-looking woman, tall, with jet-black hair and a wide smile that showed off her teeth. A trendy dresser, although Amabel trashed her short skirt.

'Fuckin' thunder thighs. Ye'd think she'd cover herself up,' her sister said when they'd been sent to fetch drinks from the kitchen.

'I think she's a nice lady,' Kay replied, thinking of the sweets she'd brought.

'Thank you, miss,' Kay had said, remembering her manners.

'Och, away with your "miss". I'm your auntie, wee doll,' she chortled, stroking Kay's cheek. 'And you're a wee darling, aren't you. Just like your mum.'

'Paws off, you. She's not legal,' her mother had laughed in that throaty way she did sometimes when she was excited.

By the time she and Amabel had struggled through with the bottles of vodka and glasses, their mother was sitting at the shiny dining table in the living-room shuffling a pack of cards.

'We going to play snap, Mum?' Kay asked, naming the only card game she knew.

'No, petal, this isn't a game. Just sit over there and be quiet now,' her mother replied, still shuffling.

'I bumped into him the other week,' said her new-found auntie.

'Him?'

'I almost choked. There's me and a new girlfriend coming out of that disco in Partick . . .'

'Thursday night then, was it?' Abigail interrupted with a crooked smile, opening her eyes wide.

'Of course, darling. Girls only night,' and her pretend auntie's eyes narrowed to slits. 'Anyways, it's one in the morning and we'd had a few drinks and there's these two polis standing right at the door. I almost had a fit. There he's there with that same wee wizened face and three stripes on his tunic.'

'Give them out for stupidity now, do they?'

'Sheesh. So, I've had a few and start to speak to him.'

'You must've been legless.'

'I'm asking him about this and that and his mate starts to chat up my pal. She's a right wee cracker.'

'They have their perceptiveness surgically removed so they can fit those stupid hats on.'

'With a straight face I'm asking what he's doing now and he's answering, all long-winded and pompous as ever, and no noticing behind my back I'm goosing my wee pal's bum. Tell you, he did me a favour. It wasn't the cocoa she was after as soon as we stepped through my front door.'

'Is he still involved with that church?'

'What you think?'

'MUMBOOO JUUMBBOOO,' her mother boomed then started dealing the strange picture cards in a pattern. The girls watched and fidgeted, feeling left out until suddenly that growling granny voice was in the room. Abigail's eyes rolled and her head rocked from side to side. She snarled and spat out words which were meaningless to Kay but upsetting to her new auntie, fat tears rolling down her cheeks so slowly you could count them.

'Abby, please. Who is it? Who's there?' Kay watched, wondering which tear would reach her auntie's chin first. 'Please tell me, is she okay?' The questions went unanswered as Abigail slowly slumped forward, her face landing on the table with a dull clump. 'Abby! Abby, are you okay? Oh dear God fetch some water. Hurry.' Kay dashed to the kitchen, pulled over a chair to the sink and filled a cup from the cold tap. When she returned with it she noticed Amabel looking fed up and bored instead of frightened like her.

A few minutes later her mother slowly lifted her head and groaned, 'What happened?' As her auntie recounted the events, all the time kissing Abigail's cheek and feeding her sips of water, Amabel stormed out of the room and as she disappeared through the door Kay heard her mutter, oh so quietly, 'Mumbo jumbo.'

Abigail had recovered enough to smoke a cigarette and drink her vodka but she wanted more, 'Listen, girls, we need a little time to talk about some things. Do you fancy going for some chips and maybe stay out for an hour or so?'

'Chips?' Amabel asked, insulted.

'And Coke,' Kay's mother bartered.

'And a wee bit extra?'

'I'll give you a fiver.'

'Done.'

'If you promise to look after your little sister.'

'Aw, Ma . . .'

'Seven quid.'

'A deal.' Amabel almost held out her hand to shake on it but thought better.

Kay enjoyed the chips and the company of the older teenagers hanging around in the light from the café's broad windows. Boys kept coming over to Amabel, whispering in her ear and she'd shake her head, pointing in Kay's direction.

'Will Mum be all right, Amabel?' Kay asked.

'She'll be very all right,' replied her sister, whispering into the latest boy's lug, setting the two hooting and laughing.

'The dirty bitch,' the youth offered. 'What a waste.'

The cold night air was having an impact on Kay. 'Amabel, need to go,' she whispered.

'Up a close then.'

'No way.'

'Well, it's that or home.' Kay nodded her head, tugging at Amabel's sleeve.

'Fine, but don't blame me, right?'

The flat was silent with no sign of Kay's mother or her auntie. Rushing to the toilet, Kay jumped up on the seat, glad to be home. As her urine tinkled on to the porcelain she worried about her mother. Maybe she'd fainted again. Forgetting to pull the plug, she dragged up her drawers while walking quickly to the door of the bedroom where her mother slept with Hans, though that night, as with most nights these days, he was staying with friends. Carefully she turned the door handle, too tense to breathe, trying hard not to make a noise. As the door inched open she hesitated, nibbling her lip and slowly edging her head into the room. Her mother and her auntie were naked and wrestling and it looked like her mother was winning. She was on top, straddling the other woman's neck, jerking up and down demanding a submission, slamming her body down on the bigger woman, rolling her over into a kind of half nelson. They were grunting and cursing and biting and pulling hair. Surely her auntie had to give in.

As Kay watched, her mother slid down on the bed sighing, 'Oooh, you're getting better.'

'Lots of practice,' was the giggled reply and the two kissed and cuddled, making up, the bout suddenly over. Relieved but unnerved, Kay tiptoed back to her bedroom, worried that she had caused the fall-out, like her grandmother always told her that everything bad was her fault.

'See enough?' asked Amabel as Kay got into her pyjamas. 'Now that's MUMBOO JUUMBBOOO.'

'Wid yese want a smoke?' The driver's voice called at her from the road whizzing towards her, line after line.

'Wha . . . what?'

'A smoke, love, or is it an athlete I've got in my wagon?' His hand was stretched towards her, a packet of Marlboro open, the cork-coloured tips splayed in a neat triangle.

'Thanks, I'm gasping.'

'Gasping now, ye'll be a heavy smoker these long years. Next ye'll be telling me yer old enough to vote.' She looked at him – pleasant, cheeky grin, boyish but old as far as she was concerned. 'Yer all right, darlin, I'm just taking the mick,' and he chuckled, though she didn't get the joke. She took a cigarette and with the same hand holding the packet he twisted his fingers and flicked a flame from an old-fashioned Zippo lighter. 'Ye learn to do all sorts of things one-handed in this business.' There was that smile again and a wink. Kay smiled back as best she could and kept on telling her tale.

'Do you have a smoke?' That's what her mother had told her to say to the young guy with the scary haircut and the sports bag. 'He'll be there near the old bus terminal. Small, green, wooden building on an island in the middle of the road. You can't miss it, love. Don't worry – he's a nice man.' Kay had been living with her mother for only a few weeks and would do anything for her. You'd never catch that old witch of a grandmother allowing her out after dark, but her mother was actually asking her to go. She felt all grown up though she knew she was only twelve and so tiny Amabel's latest name for her was 'Dwarf Features'.

Outside on the tenement-bordered pavement she immediately realised it was a different city by night. The shops she'd been in during daylight were closed, their windows shuttered, bolted, eyeless. Under the railway bridge the shallow curved arches became endless black tunnels harbouring who knew what. Two men stood in the shadows talking loudly, smoking and passing a bottle backwards and forwards.

'Oy, hen! Whit wid ye gie us for a swig o electric soup? A swally for a swally, eh?'

'Leave the wean alane, Shug.'

'If they're auld enough tae bleed . . .' Kay skipped away, faster than walking and not so panic-inducing as running – how she used to escape from The Hanging Tree. Doors banged open shooting a wave of roaring voices and a waft of smoky bitterness into the night air. Kay clung to the wall as a giant waddled out, half carrying, half dragging two men, struggling and flapping, by their throats clenched in his beefy arms. Kay pitied them as she had the trout struggling on a line when she'd been fishing with her grandfather on the lochs up in Perthshire.

'Cut it or Ah'll do yese,' the fat man thundered. 'Yese are barred. Got it? Barred – *sine die*. That's life tae you thick cunts and no parole.' The men, faces all puffy and swollen, said nothing and Kay worried they couldn't breathe. One of them kicked out, swiping through clear air. 'Fuck it. Ah telt yese.' The big man effortlessly opened his arms, swinging the two men apart before squelching them together with a dull thump. Dropping them on the ground he stamped on one's head, kicked the other in the stomach, yelled 'Yer barred' and turned back through the pub doors.

Kay edged along, her back scraping against the sandstone wall, eyes fixed on the two men crumpled on the ground. One lay still on his back, his face a mess of black-coloured wetness bubbling from his mouth and nose. The other rubbed his chest, groaning quietly, trying to make it to his feet. When his second effort failed he improvised, lying on his side kicking and punching at the unconscious bleeder where he lay.

'It's aw your fault,' he screamed. 'Ah fuckin' telt yese no tae push yer luck. Brother! Nae fuckin' brother o mine . . .' Kay turned and ran.

Just as her mother had predicted, the old bus terminal was deserted save for the young man. An angular, lanky guy dressed in a denim jacket and baggy trousers, his haircut wasn't scary, just a punkish Mohican affair.

'Vamoose, kid. Go oan, get the fuck oot o here,' he hissed without looking at her.

'Do you have a smoke, please?' she asked him, tugging at his sleeve.

'Christ, are they sending the teeny team now?' retorted the man, no older than sixteen himself.

'Do you have a smoke, please?' she repeated.

'Yer too young tae be smoking, hen. Away hame tae yer mammy.' She couldn't go home empty-handed.

'My mother told me to ask if you had a smoke, please.'

'Yer mammy should know fuckin' better then.' The young man was fidgeting and staring at something in the distance.

'It's not for me but for my mother.'

'Where the fuck did ye learn tae speak that way, man? Yese sound English or sumthin'.'

'Please, she's given me something for you.'

'Exactly who is yer mammy but?' How should she answer this? Who was her mother but her very own mother. 'Her name, doll. What's yer mammy's name?'

'Mrs Abigail Petrie.'

'Whiit?'

'Mrs Abigail P . . .'

'Naw, naw heard yese the first time. Does she have anither name cos that's pure gobbledegook shite tae me, like?'

'Abby. Her friends call her Abby.'

'Wee Abby? She's a stoater. Shame yese dinna take aifter yer ma.' Her granny, Amabel and the kids in the village had told her again and again she wasn't good-looking. She didn't need to hear it from this stranger with a weird hair-do and a face full of acne.

'Do you have a smoke, please?'

'Aye, no bad for an auld yin and a right goer. Where dae ye stay?' Kay looked puzzled. 'Her hoose? Her address, doll?'

'Flat 3/1, house 660 Ca . . .' Kay sing-songed.

'The 660 Club,' the dealer butted in. 'Aye, that's Abby's place right enough. So, whit have ye got for me?'

'My moth . . . Abby says just the usual,' and she handed over the thin fold of banknotes she'd clenched in her fist since leaving home.

'Fur fuck's sakes, man.' Without touching the money, the young man stormed away into the shadows of the redundant bus shelter with Kay trailing nervously. 'Lesson numero uno, kid. Nae transactions out in the open, get it? Try that oan me and I'll chib you right on the spot – wean or no wean.'

The dealer quickly counted the money and from his bag produced a small foil-wrapped package which he slipped into Kay's pocket. 'Lose the goods – nae refunds. Get stopped by the polis and ye swally it. Yese have never met me, right? Now get.' Kay stared at him, feeling the swell of the wrap in her jacket pocket wondering how she could swallow such a lump. 'Beat it, kid. Get the fuck oot o here,' he whispered from the shadows. She stood and looked back down the street at the ghostly lights of rolling buses and the gauntlet of people shouting and moving in some night-time ritual. It was the same road that football supporters would cheerily march down off to see Scotland play at Hampden Stadium. But at night it terrified Kay. 'Go oan, kid, doon the far side o the road. Black as the Pope's arse but ye'll no get bothered ower there.' Slowly she set off to do as he suggested when he called, 'See yese next time, eh?'

'Yeah, see you next time,' she replied, grateful for the slither of friendliness.

The regular treks for her mother's dope fostered fleeting warmth between the tiny under-age girl and the streetwise drug dealer. They'd stand around and blether about this and that and nothing. He called her his 'Wee China Doll' and told her to call him 'The Man'.

'No yer man like as in man and wife, right? But THE Man as in The Man in the Can. Goat it?' Kay didn't get it but nodded all the same. She looked forward to that time of the week when her mother asked her to run the errand and would scamper and dodge through the drunks warily, though with increasing confidence. But that first night setting off down the dark side of the street, gripping her wrap of dope in her mitt, she puzzled over what the young dealer meant by calling her home the 660 Club.

'If ye was twelve then that makes you what now?' The lorry driver had unscrewed a bottle of lemonade and stretched it across to Kay.

'Fifteen,' she croaked before taking a slug of lukewarm, sugary relief.

'Sure it's not twelve y'are?'

'No, fifteen.'

'In yer dreams,' he muttered as he pulled the lorry over, killing the engine. He explained that he had a drop nearby the following morning and they'd spend the night in the cab. 'You can take the bunk and I'll kip in here so don't go worryin' yer little box.'

'Where are we?' The lukewarm fizzy drink was making her feel sick.

'See those big gates? That's Edinburgh Zoo – the biggest in Scotland, so it is.'

Near the gates was the red frame of a telephone kiosk and it made her think of home. Was she all right? Was she dead? Maybe Kay should phone? Kay needed to know she was alive but dreaded learning she was dead. Too much too soon, the phone call would have to wait.

'Ye'll find it's right comfy,' the driver said. 'There's a curtain ye can pull so's you can take yer gear off if ye like.' Fully clothed, Kay snuggled under a greasy-smelling nylon quilt and dipped into a dazed slumber. She woke with the weight of his body leaning on her and the bristles of his chin rasping against her neck. His tobacco-scented words were empty mouth music as he licked her chops, edging a hand under her top. Kay knew what he was doing, she was fifteen after all and not a child. But she'd never done this before. The other kids thought of her as a stuck-up prude but she didn't care. She'd been saving herself but that all seemed hopeless now. Twenty-four hours earlier she would have screamed for help and fled, but too much had happened. Now there would be no husband, no house, no family, no future. She lay motionless, neither helping nor resisting, as he worked on her. Creeping fingers kept Kay suspended on the edge of sleep where her memories were more vivid than events in the cabin. As his hand squeezed into her pants, folding over her mound, she felt nothing and kept on telling her story.

'Why is our house called the 660 Club?' she'd asked Amabel.

'Why de ye think, ye daft cow?' was her sister's typically unhelpful answer. Since leaving the village for the city Amabel had abandoned the polite accent of her family for in-your-face street patter. More than that she'd become brazen and cynical. Every morning she'd put on full make-up and get her mother or Kay to stitch her into the long, fitted skirt of the day, wearing it so tight you could see her buttocks move cheek by cheek as she walked in her short-stepped, wiggly way. Blouses were always baggy and unbuttoned far enough to show a stretch of her substantial cleavage. Whenever the weather allowed she'd go out without a jacket or coat, just a dab of strong, flowery perfume.

'Amabel Petrie – the school bike,' Kay overheard a young boy talking to his friend. 'Ye were wi her last night! Whit, were ye third or fourth in the queue?'

But the 660 Club was a puzzle, so Kay persisted.

'It's a shagging club, ye naive wee bitch,' Amabel eventually condescended to explain. 'Everybody knows if they bring a bottle or a bit of puff up here they'll get laid good style.' Kay wished she'd never been told. Overnight she started watching her mother, her mind open to prospects she'd been a stranger to only months before. The secret visits by the men who lived nearby whose wives didn't speak to Abigail. Locking herself in the bedroom with some strange female she'd brought back from the pub. The nights Hans slept in the hall while a stranger took his place in his bed. Coming home from school and the fun and games already in full swing.

It wasn't just the parties and the sex that made Kay see her mother differently but also how she ruined things with Hans. The gentle man wanted them to quieten down their lifestyle with a little less drink and a lot less swinging. Her mother didn't agree and would shout and bawl, slapping out at him, smashing up his things. Abigail wanted Hans to stay and life to continue as it was but he wouldn't agree. Then came her solemn announcement that she was dying of cancer, setting her daughters wailing and the big man repentant, promising her anything. Months later, when Hans finally packed up and left, the girls discovered Abigail was fit, well and cancer-free, always had been. That's when things got worse.

By the age of fifteen Amabel hated their mother yet copied her at the same time. Kay woke up one night to her sister calling out from the living-room. She thought someone must be hurting her and nervously crept to the rescue. Through the angle of the open living-room door, Kay saw her mother with a number of men and women laughing, arms clasped around each other, happy, partying. Staring in the direction of the sofa they shouted out encouragement, 'Ride her, cowboy.'

'Ma money's on the young thing.'

'Go oan yersel, Amabel.'

'That's greedy, hen.'

Her big sister continued to moan. Naked, Amabel knelt on the couch as a half-dressed fat man took her from behind. Kay crept back to her room with only a vague understanding that Amabel had somehow crossed a line and what little they had between them was lost to her forever.

More and more Abigail was holding seances and messing with a Ouija board, calling up the spirits in that deep, growling granny voice, her eyes rolling, neck revolving, gibbering and foaming at the mouth. One night she threw a howling, terrified tantrum, insisting she'd seen a ghost in her bedroom. For weeks she couldn't sleep and refused to enter the room. Abigail went to the local council demanding a new house because her home was haunted.

'Bitch behind the counter looked at me as if I'd two heads and declared that wasn't one of their specified criteria or some such crap. Besides, I own my house. Felt like telling the snobby cunt to stuff her transfer and marching out. But I bit my lip and told her I'd take a house anywhere, anywhere at all.' Abigail was animated and happy as she packed the household goods into cardboard boxes.

'Where we going, Mum?' Kay asked.

'Arden, dear. A lovely new home in Arden.' Her mother had just uttered a contradiction, big style.

Arden, home of street gangs, murders, heroin, money lending, prostitution, gun battles and modern slums. Within months of moving into the housing scheme, Kay forced herself to become fluent in the street lingo, had taken to sniffing lighter fuel and dressed in a way that blended in. It was a case of fit in or die. You couldn't opt out and you couldn't hide. There were rules and a pecking order and girls were right in the middle, either playing an equal part or paying the price. She'd watch female classmates charge into rival gangs with razors and hatchets, deal on street corners, pulling wraps of heroin from their vaginas, pimp their little sisters and sometimes their brothers. Male or female, you were either a player or a victim. She'd watch young teenage girls pay out protection money to the street gangs then, half an hour later, stand in some derelict house with their knickers dangling from one ankle letting the same guys take their turn. That was how it was in Arden. Kay adapted but not that much.

It was as if the locals could tell just by looking at Abigail how she lived. The Arden visitors to their home were rougher, dirtier and drunker than the previous lot but they were after the same thing and they got it. No more 660 Club, it was now: 'Yer mammy's a great ride.'

'Her fanny's the second Clyde tunnel.'

'We wiz really bored and skint so we jist gave wee Abby a turn – better than standin' oot in the rain, man.'

Now they turned up for Amabel as well as Abigail. Some even turned to Kay, though she was under-age and under-developed.

'Kay, yer growing up fast, hen. Come oan have a wee drink wi yer uncle.' She knew what the invite meant and always declined, preferring to be alone in her room, obliterating her grasp of real life through the heady, buzzing intake of butane gas. Solvents blanked out the Technicolor reels of old men having her sister as others watched, her mother with her skirt in the air, young boys and old men, all comers, free for all. Kay wouldn't do that. Would never do that – not with her life.

The lorry jerked and woke her up. The last she remembered before dropping off was the driver asking her to raise her bum. Wriggling under the quilt, pulling her trousers up, she tried to remember his name and thought he'd said Joe, cracking some joke about Joseph, or was it John? All night he'd petted and nuzzled her but no more than that. All night she'd felt nothing – no pleasure or disgust – nothing. While Joe or John supervised the unloading, Kay strolled across to the phone box. Laying several silver coins on the black metal ledge she knew she couldn't phone home but would contact Jessie, the downstairs neighbour.

'Ye wee bitch, whit the fuck have ye done tae her?' Jessie took sides at random and clearly it was Abigail's turn.

'Is she okay?'

'Naw, she's very fuckin' far from okay. Ye nearly killed her.' That meant she was still alive. 'Forty stitches in her napper, man, and fuck knows whit else. She was in that casualty ward half the night.'

'She's home, then?'

'Aye, an that's where you should be, lady, right this instant. Ye've goat some explainin' tae dae . . .' Kay dropped the heavy black handset on to the cradle as Jessie ranted on. She'd learned all she needed to know – her mother was alive. Relief seeped through as another dread emerged – facing her mother now – how could she? She'd keep on running.

'England or bust, kiddo, and yer first choice destination.' The driver was straining to maintain his upbeat chatter of the night before. Maybe it was the lack of sleep or he didn't consider her skinny little body worth all this effort. The road south was etched with their silence till he turned on the radio, filling the void with cheap candyfloss pop songs and strained DJ jollity, letting her drift off into her thoughts of the night before.

'Jordo, you're a real gem,' her mother had greeted the old man at the door. 'Here's me just cracked open a bottle and looking for company.' The old man shuffled in wearing his usual threadbare ex-army greatcoat and that dirty shitty stink. His face was a wizened mixture of wrinkled folds and grey stubble. A maze of broken veins and one purple, swollen eye added colour. Jordo was one of the local sunshine boys, hanging around the patches of wasteland sharing cheap fortified wine with his mates.

'I feel sorry for the wee soul,' her mother had said one day.

'Nowhere to live and out in all weathers.' Jordo licked his scabby lips and knocked on their door every night, a leering old goat in the company of women and free booze.

Kay despised old Jordo but was determined to stay put. She was fed up of being moved out of her home to suit all comers. She slouched in front of the TV as her mother and Jordo sat at the high table behind her, drinking, smoking and gibbering. When her mother offered her a drink Kay accepted, for the first time ever. She'd no lighter fuel and the booze might help. The buzz of butane altered her consciousness, instantly zipping through her brain. The vodka tasted better but kicked in lower down and heightened her senses, making Abigail and Jordo's babble more irritating. Still Kay stayed on, accepting every vodka offered, finally sending her head into a woozy spiral.

'Ah don't know whit Ah'd dae without yese, Abby.' Jordo rehashed a speech he made every night.

'Nonsense, what's mine is yours.'

'Gets awfy lonely oot there, ye know.'

'You've no need to feel lonely, my dear.'

'There's things ye cannae dae when ye've nae hoose.'

'Like have a bath,' thought Kay to herself.

'I'm sure, darling.' As her mother uttered those words Kay imagined her sympathetic expression smiling at the old freeloader.

'Years since Ah've been wi a woman.'

'Here we go,' thought Kay. 'Everybody else has a shot at Abby so why not a drunken old wino like him.'

'What's mine is yours,' hiccupped Abigail.

'Bless yese, Abby. Bless yese.'

'No, truly. I would give you my very own daughter.' Kay tuned entirely into the conversation behind her.

'Naw, yese dinnae mean that.'

'Course I do. Would you like her? Would you like to have her? Through in the room.'

'Yer serious ain't ye?'

'Little Kay there . . .'

Kay was on her feet, screaming at her mother, rushing at her and grabbing her by the hair. Abigail leapt up and struck out. They fell over the table, smashing plates and glasses, rolling onto the floor slapping, punching, gouging, biting. Jordo crept back, cowering into a corner but remaining in the room. He loved a good scrap between women.

'Fucking's too good for you,' Abigail screamed. 'Little tight arse.' Someone's foot caught a pot of white paint. Kay lifted it, splashing it over the wall, the carpet and her mother while screaming out wordlessly. 'You little cunt,' her mother howled, grabbing her hair, pummelling her back onto the floor. Abigail's hand found a long, jagged shard of a broken plate, which she gripped and yanked round, stabbing Kay repeatedly through the knee and leg. The jolts of pain sent Kay into a frenzy, clasping at a shoe and hacking the sharp heel into her mother's skull again and again till she stopped writhing and lay still.

Clambering to her feet, Kay stood over the crumpled heap of Abigail, her mother. Shredded tights exposed blue-stained lumps of thigh on her splayed legs. One plump, naked breast flopped on its side through her ripped dress. An arm veered up her back at an impossible angle. Crimson oozed from her head, flowing into the white paint on the floor. In the corner Jordo was whimpering, 'Ah'm jist an old man. Didnae mean any harm. Honest, hen. It was a joke but. Jist a wee joke . . .' Kay turned and ran from the flat. She couldn't remember how she'd arrived on the hard shoulder of the motorway or even how long she had been on the lorry with Joe or John or whoever. The throb of the engine and the anonymous, repetitive scenery seemed to have been going on forever.

'Yooo, Carlisle in a wee while, wee darlin'. It's no bonny, sure, but it's England.' The driver was chatting again after many miles of silence.

'I'm going home,' Kay muttered, staring at her knees. She surprised herself that she'd made a decision. He pulled the lorry onto the grass verge leaving the engine ticking over.

'We could go tae Ireland, like Ah was sayin'.'

'I have to go back.'

'Sure an it'll be an adventure in . . .'

'I don't know anybody in Ireland.'

'Ye know me sure – a lot better aifter last night.' It was the first time he'd mentioned his fumbling.

'What would I do? Where would I live? Who . . .'

'Hoah, slow down would yese. There's openings for an enterprising young lass like yersel, if ye catch me drift. What disnae go on in Dublin isnae worth waitin for.'

'I don't think so.'

'Aw, c'moan.'

'No, I need to go home.'

'Ye'll regret it so ye will.'

'How do I get on the road to Glasgow?' Kay pulled at the handle and the lorry door clicked open.

'No so much as a thanks?'

'Thank you. Really, you've been a pal.'

'A pal? That's it then?' Cold anger welled up in his clear blue eyes. 'Ower there,' he snapped, motioning with his thumb.

'How do I get across?'

'Fucked if Ah care.'

'Well, see you then.'

'You and yer ma deserve each other.' Before her feet had touched the ground he crunched the lorry into gear and it jerked forward a few feet. 'Shut the fuckin' door on yer way oot,' he bawled and she was left standing by the motorway in a pall of diesel exhaust fumes.

Six lanes of fast-flowing traffic to navigate and Kay started walking. Each step hurt as her wounded knee split open, reminding her of that night. She could imagine the grief Abigail had in store for her and was terrified of seeing the damage she'd caused. It was the first time she'd fought back and her fury terrified her. She didn't want this life but soon she would be sixteen, a grown-up. She would take care of herself then and leave all of this behind her. Walk away and make things better. Life had to get better.

Govan Ways, Govan Means (1982)

'Open the fuck up, ya cunts.' The wooden frame and chains shook and rattled, threatening to give way. Inside the pub, a motley crew of stragglers lining the short bar turned and glowered. Most of the boozers were of indeterminate age and anonymous, everyday appearance. Wearing blue-grey clothes over short limbs and blue-grey faces behind half-full tumblers they were an urban pigmy tribe marked by stern glowers, spasmodic banter and facial scars. A gathering of failed hardmen, welded together by their worship of the gantry and their conspiracy to drink beyond legal hours. A tall man with long, grey side whiskers and a greasy ponytail cocked his grubby Stetson back on his head and nodded to a young skeleton-faced man clad in a turquoise shell-suit. As long as you belonged, oddities were accommodated in the place without comment or strife. As long as you belonged.

This was The Gazelle, known in the surrounding Govan neighbourhood as The Guzzle – a drinking men's pub, no more, no less. Any unfamiliar, uninvited customer would take one glance at this company and back out of the dive pronto. Yet outside on the pavement someone was insisting on entry. One drinker shook his head at the disturbance. 'Wee man wants sumfin' badly.'

'Aye, a right good doin'.'

'Cruisin' for a bruisin'.'

'Lippin' for a clippin'.'

'Shoutin' for a cloutin'.'

'Ha! Shoutin' for a cloutin'. No heard that yin afore.'

'Ah've goat tons, man. Dashin' for a bashin'.'

'He, he, he . . .'

'OPEN UP THE FUCKIN' DOORS, YA BUNCH O WANKERS.' The door shuddered and jangled with each boom. The party pooper was kicking the woodwork repeatedly. 'FUCKIN' OPEN . . .'

'Right, keep yer hair oan for Christ's sake. Ye'll have the bizzies oan us.' Irish Annie, the manager, trudged wearily to the door, puffing with the exertion and on the cigarette dangling from her lips, rubbing her potbelly in increasing irritation. The drinkers were well aware of the gaffer's potential for violence and turned to watch the show. 'What's the problem, pal?' she bawled into the panels of the door.

'LET ME IN, MAN.'

'We're shut, son. It's well past shutting time.' Irish Annie was being uncharacteristically appeasing.

'AH KNOW SHE'S IN THERE. LET ME . . .'

'Shoosh, for Christ's sake. There's naebody here. They've gone hame tae their scratchers where you and me should be.'

'SHE'S IN THERE AW RIGHT AN AH'M NO LEAVIN' WITHOOT HER.'

'Who ye going oan about, pal?'

'EH?'

'Said who is this she yer referring tae exactly?'

'MA BIRD.' Irish Annie turned to those leaning on the bar now watching her little show.

'Guy's lost his budgie. Thinks we're a pet shop. Right enough, plenty o fuckin' animals in here.' Annie grinned at her customers, her thick red lipstick twisting in a grimace of sarcasm.

'Ah blame the drugs masel,' offered the skull head taking a slug of his drink.

'Just say yes, yes, yes, yes.'

'Listen, love, there's nae wummin in here.' Irish Annie was flummoxing her regulars by maintaining her good mood.

'Yer no fucking jokin', hen,' one drinker mumbled, making sure only his companion could hear.

'AH'LL PAN YER FUCKIN' WINDAES, MAN.'

'Right ye are, then,' she replied with a sigh so exasperated it set her ill-fitting false teeth clicking. Irish Annie scooped up the hefty bundle of keys dangling from her waist by a long metal chain and busied herself unlocking the door.

'Annie, calm down now, hen,' pleaded a small man with the popping eyes of a startled chicken and a wide scar running parallel to his scalp.

'Aye, doll, remember whit happened the last time, eh?'

'Whit did happen last time?' asked the shell-suited anorexic.

'OK Corral, Alamo, Custer's Last Stand all rolled intae one, man,' replied the cowboy.

'Whiiit?'

'Pande-fuckin'-monium, ya cultureless bastard. Mayhem, man. Blood on the walls and no jokin'.' The cowboy continued drinking from his usual order of two fingers of gut-rot which other folk described as a big nippy or double whisky. Irish Annie ignored the banter and continued unlocking the doors till poised to draw the last and largest bolt.

'Come ben a minute wid ye, hen,' she shouted in the general direction of the toilets where seventeen-year-old Kay was smoking a cigarette, strictly forbidden to junior staff even in the early morning hours of a lock-in. Thinking she was in trouble, Kay dumped the cigarette into the toilet pan and rushed through the swinging doors, stumbling into the bar where she found all eyes on her.

'Stay right there, lady. Don't budge a fuckin' inch,' Irish Annie commanded, pointing one accusing finger in Kay's direction. Only then were the doors sprung open and in fell George, a skinny young guy almost as drunk as he was angry, Kay's boyfriend. As he tripped into the bar, Irish Annie grabbed him one-handed by the throat, stopping him dead in his tracks. 'Right ye are, son.'

'YE OLD BAG, LET GO O ME,' he rasped.

'Or else whit, son?' The manageress reluctantly removed the cigarette from her mouth and pulled his face close to hers. 'Whit yese gonnae dae? Should Ah be feart like?' At the bar the regulars grinned, almost forgetting about their drinks. Irish Annie smiled wistfully and put the fag back between her lips.

'AH'LL FUCKIN' . . .'

'Ye'll dae no such thing, son. So shut the fuck up an listen.' As she spoke, Irish Annie shook George by his gullet. A strangled throttling noise screeched from his mouth and his legs flapped in the air. 'Ye'd better be here for that wee lassie or ye've got a stark choice.' George slapped out and did his best to scream, succeeding only in croaking and drawing more chuckles from the audience. Kay still stood in the middle of the bar, nervously chewing her hair. 'Ye either take yon wee lassie up the road and treat her right – hear me now, treat her right – or Ah gie ye a doing on the spot,' Irish Annie continued. 'Whit's it tae be then, son?'

George's face had turned purplish-blue. Kay wasn't sure if he was choking or if his temper had boiled over with no place to go. She wished he hadn't come here. She wished she wasn't his girlfriend. She didn't know how to get rid of him. Wherever she went he followed. Whatever she did he spoiled. She'd told him to his face over and over that they were finished but it was as if he was deaf to those particular words. She'd been flattered by his attention to start with. Him a team player and her the one girl in the scheme who didn't give out. She'd thought he'd chosen her over the scores of good-looking easy lays because he wanted the same things as she did: out of Arden, settling down with someone decent and trustworthy, building a good home for their kids and the future. She soon learned that all he wanted was what he already had – drugs, effortless sex, stealing and violence. George was no different from any of the other white trash in the scheme. Trouble was, Kay was stuck with him.

'Then again, Ah could take yese ben the back and gie yese a seein' tae. Jist you an me in that dark cellar. Ye up for it, wee man?' Irish Annie slapped her free hand between George's legs, squeezing and grinning. She was in a good mood right enough.

'Let us go, eh?' George had found his voice and some sense.

'Whit's that special word?' Annie was after a final bit of humiliation.

'Gonnae let us go?'

'Naw. That's no it, lover.'

'Please?' Kay had never heard George say that word, ever.

'Cannae hear ye, son.' Irish Annie removed the dead cigarette from her mouth, spilling ash down her chest.

'Please?'

'Nuh. No loud enough, sugar.'

'PLEASE?'

'That's better,' said Irish Annie, yanking him towards her by the throat and giving him a slurping smack of a kiss, leaving a red oval smear stretching from his thin lips across his cheek. 'Fetch yer coat, hen,' George's tormentor said to Kay. 'An if ye have any bother off o lover boy jist run tae yer Auntie Annie an Ah'll fucking sort him.'

In the early morning bleakness of Govan, George stomped up the pavement in silence, his hands thrust deep in his pockets and his shoulders slouched over. Kay knew the signs of his foul moods and there was trouble brewing.

'We could catch a taxi – good night for the tips the night,' she offered, to break the silence and the spell.

'Whit did ye have tae dae for the tips?' George spoke in his tight-lipped, clipped way without looking at her or slowing his walking pace.

'C'moan, George, don't start, please?' As soon as the plea slipped out, Kay knew she'd made a serious error. Any appeal to George for reasonableness had the reverse effect.

'Fuckin' bunch a lechy bastards,' he ranted. 'Ah know whit

they're like. Slaverin at the thought o a young lassie, grabbing yer arse every chance they get.'

'No, they're nice and harmless. Really . . .'

'An ye gie them the come oan. Barmaids are aye good for a ride. Cheap slappers sellin it for a drink or a two-bob tip.'

'Nooo, George, I . . .'

'Wearing the short skirts an at.'

'I hardly ever wear skirts . . .'

'Wiggling yer arse an smiling.'

'They're a good laugh some . . .'

'Fuckin' hysterical, man.'

'George . . .'

'Really fuckin' funny.' George swung round and grabbed Kay by the shoulders.

'Please, George . . .'

'See if this is funny, ye wee cunt.' He brought his knee up sharply into Kay's breadbasket, knocking the wind from her lungs. As she bent double, gasping for air, he gripped her hair and punched her twice on the side of her face, sending her spinning into a wall. Kay gagged, spitting blood and bile as George hovered over her, shouting and bawling.

A group of men approached, but, spotting the scene, they crossed the street with one saying loudly, 'Young love, eh boys? Takes ye back.' A chorus of chuckles from his companions.

George turned to them and screamed, 'Whit the fuck yese gapin' at? Want tae make sumfin' o it? Dae yese?' The men kept walking without a murmur while George turned and kicked Kay again and again, following and punching her as she edged away, pressed into the cold surface of brick.

Kay did her best with make-up but she knew that her purple, bloated eye was impossible to hide as she limped into The Guzzle the following night. She was seventeen and the beatings had been going on since they started seeing each other two years earlier. One of George's problems was jealousy. He couldn't bear to let her out of his sight, always believing she was up to no good with someone. Yet she was faithful, deliberately choosing to lose her cherry with him on her sixteenth birthday after months of nagging and huffing and hidings from him. Sex was no big deal to Kay, who couldn't understand why other girls were so enthusiastic. Even now, when George wasn't too stoned or drunk, she surrendered to him rather than made love with him. It was hurried, rough and mechanical sex, leaving her neither up nor down. But it was to him and only him. At least it kept him quiet – for a while. But still he didn't trust her.

'Jesus Christ, doll, what happened to ye?' Bobby Boyd was whispering at her across the bar in The Guzzle. He was one of the regular customers who stood out from the blue-grey drinkers. A handful of them, like Bobby, wore expensive clothes, drove flash motors and carried the respect of the others. Even young, naive Kay noticed. Bobby had taken a shine to her, like a favourite uncle or a protective older brother. He was whispering to save her embarrassment. 'Just dinnae tell us ye walked intae a door, right?'

'Don't want to talk about it, Bobby,' was the best Kay could offer, caught off-guard with her ready-made excuses.

'Understandable, doll. But it was that wee shite George, wasn't it?'

'He'd a wee bit too much to drink.'

'Is that what happens every time?' Kay blushed, realising her previous efforts at keeping her injuries secret had failed and wondered who else knew. 'Face it, sugar, the wee man's got a problem. He'll no stop till yer in yer grave – that's how these guys are. They need stopping.' At that point a regular called Fred O'Mara came in and went straight to Kay to order his drink. Fred, a mate of Bobby's, was another who carried power with his very presence. The conversation immediately turned away from her bruised face and on to the Scotch broth of trivia that fuelled drinking hours.

When The Guzzle closed down that night, Irish Annie excused Kay duty from the extended lock-in. 'If that wee man o yours turns up the night Ah'll have him for a wee knee-trembler in the cellar. Okay wi that, hen?' Kay blushed as the drinkers chortled and hooted.

'Annie's on heat.'

'Everything has its season.'

All Kay could find to stammer quietly in reply was, 'Aye.'

When the big yellow Mercedes flashed its headlights outside the pub, Kay knew it would be Bobby Boyd. They became friends, platonic friends. It was as if he needed someone to take care of and Kay appreciated the older man's attention with nothing expected in return. Through Bobby, she developed a taste for the finer things in life, adding quality to her already developing individualistic sense of fashion. Kay felt no obligation to Bobby – a rare experience. They kept their friendship secret since no one they knew – not his wife, her boyfriend or the dogs in the street – would believe they enjoyed simple companionship.

'Fred's got a bit a business ye need tae know about,' Bobby said one night. Bobby and Fred never discussed work and Kay was clueless about how either of them earned their dough.

'What's it got to do with me?' she asked.

'Maybe everything, doll. Maybe everything.' Fred had recently visited her mother's house when Kay wasn't in. Kay was surprised he even knew where she lived. At first she'd been worried that, true to form, her mother had tried to seduce him. But he'd just stayed for a coffee and spent a lot of time chatting about her and George. When Kay cornered Fred the next time he was in The Guzzle he took her outside during her break.

'Jist trying tae dae ye a favour, hen,' he started off almost apologetically.

'What, visiting my mother?' Kay wondered if Abigail had succeeded.

'Naw, naw, nothing tae dae wi her. It was that boy o yours Ah'm goin tae fix.'

'George?'

'Aye, yon wee shite.' Kay looked perplexed and mystified. 'See tae him – permanently like. A freebie. As a favour tae yersel.'

'What?'

'Dae Ah need tae spell it oot, doll?'

'Yeah.'

'C'mere.' Fred pulled her farther away from the thin light glowing from the pub windows into deeper darkness. 'Fuck's sake, Boaby shouldnae have said nothing.'

'It's too late now, Fred.'

'Aye, looks like it.' He paused, looking away up the street for a minute before turning to face her. 'It's whit Ah dae. Kill bad bastards.'

'Fred . . .'

'Ah know, Ah know, hen. Dinnae ask me tae explain masel. That's jist the way it is.'

'No . . .'

'That yin is a cruel, cowardly fucker an he'll be like that for the rest o his days.'

'Noo . . .'

'Aye. Ye'd be better off . . .'

'Noo. Absolutely NO.'

'Ah knew this wid happen if ye got a whiff o it. Fuckin' Boaby an his big gob.'

'No, Fred. No.'

'Ah hears ye, Ah hears ye, doll. If ye say no that's whit it'll be.'

'No,' Kay was struggling in her shock to move beyond that one word.

'Right, but if ye change yer mind . . .'

'No.'

'. . . ye know where Ah'm are.'

That night Kay insisted that Bobby tell her about Fred's

background and he gave her double helpings. As youngsters, Bobby and Fred had apparently been major members of the Govan Team, one of the largest and most fearsome razor gangs in Glasgow. While many of their troops ended up dead, disabled, junkies or festering in gaol, these two graduated to more businesslike enterprises. Bobby was into rackets like protection, moneylending, clubs and drugs. But Fred did one thing and one thing alone exceptionally well. He was the leading hitman in Glasgow, one of the best paid in the country. When he offered to sort George he meant it.

Kay's friendship with Bobby tapered off after that night. She couldn't reconcile how she wanted to live her life with how he lived his. The split was accelerated when she moved to work in a pub called The Pitches in another area of Govan. The Pitches, so called because it was near the site of a huge expanse of football fields – a monument to the dominant Glaswegian religion. The pub was managed by Eddie, the then husband of her older sister Amabel, and Kay thought she might get better help in making a career for herself than under Irish Annie's spit-and-sawdust regime. A few months before she started, The Pitches had been raided after hours and Eddie held up at knifepoint. He'd been tied to a chair while the robbers emptied the safe and looted the cigarettes and spirits. What Kay didn't know was that the robbery had been carried out by George in collusion with Eddie himself.

The pub was like most she'd already worked in, being an illegal veteran employee of almost a dozen licensed establishments although she had just turned eighteen. One of the other barmaids, Fiona, was a thickset young woman with frizzy ginger hair, broad bones and thick glasses. A friendless sort of dame, she immediately clung to Kay like a lost puppy. Kay felt sorry for the graceless, myopic young woman and, though they'd little in common, would go out on the town with her now and then. Fiona was dowdy and foul-mouthed. Going clubbing with her was like cutting yourself off in a crowd. Good-looking young dudes would smile at Kay till their mates spotted her companion and pulled them away with a scornful curled lip. Even other women ignored them, warned off by Fiona's whingeing voice fucking this and cunting that. Kay was just too polite to dump her.

Fiona was seeing a young bloke, a regular in the bar, by the name of Crack Moran. It was an on-off relationship due to Crack openly admitting, 'Ah've a few babes. Take it or leave it, man.' Fiona took it when offered.

When Fiona suggested they go to a party Kay easily agreed, though her expectations were low. She reckoned the folk who chose to associate with Fiona couldn't be too choosy and were probably downright desperate. She expected to know most of them from The Pitches and some were okay.

'Aye, a wee party will be fine,' she'd replied to Fiona. 'Who'll all be there?'

'Just Crack and his mates and their girlfriends, like.'

'Might've known Crack would be there. You'd do anything he asked, eh?' Kay teased with a broad smile.

Fiona thought for a long, record-breaking second, her jaw falling open and her mouth gaping, before replying with feeling, 'Naaaw.' More perplexed looks and knitted brow. 'Naw, Ah mean aye. Aye. Aye.'

'No doubt there then,' Kay mumbled.

On the night, Fiona insisted they arrive early at the Govan flat. Kay didn't mind since street life in Govan was known to be the most dangerous in the city and drinking in a local pub could be suicidal. She noticed that she and Fiona were the only two women in the place but it was early and she felt safe with her friend, away from the anarchy of the Arden gangs back home.

Kay and Fiona had shared the cost of a bottle of vodka and a bottle of lemonade as their contribution to the party. The guy running the affair would see as far as crates of beer and a lump of dope but no further. With vodka and lemonade Kay could pace herself and take care. Not that it looked as if it was going to be a wild do.

'Sees yer cairry oot and Ah'll get ye sorted,' offered their host in the Glasgow version of warm hospitality.

'Thanks, but not too strong, eh?' said Kay.

'It's a party, hen. Let yer hair doon.'

'Aye, but it's early.'

'Suit yersel then.' True to his word he poured a weak vodka and lemonade mixer. Five or six of the regular guys from the pub turned up, led by Crack Moran. Fiona had boasted that Crack was the current leader of the Young Govan Team but he seemed such a hapless poser Kay dismissed the comment as wishful, infatuated thinking. Kay sat quietly on the couch, sipping her first drink, tugging her frock further over her knees. She'd hummed and hawed about what to wear that night and was pleased she'd opted for the longer, more subdued effort and rejected the short number with the shoelace shoulder straps. It clearly wasn't going to be a glitzy affair. On the stereo Frankie was still going to Hollywood and howling something about two tribes going to war.

Heya. Heya. Heyaaaa. Wowoowowoowow.

Kay sipped slowly at her first drink and wondered if the record would ever finish.

The freezing cold woke her. A shiver running over her skin, burrowing through her flesh and nipping at her very bones. Dry razor blades splintered in her throat, coating her mouth with a fine veneer of sticky metallic dust. Her tongue was swollen, parched and wedged between her aching teeth. She lay on her back looking at a vista of pink hills rolling one into another other endlessly. Moving, her head spun and body spiralled down and round till she threw her arms out and stared back into those rose mounds. A rattle and mumbled voices. Over the buzzing in her ears she scanned for some familiar sound to tell her where she was and give her a name to call out.

'Lick me. Fuck, aye, that's it. Jist like that.' There was no mistaking Fiona's whiny voice.

'C'mere, ya wee bitch,' Crack's patter hadn't improved.

'Aye, c'moan. Aye.' Bed springs creaked and the voices mumbled on.

Fiona, so it must be the flat and the party. All Kay could recall was arriving, sitting on the couch, sipping at her first vodka and lemonade, listening to *Wowoowowoowow*. That's all she remembered. *Wowoowowoowow*.

Her head began to steady and she moved her eyes, pulling back from the pink hills, transforming them into her own knickers draped over the top of an open door. She slid her hand over her body and felt skin cold and numb against her palm. Lying naked on the floor, she jerked up in a panic. Scorching pain seared her genitals, sending her wincing, grunting and flopping down on her back. She needed to get out – now. Shuffling her legs across the mattress towards the edge, beads of sweat sprinkled her forehead, drawing deep gasping breaths. She counted to three and swung her torso up into a seated position, slumping forward to draw wind. Circulation was returning to her limbs but with it came nausea and feeling in her raw vagina and inside, something was hurting deep inside her. The soft, white flesh at the top of her thighs was chafed red and mottled with shapeless purple bruises. Teeth marks etched the pale skin of her midriff in a dark-blue obscenity. Gingerly placing a hand between her legs, Kay didn't recognise herself. Her pubic hair was a matted, gooey mess, sticking to her fingers in tacky strips. Her lips were swollen and distended, puffing out against weals on her thighs. A dollop of thick slime spewed through her fingers followed by a stream of warm, greasy fluid. Coloured lights danced across her eyes and Kay's befuddled brain struggled to make sense of it.

'Something's not right down there,' she croaked, frightened

by the sound of her own voice. She called her vagina 'down there', cringing when she heard other women refer to their cunt, fanny or pussy. She couldn't find the words. She was ill and had to get home.

Stretching to retrieve her knickers where they dangled from the door, the muscles of her back and legs screamed out in protest. Pulling up her pants the soft gusset hurt her as it wrapped itself over her bloated lips. Scanning for the rest of her clothes she saw the deluge of the room. The naked floorboards were scattered with beer cans, bottles and cigarette butts. Puddles mixed with ash to create grey mulch in crazed patterns. Vomit was sprayed down a plasterboard wall, gathering in a drying orange mess on the floor. Razor blade, foil, burnt spoon, candle – the doings for smack – were placed in a neat formation on the window ledge. Through the curtain-free panes she looked directly into another flat twenty yards away, mesmerised by the movements of a neighbouring family going about their Sunday morning business. The only piece of furnishing in the room was an old, faded mattress marked by a series of angry red stains. Among the litter she found her clothes – slashed tights, bra tied in tight knots and one shoe filled with piss-smelling fluid. Gagging at the stink, she dressed as best she could.

Treading her way through the flat she was relieved to find her path to the front door unimpeded by other people. Turning the Yale carefully, she started as voices shouted, 'Harder. Go oan.'

'Ya wee cunt, Ah'll gie it tae yese.'

'C'moan then . . .' A picture of the two ugly people coupling in the other room made Kay retch as she slipped through the doorway.

Kay sat on the top deck of the bus smoking a cardboard-tasting cigarette, trying to be invisible. Her body was numb and dull, her senses groggy. All she could remember was sitting on that couch drinking her first glass of vodka and lemonade. *Heya. Heya. Heyaaaa. Wowoowowoowow.* In front of her sat two young teenage girls, their short party frocks and heavily smudged make-up out of place, they were oblivious to the other passengers as they chatted loudly.

'Great party, man.'

'Aye.'

'See that wee guy ye goat off wi first?'

'Aye.'

'He's a dead good snogger.'

'Aye.'

'Ye cannae stoap yersel once he starts, eh?'

'Naw.'

'But the big guy, whit's his name again?'

'Cannae remember.'

'Bet ye huvnae forgotten his tadger, but.'

'NAAAW.'

'Huv ye ever seen such a tiddler?'

'NAAAW.' The two girls shrieked and continued comparing the merits of the boys from the night before.

Kay sat and thought, 'There's something not right down there.' As if to agree the bus jolted on a pothole sending another thick squelch dribbling down her thigh.

Arriving home, Kay avoided her mother and went straight to her room. She quickly stuffed her clothes into a black bin liner as hot water steamed into the bath. Standing naked in the bedroom she parted her legs and surveyed the damage. Her labia was blistered and on one side a small jagged cut criss-crossed angrily. Her thigh bruises had darkened and the teeth marks seemed to rise out from her flesh. Black and blue dappled her neck and scattered over her breasts. Covering herself she rushed to the bath she needed more than anything.

Soaking in the suds she kept adding hot water till it gnawed at her flesh and burned a red rim around her waist. She kept trying to resurrect the night before but couldn't get further than that first vodka, the young men from the pub, Fiona's dull eyes and *Heya. Heya. Heyaaaa. Wowoowowoowow.* Her head ached and she felt sick. Abigail, her mother, would give her no helpful response. Amabel would just laugh. George would go crazy since he thought she was having a girls' night out with Fiona, just Fiona. She couldn't tell anyone. All of it was too much. Block it out. Block it out. Too much. All her own fault for trying to live another life. She should just accept things as they were. Go with the flow. It was good enough for all the other young women in the scheme so what was wrong with her? She should forget it all. Pretend it never happened. Make it disappear. She was good at that, she'd done it before. Blank it out.

Kay turned the hot tap on and lay back. From out in the hall she heard the echo of a man's voice as the bathroom door handle rattled impatiently. A low male grumble then Abigail, her mother: 'Who's in there? Kay, is that you?'

'Yes.'

'Hurry up and finish would you. Your Uncle . . .' Low voices aside as Abigail asked his name. 'Your Uncle Bert needs a pee.'

Bert. Who was Bert? Just another anonymous face in the carousel crowd of her mother's bed. A steady-go-round of half promises and drunken gropes. Round and round. Bright colours and cheerful music. Round and round. Cracked paint and meaningless jingles. Round and round. Fluffy candyfloss and cheap prizes. Round and round. All leading nowhere except more of the same. Round and round. Kay decided to step off. She decided to get married to George. She'd build a life for them and he would change. The violence and drunkenness would stop. She'd make it work. No carousel days for Kay.

The Calling (1985)

ook, Kay, you're going to have to get a job. So, why not?'
Abigail poured herself another straight gin before shoving
the bottle across to her friend, Joy.

'Yer ma's right, hen. It's good money for next tae nae work,'
Joy offered as she poured herself a large measure. 'Let's face it, if
Ah can dae it'd be a scoosh case for you, eh?'

Joy was one of those innumerable pretend aunties, but one
with staying power, sticking around like dog dirt on a shoe. A
heavily built woman with bleached blonde hair, Joy wore her
skirts short, her blouses cut low and her make-up thick. She'd
waltz in through their front door without knocking and plant
her broad arse on the chair nearest to the booze. She sat with her
knees ajar, drinking what was available and interfering in family
business. Kay grew to hate her for that and it was what Joy was
doing that night.

'Listen to your Auntie Joy, darling. She should know,' said
Abigail, who was in one of her rare solicitous moods, all cooing
and stroking. Kay didn't trust her at all. But the young woman
needed help and had only her mother to turn to.

Marriage to George hadn't been a success. The start was fine – all
white dress and three-night honeymoon, even if it was in a
borrowed high-rise flat round the corner from her mother's house.
Shortly they were allocated their own council flat, where else but
in Arden where no one wanted to live. It was in one of the better
streets and Kay loved the place, setting it up in grand style. With
George being a spasmodic earner and her limited wages from the

pub work, they relied on credit to buy household goods. With a rent book and no time or opportunity to fall into arrears, the loans and plastic cards were thrown at them. Soft furnishings, electrical equipment, fancy goods, clothes and more clothes – Kay didn't stop. One day a neighbour who had watched the procession of deliveries into the home approached Kay with a proposition.

'See if yer getting the tick, hen, there's a wee number ye can work,' she offered hesitantly, watching Kay's face for the first glimmer of disapproval. When none came she continued, 'Havin' problems in payin', doll? Ah can sort it.' The scam was easy but not so foolproof as the neighbour suggested. If anyone local wanted a new stereo, three-piece suite or whatever, Kay would buy it for them on her credit. They would pay her a cash lump sum at much less than the shop price, which Kay would use to meet some of the payments, pocketing the spare money. 'But for Christ's sakes keep tae the monthly payments exactly. Dinnae go payin' ower the odds even if yer flush.' Kay was puzzled. Surely you paid interest on money owed so paying it off early meant you paid less in the long run? 'Naw, naw. Ye'll no clear the debt and ye'll end up skint. Besides, if ye keep makin' steady, minimum payments they increase yer credit rating.' Sure enough, the more Kay owed, the more the finance companies allowed her. She utilised every dime and all was well, for a while.

Kay had a week's grace after the honeymoon then George's violence started again with extras. It was as if he believed the marriage vows entitled him to unbridled ferocity. Beatings came fast and furious, sharpened by an inventiveness she thought him incapable of. He hit her with any object to hand every night as if working to a rota. He demanded sex, making fast, desperate love then, two minutes after his post-coital cigarette, he would start a quarrel and kick her naked body all through the flat. He gouged at her eyes with his thumbs. Urinated on her bloody face. Invited his pals in to gape at her unconscious body, lying there with her breasts exposed and her knickers around her ankles.

When she went out she couldn't be sure he wasn't stalking her to humiliate her in front of a new audience. Breaking her heart as he smashed her bones.

Doctors at the casualty wards asked terse questions and probed no further. Her mother and sisters kept with tradition, sheltering her for an hour or two before sending her back to her man for more terror. Fearing for her life, Kay eventually left George, walking straight out with no more than the clothes she wore to avoid suspicion. After one night in the spare room at her mother's she sneaked home to pick up some things. Letting herself in, the flat sounded hollow. George, her husband of nine months, had stripped it bare. Everything was gone. Kay had no money, no home, no clothes and no job. She almost laughed at the irony of the last, having the week before given up bar work on her husband's insistence.

'So's we can spend a bit o time the gither,' he had argued in one of his better moods. Since she resigned they'd spent no more than a few sleeping and many violent hours in each other's company. Now she was snookered. Nothing left but what she stood in and a massive amount of debt for goods which no longer existed. She had no one else to turn but Abigail, her mother.

'See, it's five pounds for a massage. Think on it. A fiver for rubbing a man's back. Easy money.' Joy was pressing her hard. Normally Kay would have been leery but her desperation ruled that night. 'Just go tell Mr Wing that big Joy sent ye. He'll interview you on the spot. Guaranteed.'

'Go on, love. What do you have to lose?' Abigail poured another vodka into her daughter's glass and continued. 'I'll go along with you. What do you say?'

'Okay, I'll give it a go.' As soon as Kay had agreed, her mother sprang into action, handing her a dressing gown with instructions to strip off her only underwear so it could be washed and dried overnight.

'You'll no regret it, doll. Easiest money ye'll ever earn.' Joy helped herself to another drink and smiled so wide she showed a black gap at the side of her teeth Kay had never noticed before.

'If it's such good money why is she such a mess?' Kay wondered to herself, still far from convinced about the venture.

Her mother let her sleep late the next morning, waking her up with a cup of coffee and a cigarette.

'Take your time, love. I'll just run you a nice wee bath.' When Kay staggered back into the bedroom, her wet hair wrapped in a towel and her face flushed from the steam of the bath water, Abigail had laid her freshly laundered clothes neatly on the bed. Kay couldn't remember her mother ever taking such care of her, even as a young child. Any suspicions were evaporated by a gush of warmth for a mother who obviously finally understood her daughter's plight and was trying to help her.

'Don't worry, luvvie. You look great.' Abigail smoked and chatted animatedly as she drove through the city traffic. As usual she was dressed glamorously, her high heels riding her short skirt high up her thighs, flashing a glimpse of stocking top to passing drivers and pedestrians. Next to her, Kay looked like a younger, school-aged sister with her high-necked top, a pinafore dress covering her knees and pop socks. Their destination was only a couple of miles from Arden but light years away in terms of affluence, perched as it was on the boundary of Shawlands and Giffnock, full of owner-occupied mansions, large gardens, classy hotels and synagogues. These streets were familiar to Kay only as landmarks on the bus route from her home to the city centre. Now she felt embarrassed about her background and afraid she wouldn't be polite or educated enough to work in such a classy part of the city.

'Just do as they tell you, love. Everything they tell you and you'll do just fine.' As she pulled the car to a stop, Abigail reached out and squeezed her daughter's hand, smiling with reassurance. 'I'll be right here when you get out.'

The building was a small, square-shaped bungalow standing on its own in a triangle of grass and trees. 'Bubbles' was declared on the gable wall and over the front door, enhanced by a stream of fluorescent party froth. Kay straightened her clothes, coughed to wet her parched mouth and cautiously opened the door to an aroma of baby oil and perfume. Inside, a small hallway was skirted by a sea of identical doors. Behind a small reception desk sat a middle-aged woman with big blonde hair, unbelievably long eyelashes and wearing an expensive business suit. She eyed Kay up and down in a lugubrious, dismissive manner, saying nothing. Somewhere nearby women's voices spoke out.

'Ah'll do her for half price.' A cackle of laughter.

'Ah'll do her for free.'

'Fuck it, here's a fiver for ye. Let's get at it, wee sugar.' When Kay stepped close to the reception point she could see the group of women, dressed in white bathrobes, sitting against a wall behind the desk in a row beside a large mirror strategically positioned to show them everyone who entered. One woman smiled and fluttered her fingers hello.

Kay blushed and stuttered. 'Joy told me to . . .' she paused trying to finish the sentence.

'Yeees?' said the receptionist, raising one eyebrow.

'. . . ask for . . . for Mr Wing.'

'Awww, the wee shame,' chipped one of the watching women.

'He's no good at it, doll,' offered another. 'Try me.'

The po-faced receptionist asked her name and told her to take a seat in the row of five women. Sitting so closely together it was impossible for Kay to avoid looking at this group. She wondered who they were – managers, owners or customers. It never occurred to her they were the workers, appearing as they did. They all wore short white gowns tied at the waist but the similarities between them ended there. Kay's neighbour wore her hair in a boyish pageboy style and looked too young to be out of school. With an emery board she filed and smoothed at the nail of her left index finger over and over. A statuesque redhead with a long, thick mane sat back in her seat browsing through a magazine, her loosely crossed legs revealing an expanse of fishnet stockings merging into a black suspender belt and the scarlet triangle of her crotch. A slim, mousy-haired woman was crouched over, leaning her elbows on her knees, her gown falling open, showing skinny breasts with erect nipples and stretch marks. An older woman with a full figure and dyed-black hair appeared as relaxed as if at home getting ready for a night out. She looked over and smiled at Kay. When Kay smiled back nervously, the woman stuck her tongue out, running it slowly over her lips. Kay blushed and looked away, shifting uneasily in her seat and smoothing down her pinafore. It was an uncomfortable wait.

'Come. You come.' The small Chinese man had suddenly appeared through one of the numerous doorways and disappeared again just as quickly.

'Last chance, honey. It's either him or me,' the black-haired older woman was leaning over towards Kay licking her lips again.

'Is it me?'

'Sure as fuck isnae us, doll,' and the cackle of laughter rose up from the group again.

'Missy, you want job you come.' Irritation sang in the man's voice as he cocked his head out of a doorway glaring directly at Kay. She coughed, stood up and smoothed her pinafore before following who she assumed to be Mr Wing.

It was more of a cubicle than a room and was practically filled by a high single bed covered in white sheets and a thick yellow towel, a small sink, tiny table and one hard-backed chair. On each of the walls hung a large mirror.

'Take you clothes off,' Wing commanded as a form of introduction. Kay had prepared herself for difficult questions. All night she'd worried over how she would cope if asked to give someone a massage to demonstrate her abilities. Touching the naked back of a stranger is what she dreaded most about the interview. Intimacy, especially enforced intimacy, embarrassed her. Besides, she knew nothing about massage. She had certainly never expected it would be her who would be stripping.

Kay froze and gaped, the heat rushing to her cheeks and a cold tingle of sweat over her shoulders.

'C'moan. Clothes off. Chop, chop.' Kay looked at the small man in the shapeless grey suit, his too-short necktie knotted in a huge lump in a shirt collar several sizes too wide for him. He looked like a scrawny little schoolkid growing into his clothes. But he could offer her a job she needed desperately and she had nowhere else to go. Later, for years, she would struggle to explain her actions to herself.

Numbly, slowly, clumsily, Kay began to strip. Her fingers struggled with zips and buttons. Each item was shaken and folded neatly. Her stomach fluttered and heaved as she fought the urge to piss and shit.

'How you know here?' Wing asked as he watched Kay take off her clothes.

'Mum's friend Joy,' she mumbled.

'Joy! Paa. Joy no good. Come to work then no. How old you?'

'Nineteen.'

'Nineteen? You sure? Look younger. You sure?'

'Uhuu,' Kay continued taking her clothes off, looking anywhere but at Wing.

'Your mammy know?'

'Uhuu.'

'Age no matter then. Let me look you.' Kay stood with her back to him, wearing only her pants and her pop socks. Slowly she turned to face him, her arms wrapped over her breasts. 'Naw, naw. Clothes off. Clothes off,' Wing protested, waving his hand up and down. Staring at a mirror-free mark on the wall she hooked her thumbs into her knickers and edged them over her buttocks, down her thighs, then stood with her head bowed and both hands clasped over her pubic hair. 'All off. Off.' Wing jabbed his finger towards the pop socks. Kay looked up as far his chest and shook her head. 'Paa! No matter,' he decided and reached out, lifting her arms up. Kay felt the small man look her up and down, turning her round and back again. 'You give me blow job now,' he demanded, unbuckling his belt and letting his trousers and underwear fall to his ankles.

'A what?'

'Blow job. Blow job.'

'What?' Kay might have been a married woman but she had never had oral sex before. Her disgust at the prospect stuck her in a one-word groove, 'What?'

'No problem,' said Wing, unzipping his trousers. Nimbly easing himself up on to the high bed he took her by the back of the head and pulled her face towards his groin. Inexperienced and horrified as Kay was, she recognised that the man had a tiny, pointed penis. Something else, some familiar smell – deep-fried scampi.

'Lips. No teeths. No teeths,' he commanded in a high-pitched, anxious tone. Clamping her lips tentatively around the shaft of his small cock, Kay stayed stock still, too terrified to move or to breathe. She leaned over him, her arms outstretched by her shoulders lest she accidentally touch him, framing his tiny erection in her mouth, scared to budge, hoping he wouldn't notice the gagging spasms in her throat at the salty taste and the sweaty, fishy stink. He didn't notice nor did he seem to mind her lack of activity.

'I do you now, missy,' he declared, lifting her head from his lap. 'You get frenchie there.' On the table was a wide glass bowl filled to the brim with little packages of different shapes and colours like pick-and-mix from a sweet counter. Kay had never used condoms. Seeing her hesitation, Wing snatched her chosen package from her sweaty fingers. 'You watch. Watch. Next time you do.' As soon as the prophylactic was in place, Wing swung

Kay round, pushing her back on to the bed, crawled between her thighs and pushed his erection into her. Four or five thrusts later he let out a low strangulated squeal and slumped over her. His hair and forehead leant into Kay's cheek and again she sniffed deep-fried scampi. Anytime she recalled that day the memories would be accompanied by that mild, fishy smell.

Wing soon jumped off the bed. As Kay hurriedly dressed he stood wiping his flaccid prick with a towel, barking out his instructions.

'You need white gown, nice panties, sexy panties. Towels – big towels.' As he spoke he pulled a wallet from his pocket and handed Kay forty pounds. 'Come tomorrow at one-a-clock.' With that he was out of the room and Kay was leaving by the front door to a long wolf whistle from behind the reception desk. All in all it had taken twenty minutes and she stood on the pavement blinking in the sun, staring at her mother sitting waiting for her in the car.

Kay slumped back, her frantic thoughts welding her into the passenger seat. She couldn't believe what had just happened. She wanted to be sick, to punch something, to cry. Her mother drove and quizzed Kay. Forcing a staccato of mumbled half-sentences from her daughter, Abigail understood she'd been offered the job.

'Forty quid for twenty minutes work,' she sighed. 'Great money, Kay.'

'He fucked me.'

'I know, love.'

'Made me suck his thing.'

'But it wasn't that bad, though, was it?' Kay turned and looked at her mother, disbelief and disgust smeared all over her face. 'I mean he didn't ask you to do anything you wouldn't be doing anyway, did he now?'

'But I don't even know him and they'll expect me to do that every day.'

'Sometimes it'll just be massage and you'll still be paid a fiver.'

'Every day . . . to strangers.'

'But you would be doing it anyway for free with prats like George who give you nothing but grief in return.'

'I feel dirty . . .'

'He's just a man, love. Just another man like any other man.' Abigail drove her daughter to the shop that supplied the right type of gowns. Purchasing all Wing had instructed, their next stop was the off-licence where they bought bottles of Blue Bols, vodka and lemonade.

Back at the flat, mother and daughter sat at the high table drinking and talking till late. Abigail argued that taking the job was the smart move and a way of getting paid for what women do anyway. All night Kay wavered between self-loathing and fear of the future. She was broke and had to find some way out but she couldn't do that, could she? Then again, what had she done that very day – just gone along with it? Why had she done that? Had she asked for it to happen? Was it her fault? As the alcohol slowly kicked in, Abigail reminded her daughter that a man had put her in this dire position and rhymed off the numerous assaults he'd perpetrated on her.

'You'll not want to let that happen again, sugar. Take it from your mum, they'll all let you down one way or another.'

'But they want me to be a . . .'

'And what do you call having sex with a man when he wants to? And slaving to keep a home and then he rewards you by thumping you?'

'Yeah . . .'

'At least at work you'd be in control . . .'

'Yeah, but . . .'

'. . . and the men pay through the nose for it. Nothing for nothing. Let's face it, Kay, you need the money.'

'I know but . . .'

'You could have all your debts cleared and a tidy nest egg put aside in a few months.'

'You think so?'

'Enough to set yourself up in a nice flat and get a car.'

'The money's good right enough.'

'You'll not get better. You could work twenty-four hours a day, seven days a week in a pub and not get close.'

'Yeah . . .'

'For doing what? Just what you would be doing with some ungrateful man anyway.'

So it rolled on, inch-by-inch down the bottles of booze into the early hours of the morning, through every feeling and contradictory conclusion till Kay, drunk and blasé, made her mind up.

'I'm going to take care of myself from now on in. Nothing for nothing no more. Six months and I'm out of there. Well set up and not even twenty years old.' Abigail smiled and agreed. She would support Kay through her new profession, driving her to and from her work, letting her stay on in the flat. That way her daughter could live more cheaply, maximise her savings and get out of that business as soon as possible. 'I'm still young enough to start again, go to college and . . . well, live a decent life.'

Abigail smiled, nodded her head and poured her daughter another drink. 'Sure you will, love. Sure you will.'

No One's Candy

I'll have her,' the man's voice was only the next one in a long echo that had rumbled through the afternoon. All men's voices, all slightly different but finally all saying the same thing. Kay checked her watch and was dismayed to find that she'd only been in Bubbles for twenty minutes. It had seemed an age, an arduous ordeal and yet it had hardly begun. 'Naw, no her. That wan. The wee one reading the paper.' Kay lifted the newspaper even higher in front of her face and crossed her legs tighter. She'd bought the *Glasgow Herald*, a newspaper she never read, but it was big and wide enough to hide behind, or so she thought. She'd planned to conceal herself there silently as the business went on around her, listening to the comments and patter from the other women.

'It's The Cleaner,' one said and Kay keeked round the edge of the newspaper, surprised to see a businessman in an expensive-looking suit. How could he be the cleaner?

'Mmmmmm, it's The Tongue,' on another occasion. 'Hope he chooses me. Ah'm just in the mood.' Kay couldn't see any reason why that man was called The Tongue.

'Christ no him,' muttered under breath, immediately followed by, 'Oh hiya handsome come to see me again Ah hope . . .'

On and on – in only twenty minutes she was flummoxed. These women seemed to be speaking in a code, on several levels, in a language she didn't understand and felt she'd never learn. She just tucked herself in and ducked behind the newspaper.

That first morning she'd woken with a hangover and a mind full of regrets. She realised she didn't want to work in the sauna but knew she would. Obstinate and single-minded beyond belief, all her life she stuck to a decision once it was made. She had bathed and dressed carefully according to Mr Wing's requirements. Then she decided to wear no make-up and pull her long hair back in the childish way she had worn at school. Pop socks went back on her feet and she chose clumsy, thick-soled shoes – trendy in the clubs and the playgrounds but not the epitome of easy sex. She would work at the place but wasn't for enticing any of the customers to ask for extras, to ask for her. With her small frame and short height, she knew she looked like a sexless adolescent at that awkward age between childhood and puberty – neither one thing nor another. Surely, she reasoned, the men would choose the other women who flaunted their sexiness, exaggerating it to the level of randy caricature. Surely that's what men wanted?

'Naw, I'll have her. The wee one behind the newspaper.' For the first time Kay realised he meant her and a blush burned in her face, running down her neck and over her chest, mottling her skin in patches of scarlet. She stared blindly at the black newsprint and didn't budge. When this man had walked into the sauna the other women had let out a moan in unison, complaining in low whispers, 'Fuck, it's Goldfinger.' Now what could that mean? The only Goldfinger she'd heard of was a character in a James Bond movie – rich, evil, ugly. Maybe that was it.

'Kaaaaay,' the toffee-nosed bitch of a receptionist sang out. 'Oh, Kaaaay, it's you daaaaaarling.'

Next to her one of the other women nudged her gently in the ribs, muttering out of the side of her mouth, 'Better go sharpish, wee sugar, or Wing will hand ye yer books.' She'd learned that woman was called Rita, though her working name was Samantha. An older, handsome woman, she'd been there the day before. With long jet-black hair, a full figure and a penchant for fishnet stockings, she appeared more relaxed and at ease than the other younger women who constantly chatted and teased each other, fidgeting in their seats. Rita had frightened Kay the day before when she'd smiled at her, running her tongue along her lips and suggesting a lot more than testing her lipstick. But today Kay was already getting a different feeling – that Rita was okay, was somebody she would come to like and rely on. 'Go on, hen. Sooner started sooner finished,' Rita muttered again, all the while staring straight ahead at Goldfinger, a broad lascivious smile spread across her face.

As Kay slowly folded the unread *Glasgow Herald*, the comments from the other women rattled out less furtively than Rita's supportive advice.

'Get yer fanny ready, Teddy.'

'Ooooo, yer for it now.'

'Hope you washed yersel this morning.'

Carefully placing the neatly folded newspaper on her seat, Kay turned to face Goldfinger, her first customer. He seemed ordinary – not rich, evil or ugly. A working man in an off-the-peg suit. Slightly built with mousy hair cut in an old-fashioned side parting. Facial features even and uninteresting. Plain. Unremarkable. The kind of guy she'd pass on the street and not notice. Maybe the other women were making up the nicknames just to tease her, a kind of initiation ceremony for the new girl, like being sent for a bucket of blue steam in the shipyards. The man seemed innocuous, innocent and suddenly she felt more at ease. Not entirely confident and still unhappy but not as frightened.

In the cubicle, Kay quickly stripped in the abrupt routine she'd gone through with Wing the day before – the only routine she knew. Goldfinger smiled, discarding his clothes, and chatted, 'I've no had you before.' No answer from Kay. 'First day is it?'

'Yes,' she replied. What else was there to say?

'Been busy?'

'Emmm, not really.'

'I'm surprised, a good-looking young lassie like you.' No answer. 'How old are you?'

'Nineteen.' Easy questions she could answer.

'Really? You look younger. A lot younger.' Kay blushed, remembering her efforts that morning to dress down her appearance. She knew what she had been doing but it was going to get her into trouble. Here was her first customer already complaining, or so she thought. 'When did you start?'

'About an hour ago.'

'Right. You had any johns?' This elicited a puzzled look from Kay, who by now was standing naked before the man, covering her breasts with one arm and with a hand clutching her pubic hair. Naked, that is, aside from the pop socks. 'Punters?' he tried again with no greater success. 'Clients. Have you had any clients?'

'No.' She was in trouble now and feared the guy was going to throw her out of the room and ask for a more popular girl. 'But I've just started.'

'Aye, you said.' The man was naked and smiling a beamer. He still looked like any straight Joe – the bank teller behind his counter, a schoolteacher, a salesman.

'Would you like to lie down?' Kay asked.

'Eh?'

'On your front. So I can massage you.'

'That will be nice. Yeah, nice one.'

As she oiled and stroked the man's back Kay was caught between disgust at his collection of fat, yellow-headed pimples and her hopes that if she was good at the massage that was all she'd be asked to perform. It was the first time she'd massaged any back and she soon ran out of ideas. Stroking up and down was all she could fathom and she worried that her client was going to get bored. He didn't leave her to worry too long. Flipping over on his back, his erection pointed at her, poking into the soft flesh of a breast. She knew what that meant and 'no teeths' as Wing had commanded. She was surprised that Goldfinger's cock didn't taste of deep-fried scampi. Surprised and disgusted at the taste of salt and sweat and something decidedly cheesy. She gagged again and tried to think of something, anything else and failed. Goldfinger thrust upwards with his crotch, forcing his hard-on deep into her throat, making her retch and struggle for breath. Goldfinger didn't seem to mind or care.

'There's a little thing I like to do,' his voice was hoarse, matter of fact. Kay was relieved that he'd slipped his penis out of her mouth but still she felt sick, as if he were still ramming it down her gullet. 'It's just a little thing all the girls do for me.' Goldfinger slipped off the couch and instructed Kay to get up on it but on her hands and knees. She knew enough to expect him to mount her from the rear, doggy style. Clenching her teeth and gripping the sheet, she waited for him. Instead he kissed her buttocks, tickling her and making her feel somehow more exposed. When he gently prised her arse open she felt vulnerable and used but still relieved that the oral sex had stopped. When his finger slipped in to her anus she wasn't so sure. It hurt a little but, more unsettling, it made her want to shit. What if she did? It felt like she was already shitting as someone ogled her backside and she didn't like it at all. Goldfinger. Now she understood.

He hadn't lasted long after that, the excitement of his little extra driving him to orgasm quickly and noisily. They had dressed silently with Kay looking anywhere but at him. Outside she took her seat as the other women, curiously silent, eyed her warily. At the desk, Goldfinger halted and addressed the receptionist, 'Very good. Excellent. Here's something extra for the little girl. Eh, what's her name?'

'She's not decided yet,' the receptionist explained.

'Excellent. Excellent. I'll be back. Soon.' He whistled a tuneless, jaunty ditty as he swung through the doors and away.

'Looks like you've got a fan.' The receptionist had joined the women and handed Kay Goldfinger's tip of ten pounds. 'Not a bad start.'

'Never mind that,' blurted Rita. 'Whit did he make you do, Kay?'

'Well . . .' Kay hesitated, reluctant to talk of sexual matters to women she hardly knew.

'Whit she means is did he stick his finger up yer hole?' It was one of the young women, the wild one with spiky hair who wore her gown loose, showing off her naked body to anyone who glanced.

Kay blushed, hesitated and stammered, 'Well. Well, yes.'

'Ye filthy clart,' Spiky howled.

'Jesus, ye'll no shit for a week,' another joined in, her face full of disgust.

'Shut yer fucking faces, you lot,' Rita growled. 'Kay, doll, ye didnae need tae dae that.'

'But he asked and . . .'

'Aye, but ye dinnae have tae dae everything a punter asks.'

'That's for fucking sure,' agreed Spiky. 'Or Ah'd be well deid by now, man.'

'You only do what's reasonable. What you want to do. What you are willing to do.'

'Silly wee cow,' another of the women offered.

'Leave her alane, you,' Rita growled. 'She's just new. You were new at the game once.'

'Aye, right. Fair do's.'

'Jesus, Ah remember ma first time,' offered Spiky. 'Blow job up a lane for two pound and his dick tasted like gorgonzola.' The women laughed and nodded. 'And he paid me in two bob bits. Think he'd robbed his wife's gas meter.'

'Talking about being new,' butted in the receptionist, who had been standing listening to the conversation. 'You'll need a name.'

'I've got a name,' replied Kay.

'A working name, dear,' the receptionist muttered, returning to her condescending tone. 'Rita is Samantha. Mavis is Susie. Rosemary is Rocky. Who will you be?'

'We dinnae have a Candy in here,' offered Spiky, who Kay now knew to be Rosemary or Rocky. 'Ye can spell it with a K like Kay. That way if yer boyfriend or the social catch ye oot ye can just claim it's a nickname annat.' At that the door went and a new customer walked in, drawing the receptionist back to her duties with one final comment, 'Think about it, okay?'

In the mirror Kay could see that the man was older, silver-haired and slightly portly. Immaculately dressed in an expensive black suit, his shirt seemed ultra white, his tie knotted impeccably. A man of taste and wealth, he looked like a doctor or a judge or a high-powered businessman. Kay bet herself he would choose Rita – tall, sensuous, classy.

'I'll have her,' he said, nodding in Kay's direction. 'The petite lovely, second from the right.'

'Your lucky day right enough,' Rita whispered discreetly from the side of her mouth.

As she closed the cubicle door behind them, the customer reached out and gently took hold of Kay's hands.

'How old are you, my dear?'

'Nineteen.'

'Never that old.' Then with a sly wink, 'Still we'll just pretend that you are.' As he slipped off his jacket he paused, 'One more thing, my dear. What shall I call you?' She didn't hesitate.

'Kay. My name is Kay.' She was no one's Candy and never would be.

Mother Pimp (1987)

For months now something had been worrying Kay. Here she was almost a year into the business and still her debts were not cleared and she was no closer to walking away and setting up a new life in her own home. It didn't take many sessions lying on her back, blocking off the distress of some punter's condition by working through her finances in her head to realise that the sums didn't add up. Something was wrong.

Kay was popular at work and the highest earner she knew. Five days a week, sometimes seven, at the sauna and home visits to regulars as well as new clients who had heard of her. She knew that they liked her small girlish build and played the role with increasing perfection. She had shaved off her pubic hair, learning that most of the punters preferred that, but it was also an added spice to those who wanted their women young, very young. Her wardrobe had been augmented with designer clothes. When called for she could appear as a sophisticated lady dripping sex appeal. When they wanted her young, the pinafore and its newly purchased replicas would be brought out. In her own time she looked like only Kay could in an esoteric collection of outfits and a larger gathering of shoes that suited her and were distinct, unique, seldom seen on the streets except on her body. All that cost money but not enough to rook her. Something wasn't right.

For nine months she had been working at every opportunity. In spite of her horror and disgust she refused no punter – even the ones the other women warned her off. She had reasoned that she was only doing this for cash, was only selling herself for a short time and the more she earned as quickly as possible, then the sooner she could walk away and start her own life. Some weeks she was earning a thousand pounds – not bad at 1987 prices for a woman not yet twenty-one. Still she was broke. Something had to change.

Since that very first morning, when her mother had driven her to the sauna and waited to drive her home, they had had an arrangement. Whatever Kay earned she paid her mother thirty per cent plus a fee for the taxi service. At first this had seemed only fair. For a start, Kay didn't want any taxi driver to know where she worked. Those guys tended to be local, neighbours even, and Kay had a secret to keep. Anyway, she knew that one or two drivers passed information on to the police, others worked for firms who ran saunas elsewhere and there was the occasional rogue who expected regular sex in exchange for keeping quiet. Abigail's car was a far safer option.

The percentage payment to Abigail had also seemed to be reasonable. After all, Kay's mother had taken her in when she had nothing apart from the clothes she stood up in. She was willing to give her accommodation, feed her, look after when she couldn't pay a bean. As soon as Kay started working, it seemed fair that she paid this back to Abigail pro rata.

Then again, Kay had been with her mother precisely two days before she had started work at Bubbles. Not exactly a long period of dependence. And there was something else bugging Kay.

'You're gonnae get approached by men,' Rita had warned her one day.

'Is that not the point?' Kay had joked.

'Men that will offer you better money,' continued Rita, not smiling.

'Good . . .'

'Not good,' interrupted Rita. 'They'll want ye to work with them. Tell you they can get you better clients, easier work, classier areas, more money. They'll probably come in as a punter to start with and be dead nice to ye. Pay ye a bit extra, be good tae ye sexually.'

'Sounds okay so far,' replied Kay, wondering what the point was.

'Aye, until ye work for them. Then it's take any trick they tell ye, working seven days a week, half the money, maybe more, goes tae them.'

'Half, that's not fair.' Kay was getting the point but Rita wasn't finished.

'They'll tell you that you're tae bring in a certain amount every day. If ye havnae got it they'll gie ye a doing or maybe rape ye. And later they'll make it up tae ye, being sweet and that. Early doors they'll give ye drugs pretending aw they're doing is showing ye a good time. Afore ye know it ye need the smack and ye're working for the daily hits – aye an tae pay yer fucking pimp.' It was one of the few times Kay had seen Rita angry.

'A pimp?'

'That's what they are – men that live off a working girl's earnings – BASTARDING PIMPS.'

'I'll never do that, Rita,' replied Kay, 'I wouldn't be so stupid.'

'Ah hope no,' replied her older friend, 'but many a smart lassie's working a rainy street corner for them right now.' Rita stopped and lit a cigarette. 'Men! Never work for the fuckers, Kay, they'll only ruin ye.'

'No way,' replied Kay and she had meant it sincerely.

Now months later Kay was beginning to wonder if she hadn't become one of those smart lassies working for someone else. Maybe her good friend's advice fell a bit short of the mark in failing to warn her that women can also be pimps, that mothers can be pimps. In a good week of earnings of a thousand pounds, Kay had to hand three hundred to her mother as her percentage and an additional two hundred for the taxi service of the few miles between their home and the sauna several times a day. That was five hundred quid and half her earnings in anyone's book. In a bad week of, say, five hundred pounds, she still had to pay Abigail the money for the lifts plus her cut. In those weeks her mother took almost three-quarters of her total income. How could she have been so stupid?

Kay bought a bottle of vodka and decided to have a heart-to-heart with her mother. The first drink hadn't been consumed when Abigail butted in.

'You ungrateful little cow,' she had started.

'I'm not ungrateful,' pleaded Kay, 'it's just . . .'

'You had fuck all when you came here. Now look at you.'

'But remember,' Kay persisted, 'remember that night sitting here talking. The night before I started . . .'

'I spent half that night up with you, supporting you . . .'

'I know, but . . .'

'. . . and in the morning I had all your clothes washed and ready. What thanks do I get?'

'It's just,' Kay persisted, 'I was only meant to be a working girl for a short time. Remember? Clear my debts and get my own house . . .'

'A short time?' laughed Abigail. 'Don't be so fucking stupid. You're a whore for life.'

'Mum, no.' Kay wanted to cry, to slap out. All those months, punter after punter, she had clung on to the one fact that made it all acceptable – getting out. 'Nooo, I'm going to stop, and to do that I need more of my earnings – not it all. Maybe we could discuss a set amount I pay each week . . . say a couple of hundred and I'll start getting taxis to work, eh?'

Abigail didn't need the time to think. She recognised the vast reduction in her income. 'Fine!' she bawled. 'If that's what you want then clear up and fuck off out of here, you ungrateful little cunt. You'll never cope on your own. You'll be back here in weeks. Now get out – go on, fuck off.'

Rita had also omitted to warn Kay that one standard trick of the pimp is feigned rejection. Maybe Abigail thought she was playing that trick. The problem with her strategy was her working girl was no junkie and had no sexual relationship with her, and she had failed to notice one other important factor – Kay had changed a great deal since she started selling her services. This was not the Kay she thought she knew.

Within days Kay had rented her own flat in the south side back in Arden. Within a week it was decorated and furnished to her own taste. By week two she found herself dolled up in her Yves Saint Laurent suit – a little black number with a box jacket and a split up the back of the tight skirt – five-inch heels and perfume, nothing else. Her appointment at the Tropical Palms was agreed in less than twenty minutes. This time she didn't need to prove she could do the business, the proprietor having already heard of her by reputation. The twenty minutes were spent negotiating her fees, how much above the standard rate she would be paid. The managers were a male and a female, partners in life as well as in business. The owners were a large group of brothers well known as gangsters who had come close to running the city streets twenty years earlier. After reassurances that the brothers never stepped inside the premises, Kay got down to business.

The managers wanted her to be available for overnight stays, usually in the hotel rooms of businessmen passing through. They wanted her to be up for weekends and longer visits, even if it meant trips abroad. They wanted reassurances that she could hold a conversation, knew which cutlery to use, had a wardrobe of outfits for every occasion. They were keen to have an idea of the number of her regular clients likely to follow her. She hadn't thought of that prospect and, caught on the hop, gave an estimate – an embarrassingly low estimate as it turned out. But it was enough for her prospective employers. They doubled her rates, gave her a few hundred pounds up front and shook hands on the deal.

Kay left, much better off, and celebrated by buying her first car. Okay, she had sworn never to take on more debt and had just breached the promise by buying the car on credit. But having rid herself of her mother's leeching and increased her income by moving from Bubbles to the new, higher-class salon, she was confident of being able to afford the expense. Besides, she had learned Rita's lesson well about avoiding becoming the wage slave of some pimp – of whatever gender. The car offered control, freedom, flexibility. Kay had decided if she was going to sell herself for sex she wasn't going to be a prostitute, a whore, just another working girl. She was going to be a top-class call girl, the best. She was no one's plaything and that was how it was going to stay.

The Professional (1991)

'Come oan in out of that rain. Ye'll catch yer death.' Rita threw her front door wide open and Kay stepped over the threshold into a sea of soft light, enveloping heat and an aura of sweet jasmine scent. Kay loved that house as she loved Rita. 'Here, get yer coat off and Ah'll get a towel for yer hair.' It was a typical Glasgow winter's night with low clouds blotting out the moon and hard rain lashing at every turn. Kay had got soaked in the short walk from the street corner where the hackney cab had dropped her at the off-licence where she had purchased wine for the visit. The taxi driver had offered her a free fare in return for her phone number – an offer she'd refused delicately but assertively in a well-practised routine. As she had discovered her sexuality through her work over the last five years so all the men she'd met seemed to tune into her awakening, her availability.

'I've brought you some wine, Rita,' Kay called out. 'Will I put it in the fridge?'

'Lovely, we'll have that after we finish this aff.' Rita entered the room with a tray of wine and glasses balanced in one hand and a thick bath towel draped over the other. 'But c'mere and sit down – there by the couch.' Glasses full and clinked, Rita gently dried Kay's long hair, the younger woman sitting on the floor at her feet.

'Do you remember when I would've gone all weak-kneed at this?' Kay asked with a giggle.

'Ha, aye. Ye silly wee midden.'

'God I was that . . . that . . .'

'Naive?'

'Aye, naive.'

'And lovely too. It was a big compliment, so it was.'

'A reddy it was that embarrassing.'

'Well, ye had tae fancy the only straight working girl Ah know.'

'I know. All the other girls in that Bubbles going at it with each other all the time and here's me thinking it was only you that fancied ME.' The two women broke into loud laughter.

'They used tae try and get you into bed aw the time, Kay.'

'I realise that now.'

'Christ, they weren't exactly that subtle, hen.'

'No, true. I'd more free eccies and blues and dope and speed than I could cope with.'

'Must've cost them a bloody fortune.'

'Haa, aye. And it never worked.'

'An what aboot the wee shows?'

'Whaaaaat now?'

'Did yese ever wonder why it was always you that was the second girl?'

'Aye. Oh no . . .'

'Oh aye. Mean ye were always popular wi the punters wi that wee girl lost look but it was the other lassies that made sure tae suggest ye.'

'Christ. That first time. It was worse than the interview with Wing. Fat guy in the corner wanking off and I'm meant to get it on with a woman.'

'Every man's fantasy, so they say.'

'Not mine. I just didn't know what to do so I followed her lead.'

'Just what she'd hoped for, ye wee soul.'

'But the dirty cow was manky. Hadn't washed for weeks. Oh Christ, she was humming.' Rita shook her head in sympathy and laughed at the same time. The poor hygiene of others was just one of the common pitfalls of their profession.

'They was that desperate for yese, Kay honey, because they couldn't have ye.'

'Aye, but not very nice. Like you were nice. Very kind to me.' The two women lapsed into silence, the only sound in the room being the low voice of Frank Sinatra doing it his way again from the stereo. Kay broke the spell, 'Well, now you know two.'

'What? Eh, two what?' Rita started, her thoughts suddenly interrupted.

'Two straight working girls. There's you and there's me.'

'You sure, Kay?'

'Ha ha, absolutely bloody certain.'

'What was all that about then – you 'n' me annat?'

'Truth?'

'Of course, doll. Always the truth between pals.'

'Well, I was lonely and scared and, well, other stuff.'

'Other stuff like yer mammy?' Kay twisted round to look at her friend, surprised and unnerved at the accuracy of her observation.

'How did you know?'

'Ah've know a few mothers to act like pimps but she was the worst Ah've come across.'

'She took her cut . . .'

'Aye an the bloody rest.'

'Didn't realise at the time but her and her pal . . . they talked me into going along to Bubbles.'

'Aye?'

'Well, my mammy's pal was a hooker for years – street girl – I know that now. Mind it would've had to be dark streets for anybody to take on the ugly bint.'

'How long you been on the game now? Three years is it?'

'No, four years past.'

'And you still believe that crap about hookers havin' tae be gorgeous?'

'Well . . .'

'Trouble is, now yer working at the top with the best-looking girls and for fancy dough. Most of the girls are just ordinary-looking women . . .'

'Aye, I know, I'm just angry at her.'

'Ye've every right tae be.'

'And my dear mammy helped me out over that first year.'

'Aye?'

'No, she charged me.'

'The greedy bitch.'

'That's why I moved on – suppose it was good for me, though it wasn't intended to be.'

'Yer mammy – pimping ye. Ye would've been cheaper working for some gangster, hen, an Ah'm no jokin'.'

'But while all this was going on you were being so kind to me I became a wee bit infatuated. Sorry.'

'Hey, like Ah said it was a big compliment and didnae half get they other besoms jealous. Ha, thought the wee spiky one was goin' tae knife me one night. Daggers in her eyes.'

'There were some laughs though, eh?'

'Always are in this game when yer winning.' Kay thought of Rita as one woman who had made the business work for her. Happily married, three healthy and successful children, a good home and her health all intact. She was a winner all right.

'Remember Trigger?' Kay took to a fit of the giggles just thinking about the punter.

'How could Ah forget? Aw skin and bone wi a dinger that would make a darkie green wi envy.'

'First time I did him I thought it was a joke.'

'Disnae look real does it, sticking oot a foot and a half frae that emaciated pile o bones?'

'Thought I'd never get it in me.'

'But ye did, eh, ye greedy wee muffin.'

'Aye, but I didn't like it.'

'Why is it that the guys wi the biggest cocks are the least able tae use them?'

'God works in mysterious ways . . . so she does.'

'Then that other guy . . . nice-looking bloke used to come in every Thursday. Drove a wee red sports car?' Rita poured more wine.

'Bender!'

'He wisnae! He loved his fanny,' Rita teased, knowing Kay still fell for it every time.

'No, we called him Bender cause his dick bent in the middle at almost right angles. Remember?'

'Aaaaye, how could Ah forget him. Christ, he used tae rattle ma ovaries when Ah did him.'

'The biggest laugh I used to get was at the Cleaners.'

'Fuck, aye, they're easy money. Always wondered about offering tae dae them here. Save me hours of boredom and keep the place real spick an span.'

'My first one was a real toff. I think he was a judge or something.'

'They lot are always well perverted, hen.'

'He looked so well-to-do I thought he'd be after nooky. There's me throwing my kit off and being all seductive and he's looking like I just shit in his mouth.' Together the women howled in glee, simultaneously remembering another client with specialist tastes.

Rita gasped, 'Christ, Scat, he was the clartiest bastard Ah ever did meet. Ah never did him, did you?'

'No way.'

'It was that wee spiky bitch volunteering aw the time. Man-hater that she was. Ah couldnae work oot how she could manage tae shite on demand. Every bloody time he came in!'

'But she did.'

'Aye, an used tae boast tae her girlfriends how she couldnae shite without pissing at the same time. A turd in his gob an a golden shower up his nose . . .'

'Wonder he didn't suffocate.'

'Wing would've charged him extra if he'd known.'

Kay and Rita drank and reminisced with a frankness denied them elsewhere. Even with knowing and supportive families, prostitutes don't talk about their work. That would be to rub salt in some barely healed emotional wounds or, at the very least, invite disgust and misunderstanding. Caution also had to be adopted with most of their colleagues, in case the greedy ones sussed a bit of trade and tried to undercut them in price or offered to go even further with the clients. Besides, the turnover of women in the business was so huge that a chatty work associate one day is a stranger never to be seen again the next. Now and then a former working girl with a grievance against a sauna owner or some of the other women would go to the police or a journalist on their favourite tabloid. Kay and Rita knew only too well that loose talk could lead to a visit from the CID or, worse, find its way on to page three of the newspapers, complete with names, addresses and photograph. But tonight they were two friends in private. Tonight they could talk and laugh.

'God, mind Daddy Bear?' giggled Kay.

'Aye, he was nice.'

'Maybe, but see that first time with him, I thought you really were going to thrash me.' Kay slapped her friend lightly on the thigh.

'Maybe Ah should've, an' chased ye oot o this business.' It was a constant undertone between the two, mentioning issues which might make them leave the sex industry.

'But what was that all about – getting you to pretend you were spanking me, punishing me?'

'God knows, but he was harmless enough.'

'Aye, but do you never wonder what makes some of these men do what they do?'

'Aye, Ah used tae but gave it up a long time ago as a lost cause.' Rita poured more wine. 'And Ah recommend you dae the same. Ye'll just waste yer energy.'

'But you have to be curious,' Kay persisted. 'These men behaving like that with us yet their wives and kids and workmates not having a clue . . .'

'We're the waste bins for their secrets, their perversions, their little tastes that would see them drummed oot o the Brownies.'

'That's for sure.'

'By coming to us once in a while they can go on as normal in their day-to-day lives.'

'Aye, but wouldn't it be better if they could be open about their peccadilloes?'

'No, it would do us oot o business,' Rita laughed. 'An hey, that's an awfy big word for a wee woman. Peccadillo . . .'

'Talking o peccadilloes,' Kay giggled, 'I love the Trannies.'

'Aye, now their secrets are a shame.'

'First one I had looked like someone out of *Psycho*.'

'Whit?'

'You know, grown man dressed in his mammy's old-fashioned clothes.'

'Aye, wee souls struggle tae buy their outfits openly.' Rita nodded her head in sympathetic agreement.

'I still visit one I met when I was at Bubbles,' confessed Kay. 'I buy him clothes that fit and suit him. Some nights all he wants me to do is teach him more about make-up or restyle his wig.'

'Easy work if you can get it.'

'Aye, but I'm fond of him,' replied Kay in a more serious tone. 'Besides, he pays me well, whatever we do.'

'Better no let Wing find oot,' warned Rita, 'he'll want his commission.'

'Yeah,' agreed Kay, 'and backdated too no doubt.'

The two women moved on to the topic of Wing and his meanness. How he'd started by charging them for the laundry service for the towels, then a hefty contribution towards heating and hot water and eventually condoms – a move that resulted in some of the women forgoing the use of protection in some sort of industrial action. It was a strike Kay didn't join in – she knew the risks. Instead she accepted an offer from another sauna owner, moving on and up.

'Ye were dead right tae move, ye know,' offered Rita. 'Literally dead right. Two o they lassies that Ah know of have the virus.' The two women held their silence for a moment as if in respect to fallen colleagues, paying homage to the daily risks they knew their work entailed.

'And you were right to retire, Rita.'

'Aye, past ma sell-by date, hen. But you, you've the future right at yer feet. Well, maybe a wee bit higher up, eh?' Kay had changed work premises several times, always moving on for higher fees and a better class of clients. Wherever she went, a host of her regular punters followed. All she knew was the sex industry but if she'd been bothered to find out more she would have learned that she was working for members of Glasgow's underworld of organised crime. She knew nothing of that and didn't care.

'I'm glad I've moved on. You know I had planned to chuck this after a year and now it's been four. But, I feel as if I've found my calling, know what I mean? Discovered what I'm good at. As if I'm in control.'

'Yer at the top.'

'Aye, suppose I am.'

'But what about you, ma wee Kay? Any boyfriends or that?'

'No, not just now.'

Rita threw her a questioning look. 'Not for a long while, eh?'

'Rita, can I ask you something?'

'Course, doll.'

'There's some punters, the ones that are good at going down on you, I get off on. You know, orgasm. You think that's weird?'

'It's no unusual, pet. But dinnae let the bleeding heart liberals hear ye say that. We're aw supposed tae be deprived junkies that get beaten up by oor pimps if we dinnae earn. Oh, aye and frigid.'

'Did you then . . . get off on some clients?'

'Aye, of course, but Ah always knew it wisnae . . . well . . . no enough. Ye have tae make yer ain life.'

'What do you mean?'

'You need yer ain life. Settle down. It's time ye got yersel a man, Kay, unless ye've changed yer mind aboot the dykes.' Rita smiled, trying to lighten the serious tone the chat had fallen into.

'No, I've not changed my mind. But men, well, they change you.'

'Sometimes for the better.'

'Sometimes for the worse.'

'Men are no aw users, Kay.'

'No, I suppose not. I suppose some men are okay.' Kay believed what her friend was saying but was unnerved by some niggling doubt she couldn't put into words. Like The Hanging Tree of her childhood it was always there, always waiting. 'One more glass of wine then I'll get off up the road and let you get to bed.' Kay filled their glasses to the brim with by now lukewarm white wine soured by the heat from the bubbling gas fire.

'Grand, a toast. Let's have a toast.'

'Yeah, go on, make a toast.' The little girl that was still in Kay sat up brightly, watching her older mentor with keen bright eyes.

'Here's tae the future. Our future and whatever it may bring.' The two women clinked glasses and drank deeply for the last time.

Within months Rita would be dead, battered to death in a crumbling back alley of an English city during a brief lapse in her retirement. Within months Kay was to make an acquaintance that would begin to change the shape of her life forever. But that night they drank and hugged. Real friends in a cold world.

Puppy Love

Turning away to slip her dress over her head, her unexpected and unusual shyness caught her by surprise and set her giggling. For five years on a daily basis she had carried out every possible sexual function, faced every deviance, met every taste and always with strangers, so why had she suddenly turned coy?

He was different. A first. For five years her sex life was predominantly professional, peppered with an occasional one-night stand, usually some working girl's brother or a friend of some boss. All set up, expected and short-lived. All marked by a prior knowledge of her profession and the assumptions that tagged along in its wake like a bad smell following sewage. Till tonight.

'Please, just one dance,' he'd smiled for the umpteenth time and she'd refused again just so she could hear him ask nicely one more time. 'No? God, you're a hard woman to please. Drink . . . how about a drink then?'

'Okay.'

'Okay? Really? Smashing.'

'Vodka and Coke, please.'

'Voddie and black it is.' He smiled again and waltzed off through the crowd of dancers and loiterers, heading to the bar. He stopped and turned back, 'You won't run off will you? Please?' Kay wasn't going to run off. She was enjoying his attention far too much. He was slim but strong looking. Handsome in a boyish way. Wore fashionable gear showing individual taste and care. She liked that, having become a fashion

102

freak in the last few years – a fashion fiend with her own particular style. He didn't even know her name and yet here he was chasing her of all the other women in the place. Lenny Lovat he said his name was and, for a second, she wondered if he'd made that up.

'You're too suspicious, Kay,' she'd chided herself. 'Spent too much time surrounded by pimps, punters and pros. This is just a normal guy. A sweet, straight normal guy.' When he came back he'd handed her the drink with a smile and she'd grinned and offered him Ecstasy. Straight, yeah she wanted that, but boring no. He took it and tongued it. It was a symbolic exchange and from then on they were together.

Danced out, back at her place in the early hours she was laughing at her shyness. The number of men she'd simply stripped off for even that day without giving two hoots. For once she wanted to watch her man undress for her, felt warm with anticipation at the thought of him naked. Kay dropped the hem of her dress, turned towards Lenny and watched him as she slowly unbuttoned and unzipped. 'This is how it's meant to be,' she thought and felt an unfamiliar tingle of anticipation. As she watched him undo his buttons and unzip his fly, her heart was racing, fluttering with a blend of nerves and lust she found unsettling. She was just twenty-four years old, a sexual artisan of the highest grade and here she was feeling like a virgin bride on her wedding night. The eccies had long since kicked in, making her loved up, eager. As his trousers slipped off his hips she ogled his crotch, looking for a bulge in his boxers, better – no underwear at all. They slithered to the ground revealing . . . another pair of trousers. And under his shirt, another shirt. Kay thought she'd seen everything in her profession but this was new.

'Why you wearing two outfits?' Her question was obvious and plain.

'Aw, it's my joab,' he replied absent-mindedly, continuing to undress with absolute concentration.

'What the hell do you do?' She was lost for any possible explanation. Her life was about wearing as little as possible and getting out of it and into it as quickly as possible. Wearing two sets of clothes was entirely beyond her ken.

'Ah'm a joiner.'

'Right.' He looked up and saw she meant that she still didn't understand. 'Sometimes it gets really cold out on site.' He looked away and fiddled with his second set of shirt buttons.

'Oh, right.' Relief tinged her voice. A joiner, now that was straight and honest. A joiner was a good thing to be. 'Don't want you getting cold now, do we?' Kay padded across the room wearing nothing but her chemise, which she knew clung to her body, and the silk swished softly with every movement. 'Kay will keep you warm.' And she did. That night and for a long while to come.

Tell Her Ah'm Tied Up

'CUT THE FUCKIN' LIGHTS OOT, MAN.' The road went dark as soon as she flicked the switch. Tree ghosts and grey hedges slowly emerging as she drove from memory and, as ever, fast and furious. What was it he'd said that first time? Oh yes, 'Yese have tae have the eyesight o a cat, man. Fuckin' magic eyesight.' He was wrong. She couldn't see a thing. She didn't look at the road, even in broad daylight. She sensed it. Felt it there in its bends, twists and turns. If it bevelled more steeply she leaned as it went over. The tarmac shrilled out to her as a soul sister, a saviour. The road belonged to her in dark or in day. And she only drove one way – flat out.

'FUCK'S SAKE SLOW DOON, YE'LL FUCKIN' KILL US.' Once, always once, he bottled it on every expedition. Kay heard but never listened. He'd soon relax again. This was where she was comfortable, felt at ease. For years she thought it was the skin game she controlled till she discovered driving. Not just any driving but getaway driver for the top tie-up man in the country. She wished it wasn't this way, but it was, so she embraced it with open arms.

'Where do you get your money, Lenny?' she'd asked, more out of admiration than curiosity. For a year they'd been together, living like nobility, but he never did a nine-to-five in all that time. Every couple of weeks he'd stay out late on his own, warning her in advance. At first she thought that he was bored or seeing someone else because all the men that she knew did – except for Lenny. Things were too good. She'd let her guard down and shown her real self, her feelings and her passions – all that she knew never to do when doing the business. Muffling the shrill release of an orgasm was hard learned but wise. Never let a punter feel your pleasure or they'd think you owed them something. With him she screamed to the rooftops and clung to his back, her legs wrapped tight around his waist, never wanting to let go. Falling in lust – obviously a big mistake. Just she couldn't help herself. Now she'd pay the price as he warned her not to stay up. Every time she expected him to disappear forever. But no. He'd crawl back into bed in the early hours just before dawn. Tired and sweaty but sober and horny, seeking her out through the veil of her slumbers. It wasn't another woman or man he'd been with so she'd asked, 'Where do you get your money, Lenny?'

'Don't ask, hen.'

'I just did.'

'Naw, seriously, you dinnae want tae know.'

'But I do.'

'Naw, ye . . .'

Three, four, five times and more she'd asked and dropped it after the same conversation. He'd tell her in his own good time she reasoned and cuddled in, silent and happy with a good man.

But he didn't tell her so she asked again, 'Where DO you get your money, Lenny?'

'From thieving.' The words seemed to reverberate through the smooth skin of his chest and into her ear, a muffled echo but deafening nevertheless.

'What?'

'Thieving. Ah get it frae thieving.' Kay couldn't balance his persistent statement with the polite, loving man who treated her with nothing but respect. She knew thieves. Had grown up in a den of them in Arden. They were slimy, edgy lowlifes who'd pinch their mammies' purses on giro day. Nothing like Lenny Lovat. Nothing at all. He must be teasing her.

'You winding me up?' She nipped his nearest nipple and

scrunched her fingers into the flesh at his side where she knew he was deliciously tickly. His knees jerked up and he twisted to one side, but instead of the playful retaliation she was used to he pushed her hands down and held her by the wrists.

'Listen, Kay, Ah'm a thief,' he said, now looking straight into her face. 'Ah steal frae hooses.'

'No you don't.' Even as Kay shook her head she could tell that she was wrong and he was telling the truth. His eyes had the look of desperation and relief. It was exactly the expression she imagined Roman Catholics had as they unburdened themselves in the confessional. Lenny just nodded his head and stared at her po-faced. She stroked a strand of hair off his face, wrapped her legs around his and instructed, 'Tell me about it. Just tell me what you do.'

They didn't get much sleep that night. Even when he'd finished speaking Kay couldn't sleep. Her head was buzzing with the new part of her man she'd just learned all about. She thought she knew him. Touch him there and that happens. Stroke him here and something else. Dress with a short skirt and that perfume, he'd smile all night. His drug preferences. His time for shitting. The noise his breath made when he was in a deep sleep. Tea with milk, coffee with two sugars. Hair going frizzy if he let it dry naturally after a shower. The feel of his skin – everywhere. Laughs and how they changed depending on his mood, the company, the reason. Those expressive eyes and their different meaning, one look for every occasion. She thought she knew him but realised she hadn't a clue.

Long after his breath had fallen into the regular, heaved sighs of sleep she lay beside him and thought of all he'd told her that night. Not just any old type of thief but a specialist. A robber of antiques from large houses. A tie-up merchant. Planning his raids with precision. Risking being identified by the victim. Securing them with rope then brandishing a shotgun into their faces. Her Lenny? Threatening? Judging the old couple's fear till he reckoned they'd told him all about the valuables in the house. Not pushing it too far lest they die of a heart attack or suffocation or hysteria. Intimidating without having to deliver the blow. Pushing them to the limit to reveal where they'd secured the goods they'd spent their lives earning or stealing.

Then getting out of there in one piece – fast and efficient, praying that he hadn't triggered an alarm beam too sophisticated for his knowledge. Dumping the stolen car. Stripping off his top layer of clothes – joiner, a fucking joiner – he's a thief and careful with it. Car and clothes set on fire and off on the legitimate motor. Stopping off at a pay phone and alerting the police – anonymously, of course. Hoping that the boys in blue wouldn't hover over their unfinished cuppa and arrive when the old dear had smothered on her gag. Lenny wasn't just a thief. He was a tightrope walker with no safety net. By the time he woke hours later Kay had made a decision.

'Let me come along with you on a job,' she'd asked her tired, still shame-faced man over that first cup of coffee and cigarette.

'Aw, Kay, it's dodgy. Risky.'

'I know but I want to see what you do.' He'd thought about it, wavering on the precipice of saying no and a row with his woman. An experience he hadn't had often but often enough to want to avoid.

'We cannae have tourists on these shows.'

'I know.'

'Ah work alone. Always have.'

'Okay.'

'So what can you do if you come along?' She thought and had no ready answer but found herself replying nevertheless.

'Well, I can drive.'

She didn't need lights. From that first night on that bending, unlit country road in the wilds of Ayrshire she knew she was good at the driving. So did he. She had grown to depend on that man who'd turned out to be a tie-up merchant. She couldn't drown her feelings because of something he did. He was still Lenny. She was still Kay. They were still Kay and Lenny.

She'd gone along terrified, desperate to learn more about him, and ended up addicted to the crime and more knowledgeable about herself. Kay loved the excitement. It was as if she was a free adolescent, the way it should have been. The risk taking, the chance of capture, just knowing she was breaking the rules. She was hooked but also good. An addiction to speed behind the wheel had finally paid dividends. Even Lenny conceded she was a better driver than him, better than most he'd hired from time to time. As a partnership, they increased their workload. Lenny the tie-up man and Kay the getaway driver. She was good. One of the best and, besides, as long as they didn't get caught nobody would ever know. Or so Kay thought.

Down in the underworld, Lenny Lovat was renowned as one of the best in a difficult line of business. Everybody watched him. Now they were watching his new partner. Very good she was too.

What Goes Around

The day Lenny got arrested she flipped. Her man was in jail. Everything in her life turned sour. What would she do without him? What would she do without him? Kay did what she always did and pulled herself together, dressed in her best and set off to visit him. Lenny was smart, always ahead of the game. He would know a way out.

'Ah'm well fucked, doll.' He looked pale and wan in the white light of the prison visiting room. 'Seems like they've IDd me and traced the goods. A double fucking whammy wi jam oan it.' He'd been fingered for a raid he'd carried out on his own in the town of Gourock – a middle-class retirement hole down on the Clyde estuary. Lots of big houses and much money in the keeping of grey-haired custodians. Lenny had been a regular visitor to Gourock.

'What happened, Lenny?' Her question wasn't as pathetic as it seemed. Mr Lenny Careful Lovat getting caught was an aberration of the nature of life.

'They raided the goods handler the day after Ah'd delivered. Got him on a stack o stuff. So he grassed me up.'

'Bastard.'

'Aye, but it's the way of it these days, hen. Trading bodies for charges – he's jist doing whit most folk do and no as bad as most, eh?'

'But . . .'

'But nothing. It's just ma Donald Duck. Ma turn for a wee spell.'

Lenny explained it could have been worse. At least on that

particular job he had been after goods to order. A painting.

'Widnae mind but it wisnae even hauf decent. Jist some auld foggy bastard in fancy dress.' Kay wondered if it had been a famous Picasso or a nice painting of a small child with an angelic face crying large crystal tears whether he would have felt any better. What did her man think of pictures, of art, of dance, of music not blasted at your drug-sodden head in some club? She didn't know. 'Didnae have tae threaten much. Straight in, grabbed the old dear, tied her up and wheeched that picture right oot the door. Easy-peasy.'

'But they've got you and a witness,' Kay couldn't understand his sense of optimism.

'Two witnesses but. Aye, they've got me but only for one. And this one – nae arms. Nae shooter.' Lenny pulled on his roll-up and smiled.

'They've still got you though.'

'Aye, for a week.'

'One week?' Kay had convinced herself that he'd be going to prison for years. This was all new to her.

'Ah've a bail hearing next week. Solicitor says it's a scoosh case. Ah'll be back in your bed that same night.' Kay didn't understand this life. Didn't understand it at all.

At Lenny's court hearing his lawyer's prediction proved to be accurate. Sitting in the well of the court house, Kay couldn't hear or understand anything that was going on. When Lenny turned to her and beamed a broad smile, only then did she understand. They waltzed out of the court building arms wrapped round each other, stopping every few steps to kiss and nuzzle each other. The granting of bail was good but his lawyer was predicting a prison sentence at trial. They needed a plan.

As Kay was reversing her car out into the main road she wracked her brains for something that might help. There was nothing there. She simply hadn't a clue about what was important in this world of Lenny's. So she tried to lighten the conversation.

'Here, I saw someone in court I recognised.'

'Aye, me.' Lenny squeezed her knee and dragged on his first real cigarette for a week.

'Aye, and someone else.' He twisted round to gaze at her face. 'From my working days.'

'Aye, right.' Lenny had dealt well with Kay's revelation that she'd been a working girl but was still raw at the memory. He'd asked her to give it up a week after they'd met and she answered with a hug, covering his face in wet, sloppy kisses.

'That guy in the black gown.' Now she had his attention.

'Whit guy?' There had been about nine in the court including the sheriff.

'The guy on the right. At the opposite side of the table from your solicitor.'

'The prosecutor?'

'Tall guy, skinny, big nose with broken veins and a bald patch.'

'Aye the procurator-fucking-fiscal. Ya fucking beauty. Tell me aboot him.' Lenny's enthusiasm frightened Kay. She was only trying to lighten the chat and hoped she wasn't about to disappoint him.

'He was a regular when I worked at the Tropical Palms. You know the one in Holland Street run by that fat guy called Davie.'

'Never mind that, what did the PF want? Mean what was he intae?'

'Oh, right. He liked them young. Younger the better. Took me a good few times but see if a wee lassie started . . . well he was their man.'

'Yeeees. Fucking yeeeeceees!' Lenny grabbed Kay and kissed her face.

'Woooah, watch it you or I'll crash.'

'Ye wee smasher, Kay. Ah think ye've just saved ma life.'

Free the Gourock One

The Polaroid camera made it more obscene somehow. God knows she'd lain on her back with her legs wide open on many occasions. But that click-whirring-thrimp that the camera made put an edge on it all. She didn't think it would work. The message was too obscure. 'One fanny's much like another,' is what she thought but dared not share with her man, Lenny. His enthusiasm was so infectious.

'This'll sort him, doll, just you wait and see.' And he clicked-whirr-thrimped again and again. They had a collection of pictures and he took his time choosing the best one. To her they all looked the same. No face, no place, just her legs akimbo and her sex winking back at the lens.

'You write the message – but print it mind,' he'd ordered.

'What'll I write?'

'Jist this – REMEMBER ME? WE REMEMBER YOU! – Okay?' Lenny drank a deep draught of his lager and downed another couple of blues. She worried about how much Valium he'd been taking since he made bail. Always a regular user, he was on fifty, maybe sixty tabs a day and wandered round with that stupid, wet grin on his face. He even grinned while he was sleeping, so no consolation there.

'Too obscure, Lenny.'

'Too whit?'

'If you write that he'll no know what you're on about. No know that it's your case he's got to be careful about.' Lenny rubbed his face, the weariness of the blues washout showing suddenly in his bloodshot eyes.

ARMED CANDY

'Aye. Aye, ye've goat a point there.' He thought for a long moment, then, 'Just add FREE L.L. THE GOUROCK ONE – how's that?'

'What if he susses and calls your bluff?'

'Ma whit?'

'There's not that many people with the initials L.L., is there?'

'Nuh.'

'Well . . .'

'Well fuck all – jist write it wid yese?' Kay wrote the message, wondering if her man had lost it.

Lenny broke into the procurator fiscal's home while he and his wife were sleeping in bed. A few objects were moved around and the photograph-cum-message left. Days later, Lenny was arrested not for the break-in but for new charges which had come to light courtesy of the grassing dealer. The fresh charges involved a shotgun and one old dame who had died of a heart attack soon after her tie-up. Lenny was in trouble.

Awaiting his trial the two came to an arrangement. 'Ah cannae get through this without some help, hen,' he'd explained during a visit. 'Need ma little helpers, know? You remember Kathy? Mind? Big Eck's bird? Go see her an she'll explain.' Kathy taught Kay all there was to know about smuggling drugs into prison. Cheeking the drugs at both sides of your mouth so your face looked symmetrical. The French kiss exchange was simple and straightforward but wide open to a random search. Greetings cards were the best and the safest option. Fancy, padded cards were the easiest. A new razor edge and slice the cardboard open. Mincing the Ecstasy or the speed or the blues – grinding them down finely till there was no bulge in the wrap and then gluing it back together, preening the excess off neatly with a new blade. Wearing rubber gloves throughout so her fingerprints could not be traced. Left-handed writing from non-existent girlfriends of Lenny's or his named associates. One hundred speed balls in one card – or any drug of preference. Kay practised and practised till

114

she became the best. Word spread and other cons' wives visited her asking her to prepare a wee present for their menfolk. She always obliged, of course.

As Lenny's trial approached he was being warned of a long stretch. Though he was still convinced he'd nobbled the PF he wanted more insurance. When he was found guilty he wanted a plea of mitigation in favour of a non-custodial sentence. Kay wasn't pregnant. None of his family were terminally ill. He didn't have an essential job and finding Christ all of a sudden didn't wash with the beaks these days. There was only one thing left to do – promise to settle down and, what was more, prove it by getting married. You never know, it might just cut a few years off his sentence.

It was put to Kay like an obligation. Nothing like the romance she'd once felt with this handsome young man. But why shouldn't she get married? They had been living like man and wife anyway and, besides, it was just a piece of paper. Anything to help him stay free. Anything. So they were wed in Perth Prison three days before his trial.

The minister was very kind and caring. Lenny looked good, though thin and pale. Kay looked utterly gorgeous. She didn't care about the ulterior motives. She was getting married and this was how it would be. Take me or leave me, here I come. My name is Kay, how do you do?

Though strictly against the rules, protocol allowed for the newly-wed couple to spend some private time together in the minister's vestry. Marriages can be declared null and void unless they are consummated – this was their chance and everyone knew it. Alone in the vestry, Lenny went straight for her breasts. At first Kay thought that absence had made him clumsy and desperate in his passion. Then she realised he was only trying to scoop out the drugs she had secreted there in her bra. She watched him unwrap the foil, tongue and swallow the little helpers then, and only then, smile. When he fumbled at her stocking top she saved him the trouble and whisked out that little package tucked into her panties. He took some more. 'Fuck it,' she thought, 'if that's how it's going to be,' and gulped down some speed.

By the time they joined the others twenty minutes later, Kay was high and giggling. She noticed that the minister was drinking heavily from his glass of lemonade. A little crushed speed, some eccies and away she went. By the time the screws called the proceedings to a halt the reverend was on a table singing boisterously.

At Lenny's trial the procurator fiscal didn't blink or waver. Twelve years in prison was the sentence and Kay howled for a month. Then she realised that Lenny's letters were all becoming coded shopping lists for drugs and nothing more. The only time he kissed or touched her during visits was to collect those little packages. She paid for some glamour photographs of herself to be taken, a wee bit saucy, for his cell wall. He sold them to other cons for tobacco he didn't need. Lenny was becoming top dog in jail because of her supply of drugs. No problem there but he was making it clear that this was his life. Then Kay discovered that a short while after their wedding their nice wee minister had been sacked from his post in disgrace. Alcohol and personal problems went the official announcement. Maybe the Mickey Finn she put in his drink hadn't helped? Kay realised she felt more for that poor minister than she did for Lenny. She had always promised herself not to follow that downward route. To make something of her life. She recalled the small girl she had been crying herself to sleep as men buggered her sister next door. A bit of the disgust of that time re-entered her soul and she couldn't allow it. She'd be nobody's pusher, no one's whore. Time to move on.

Kay was torn in splitting from Lenny. The good times had been excellent and perhaps the changes in him were an inevitable consequence of jail time. How would Kay know? She'd never known anyone who'd served serious jail time before now. Her resolve to break up their relationship was a slow nagging process worn out of her by his constant demand for her smuggling skills and little concern about her. Perhaps it was inevitable with the young man put away for so long but how was Kay to know that? How is any prisoner's wife to know that?

In truth she'd started to wonder about Lenny many months before his imprisonment. Months before he had asked if he could hide a guy on the run from prison in her house. Not just any guy but a murderer. Andy Gentle was his name, his real name. Kay had said no. A murderer, for Christ's sake. In her house. What was Lenny thinking of?

She had asked for details. Andy Gentle had been jailed for eight years for murdering a guy in a knife fight at Charing Cross in Glasgow back in the 1960s. Released on parole he'd been out for a few months when he and a mate had killed an Easterhouse woman during a heavy drinking spell. A week or two later Andy Gentle had murdered his accomplice, strangling him to death to stop him blabbering then dumping his body in a shallow grave in the nearest tenement back green in Springburn. Not just a murderer but a triple murderer. Lenny had been paid to kidnap him from a period of home leave at his daughter's house in Maryhill. Kidnapping with Gentle's entire cooperation – he was going on the run. Lenny needed a safe place to hide him and asked Kay.

'Jist a few days, hen,' he'd pleaded as she weighed up the difference between sleeping with a robber and sheltering a murderer. After a barrage of insistent reassurances from Lenny she said yes just to shut him up.

When they brought Andy Gentle to her door she was shocked. He was not the man she had expected. Gentle was small, skinny, with a mild face and a warm smile. The kind of face you'd leave your children with. For five days and nights he was her guest and he sat there drinking endless cups of tea and chatting with her about astronomy, astrology, politics and psychology as Lenny and his handlers paced up and down the room, stopping every now and then to peer out the edge of the curtains. Gentle by name, gentle by nature. He was the best company Kay had had in a long while. One night late, when Lenny and the others were asleep, she and Andy Gentle had talked. The man craved company of his own choosing and luxuriated in the presence of a woman.

'Know, Kay, they'd better not catch me,' he'd said on his last night in her home.

'They'll no, Andy. I'm sure they'll no.'

'If they catch me they'll kill me, hen. Mind what Ah've telt ye.'

Kay hadn't known what to say. Gentle had left for his bed soon after giving his hostess a warm cuddle of gratitude on his way to the door. He was captured a short while later. On 22 April 1996 he was found dead in his cell hanging by his neck. Suicide, they said, but he was only a short time away from being released. Why had he escaped? What was he so afraid of? Did Andy Gentle kill himself? Or did they kill him? Who were they? Kay had gained the impression Gentle had meant the authorities but that couldn't be right. Could it?

A Gentle Requiem

In future years information was to emerge that would have terrified Kay had she been aware of it. Information concerning of all people the gentle Andy Gentle. It was information that would have made her question her feelings for Lenny and her belief that she knew him.

Released on licence following his period in jail for his first murder, Andy Gentle had taken up with a well-known Glasgow crime figure, Ian Waddell. It was with Waddell that Gentle drunkenly murdered the hapless Josephine Chipperfield in Easterhouse during a drinking session. It was Waddell that Gentle then murdered to prevent him from talking – or so it was argued.

Before his death, Waddell's name had been coming up in interesting quarters. A man called Paddy Meehan had been sentenced to life for the murder of Rachel Ross in Ayrshire in 1969. Ross was an old woman and rich. She'd been tied up by the raiders before they looted her house and died as a direct result. Many people believed that Meehan was innocent of this murder, including some of Scotland's most prominent criminal lawyers like Joe Beltrami. Beltrami was being told by one of his clients, Tank McGuinness – well known for his violence on Glasgow's streets – that he had been responsible for the Ross death, not Meehan. This information was being backed up by another of Beltrami's clients, Arthur Thompson, the so-called Godfather of organised crime in Glasgow. Beltrami couldn't use the information as it would breach the confidentiality of his lawyer–client relationship with Tank McGuinness – well, he couldn't use it while McGuinness was alive.

In 1976 several assassination attempts were made on McGuinness. They all failed till one dark rainy night in Glasgow's Janefield Street when he was battered to death by one of his friends, Gypsy John Winning. Winning confessed to the murder but died himself soon after. Beltrami was now free to reveal the information about the real cause of Ross's death. He was aided and abetted by luminaries such as Ludovic Kennedy, the writer and TV presenter; Malcolm Rifkind QC, who would go on to be Secretary of State for Scotland, and Ross Harper, who built up one of the country's largest legal firms and became chairman of the Conservative Party in Scotland. The powerful campaign rightly achieved a Royal Pardon and freedom for Meehan. Unfortunately, Meehan showed an ungrateful streak and spent the rest of his life berating the very people who had won his freedom against the odds.

A few years after McGuinness' murder, a former police officer recounted how, in spite of having an outstanding warrant for McGuinness' arrest, he and a colleague had been ordered by Charlie Craig, then in charge of CID in Glasgow, to stay back from him on the night of his death. Meanwhile, Arthur Thompson's son, Fat Boy, was quietly letting it be known to those who would listen that McGuinness had been killed on order of his father. There is no doubt that Fat Boy lied a great deal, but it is also true that Arthur Thompson himself was responsible for dispatching many a soul. Somebody had been determined to murder Tank McGuinness.

Street players have the view that Thompson arranged to have his old friend McGuinness murdered not to help free the wrongfully convicted Meehan but to protect another, more important ally – Charlie Craig, then the most senior detective in Strathclyde Police. Craig was notorious for his willingness to flaunt rules. There had been serious misgivings about his handling of the Ross murder along with a whole raft of other cases. Thompson's investment in keeping his old collaborator

Craig in his senior position of influence was obviously a lot more important to him than Meehan's freedom or the life of an old friend – Tank McGuinness, the man whose murder he arranged.

With McGuinness safely dispatched in 1976, the campaign for Paddy Meehan's freedom proceeded apace until in 1982 the story took another twist. Ian Waddell let it be known to a journalist that he was the second man involved in the murder of Rachel Ross along with Tank McGuinness. So Waddell was a tie-up merchant the same as Kay's Lenny Lovat. Waddell had a story to tell that others like the powerful Arthur Thompson had gone to great lengths to conceal. Waddell had hardly made the statement to the journalist when he was knifed to death by Andy Gentle. Coincidence or contract?

Contrary to Kay's experience of him, Andy Gentle was no choirboy. Jailed for the murders in 1982, he entered the prison system just as the lid came off. Gentle was a main player in the riots in Peterhead Prison and elsewhere. He repeatedly settled disagreements with other cons with violence and as late as 1993 he stabbed the same prisoner twice while in Shotts Prison special unit. Andy Gentle was no angel and no pushover. So who was he so afraid of?

Why was a tie-up merchant like Lenny asked to smuggle Andy Gentle away? It was a curious choice. After his few days in Kay's house, Gentle was taken by Lenny to another place then on to a so-called safe house in Greenock in the shadow of the prison he had just escaped from. He was captured within hours. Back in Greenock Prison he re-entered an institution under scrutiny. The jail corridors were full of deaths with seven alleged suicides in eighteen months. Yet everyone agreed with Kay that Andy Gentle was not suicidal. The official version was that he became suicidal after a fall-out with another con. Could this be the same Andy Gentle, veteran of brutal riots, feared nutter of every hall in every prison in Scotland?

The night Kay last saw him, Andy Gentle predicted that if

'they' caught him 'they' would kill him. Why did Lovat take him to the front door of the jail he had just escaped from? How did Gentle get captured within hours of moving to the new house? Why would Andy Gentle kill himself after his years of prison time and when freedom was in his grasp? Why did he escape in the first place? Why did Lenny Lovat agree to hide Gentle?

Kay didn't know it but she had been living in a nest of vipers. Nothing about Lenny Lovat was as it had seemed. Had she known half of all that maybe she would have taken fright and changed her life completely – if she could. Certainly she wouldn't have wasted those nights and those tears feeling guilty about her separation from Lovat. One thing was clear: through all those events Lovat was being watched carefully by bigger players. Lovat and Kay were being watched and the observers liked what they saw in the young woman. She would meet her secret admirers soon.

Meaning of Life (1995)

Keep sending the dolly mixtures though, babe. Promise?' No tears, no pleas, no regrets. The supply of drugs was all Lenny was interested in on the day they had agreed to separate. She had kept delivering for a while and then stopped that too. He could get someone else to provide his prison currency and a short while later she learned that he had, through some former girlfriend – young, good-looking and, in Kay's view, with absolutely no self-worth.

'Good luck to her,' she thought. 'She's in for a long, loveless trawl.'

Kay had to support herself and went back to her old profession exactly where she'd left off – at the top. Now she had more self-assurance. Somehow dealing with the men who used her services didn't seem so frightening. She worked for them because she could imagine no other way to earn a living, but she resented the sex. Always had and now more so since she'd had her first real relationship where making love was part of a bond rather than a cheap transaction. So she set her limits.

At one time she even refused to have intercourse, telling her punters, 'Look, I don't go the whole way. Reverse massage and a hand job is all you get from me.' If they grumbled she simply passed them on to another girl. Most didn't grumble so the sauna owners had no reason to complain. Eventually she gave up the restriction simply because she could. It was her decision, her choice, she was in control. So she did.

Kay was still getting the top offers. Overnighters at five hundred quid a session. Regular punters who'd pay her over the odds and buy her presents – clothes, a car, holidays. So she wasn't surprised when she was offered funny money to do a show in a city-centre club one night. It was a two-girl, lesbian floorshow and she wasn't looking forward to it much. But the money was good and extras were promised. One night's work and she would have made her week's wages. It was too good to refuse.

When she turned up at the venue she went weak at the knees. The private party was for one of Scotland's football teams who were celebrating the end of a successful season. It was the football team she'd supported since she was a child. There were her heroes all sitting round watching her rather than the other way around. Kay would have performed for them for free – a fact she didn't share with her boss. Instead she vowed to put on the best performance of her life, not without personal cost.

As the music beat out Kay French-kissed her performing partner and caressed her thighs.

'Get down oan her, girl.'

'Off wi her knicks.'

'Can Ah join in?'

The shouts of encouragement from the audience all seemed to be in broad Glaswegian. Maybe the foreign players had picked up the type of English they heard day-to-day and she worried for them when they moved on to London or Manchester – would anyone understand them? She wished the fat guy who'd arranged the event had chosen another partner for her. This one was getting all the best jobs because of her enthusiasm and willingness to do absolutely anything with absolutely everyone – including the boss. But she was a dirty bitch.

'You are a clarty whore,' Kay whispered into her partner's ear while slowly removing the woman's panties. 'I can smell you from here.'

'Go oan, gie ma fanny a good lick, ya snotty-nosed fuckin' wee bitch,' the woman replied while smiling broadly and tweaking Kay's nipples, much to the pleasure of the raucous footballers.

'Do you never wash?'

'Why bother when you'll do it for me?' she sniggered in Kay's ear, stroking her fingers through her hair in some parody of being lost in lust.

'Think so?'

'Aye.'

'No!'

The cheer was spontaneous and loud.

'GOAL, ya rasper.' One of the Scottish players applauded the sudden progress as Kay forced the other woman to her knees and straddled her face. Heroes or no heroes she wasn't going down on that woman. God knows what she'd catch.

After the show the men surrounded the women instantly. The Scotsman who'd called out sidled up to her and whispered, 'Fancy moving on to a club later? Just you an me, okay?'

'Sure,' she replied. 'Love to.' This would be a pleasure. A kind of one-night stand with someone she'd idolised for years.

'Fancy some Charlie?' he asked and Kay immediately agreed, following him. The bath was full of bottled lager on a bed of ice – the official reason why all the men were disappearing into the private suite on a frequent basis. Bodies of those sporting stars crowded the large bathroom queuing up for a space at the smoothly tiled ledge. Kay was feeling giddy in such company and awash in the expensive scents of these powerful men. One by one they took their turn, chopping the cocaine and blasting it up their noses.

Kay knew that she wanted to tell someone, anyone, about her company but couldn't dare. Not only was that unprofessional but, put simply, no one would ever believe her. This was one of the cleanest sporting organisations in the country. No one ever stepped out of line, publicly at least. There was no filth on these guys. They were so gossip-free they were almost boring. In the corner a big, angry-faced guy was fucking her performing partner up against the wall. Kay hoped for his sake he was wearing a condom. The coke hit her like a delicious dream. A familiar wave of warmth swept her limbs and she shuddered. This was going to be a great night.

Out in the main room, Kay sat and chatted with her heroes. Their talk was flirtatious, harmless, fun. Confidence bred on cocaine. Everybody was invincible. She watched her performing partner disappear with men one by one, only to return and invite yet another for a little extra. One player repeatedly refused the woman's approach and Kay had noted he had seemed awkward, ill at ease during their stage show. She couldn't decide if she thought he was a good man or just someone who got up to his games strictly in private. Did that make him more or less honest than his teammates she wondered?

'Want more Charlie?' It was her date for later in the night.

'Yes please,' she smiled.

'Here y'are then,' and he handed her over his wrap which she knew from her time with Lenny held several hundreds of pounds worth of coke. 'You go ahead, Ah've tae have a word wi the boss. Catch up wi yese in a minute,' and he leaned over and pecked her on the cheek. She had a date all right.

In the bathroom a few men were sniffing the coke and washing the burn away with the iced lager. Kay had no sooner taken a hit when she was grabbed from behind. The angry-faced guy had decided it was her turn and wasn't taking no for an answer. She pushed and kicked at him, trying to scratch at his face but she was like a powerless doll being bent this way and that in his thick, muscular arms. When her date bounced into the room, he was in time to catch her heaving a sobbing orgasm against her will. Cocaine works in different ways for different people at different times. That night it turned her on beyond her own definition of decency. She was taking responsibility, blaming herself for letting her date down. Cursing herself for acting like the cheap whores she despised. Her mother was in her and there was nothing she could do about it. He would want zilch to do with her now and she didn't blame him.

Lost among the throng back in the main room, Kay was polite but the joy had gone out of her night. Her escapade with Angry Face troubled her and she was too stoned to blame the drugs but not too stoned to blame herself. On her way to the toilet, a hand tapped her on the shoulder.

'Trying tae sneak away, eh?' Her date had followed her out into the corridor.

'No, I was . . .'

'C'mere,' he pulled her into a room, a bedroom where her performing partner had been entertaining the line-up of troops. The sheets were badly, freshly stained and the room stank of sex. 'Why did ye let that big ugly bastard do yese afore me?' He was unbuttoning his trousers. 'We had an arrangement.' He was pulling her pants down. 'Hate that big bastard, so Ah dae. Thinks he's a fuckin' smoothie.' He was shoving his erection into her.

Kay lay on her back, as detached from his bucking and thrusting as she was with any john, any working day. She thought she'd had a date but all she had was just another man wanting his end away. She felt nothing, wasn't there, her mind carefully counting how much she'd earned that night and how she would spend it. Coldly, calmly, she acknowledged to herself that the smaller Scot had a much larger penis than the hulking giant. Not only that but his method was better. 'A right good ride,' her day-to-day colleagues would call him. Maybe so but Kay felt nothing. The world hadn't changed. When he'd finished and pulled his trousers up, he went for his wallet and threw five crisp tenners down on the bed. Not only was he just another john, he was also a cheapskate john, earning hundreds of thousands of pounds a year. All he wanted to do was empty his sacks and she was his body of choice.

Bouncing through the Glasgow streets in the back of the cab in the early hours, Kay ignored the constant patter of the driver. He didn't seem to notice or care or draw breath.

'Ah think they get paid too much these days. Mean when Ah was a boy, ye'd see the big-name players just walking doon the street. Jimmy Johnstone, Pat Stanton, Denis Law – seen them aw. Wan time I was in a chip shoap on Paisley Road West, hanging around scrounging a bag o scraps, when in walks big Slim Jim Baxter. Tae buy chips!' He roared the last statement of his obviously oft-repeated tale with a mixture of surprise and shock as if the footballers should be doing something else in a chip shop. 'Stood ootside eatin his supper annat. Ah'm standin next tae him, eatin ma wee poke o batter and scraps o tattie feeling like a million dollars, know? Slim Jim leans ower tae me an asks, "Thirsty, son?" and passes me his bottle o Irn Bru. Not a word o a lie. Baxter, God oan legs hissel, gied me a drink o his scoosh.' The driver was silent for a rare moment, contemplating the supreme moment of his childhood. Then, 'Tell ye, these days they so-called fitba stars widnae gie ye the dog shite aff their shoe without picking yer pocket for yer dosh.'

Kay pondered on the philosophical point of the cabbie's story and cursed herself for being so naive after all she had been through. He was right. It was an exploitative mean world and everybody was out to get everybody else. Tonight she had been star struck as if she was in some special company. But she wasn't even in decent company. Just ordinary men, ordinary people who took what they wanted at the cheapest price. The driver cursed loudly as he crunched the old Hackney's gears painfully and moved on to the topic of religion. Before he pulled outside her home he'd also dealt thoroughly with politics – no bars to any theme in a late-night Glasgow taxi. By that time Kay had decided that from then on in she was going to be in charge. Take control of every possibility that came her way. No more wee Kay. She handed the driver a fat tip. She owed him though he didn't know it. From now on in people would owe her and she'd make sure they paid. From now on she was going to exploit the exploiters, just you wait and see.

Fly in the Soup

'Ah'll pay for yer lunch, hen.' Kay turned round in her seat and stared at the intruder. Who the hell did he think he was? She had searched out that restaurant-cum-bar, deliberately choosing it as a quiet venue away from the streets, the wise guys and the hustlers. And here he was hassling her from the next table. 'For you an yer pal,' he persisted. 'Straight up. No strings.' The stranger smiled a not unpleasant, boyish, gormless grin. Kay found him as threatening as limp lettuce.

'Do you mind?' she replied, throwing him her fiercest look. 'This is a private conversation.' He held his hands up, palms out, and shrugged an apology. Kay glowered at him once more, turned away in her seat and continued talking, just more quietly, into her mobile phone. She was talking with Lenny Lovat's sister. Just because she had split from him didn't mean she held any grudge against the family. She was fond of them all and was telling Lenny's sister of the nice bar she had found and promising to take her there for lunch sometime soon.

The Dovecote, we'll call it, was based on the periphery boundary of the Glasgow schemes that Kay grew up in but might as well have been in the middle of the country. It took advantage of a peculiarly Glasgow phenomenon where, on all sides of the city, urban jungle turned to rural idyll, suddenly and dramatically. The Dovecote, pronounced 'doocot' in the vernacular, had recently come under new ownership, been refurbished at considerable expense and was aiming at a more exclusive clientele from the middle-class enclaves that bordered the wild council schemes. If it worked, The Dovecote would offer

Kay what she wanted — a safe haven from her neighbours, punters and the teams of Arden. In spite of the man coming on to her as soon as she walked through the door, she still believed the bar offered her that respite. Men came on to Kay wherever she went — she knew she couldn't hide from that unless she were to discover a place without men.

'Yeah, it's really nice,' Kay was saying to Lenny's sister. 'What about next week? Tuesday? Good. It's a date.'

Kay watched the small man out of the side of her eye as she spoke into the phone. One of the lessons of years as a working girl was never to trust anyone, regardless of how innocuous they looked. Small, thinning hair, expensive but dull grey suit, smart tie and glasses. No threat there then.

'How's Lenny doing?' Kay said into the phone. There would always be a little of her that would hope that Lenny was all right. Besides, his family worried about him every day and she cared about them. Prisons anywhere are dangerous places to be, particularly if, like him, you were involved heavily in the drugs scene. The sister reassured Kay that Lenny was doing just fine and gave her a rundown on the latest visits and small minutiae of developments around his prison life. 'Okay, good,' said Kay, rounding off the conversation. 'So next Tuesday then? No, no lunch is on me. My treat as long as I'm no skint,' she joked, knowing that these days she was never broke but also knowing that Lenny's sister was going through a hard time and not wanting to sound as if she were showing off or, worse, taking pity on her. 'Look forward to it. Byeee.'

No sooner had Kay pressed the off switch on her mobile phone than the wee man at the next table leaned over again.

'Couldnae help overhearing,' he started, 'but is your man Lenny Lovat?' Kay looked at him with new eyes. He had overheard Lenny's name but how did he know of him? Was it just a case of remembering him from the press coverage of his trial? Was he a policeman? No, too small.

'My ex-man actually,' Kay answered while wondering why she was giving the wee guy the time of day. 'What is it to you?'

'Aw, Ah know him a bit,' the man replied. 'We're frae the same area.'

'That's nice,' replied Kay while turning away from the man and crossing her legs. The tone of the words and her body language screamed, 'FUCK OFF. I'M NOT INTERESTED.'

'And Ah know his work a wee bit,' the man continued. Kay looked at him square on. Weak, soft eyes staring at her through his lenses. A receding hairline leaving his forehead looking overlarge, shiny. She immediately christened him Joe 90 after a kids' TV show puppet of similar appearance. Kay sipped at her drink and ignored him. 'Look, Ah was serious aboot buying ye lunch,' he continued. 'How about it, eh?'

'My mum always told me never to speak to strangers,' Kay answered coldly, irony dripping through her voice and her spirit as she recalled how her mother would advise and do exactly the opposite.

'Here, whit am Ah thinking?' Joe 90 slapped himself theatrically on his shiny forehead. 'Ah've no introduced masel.' He stood up and moved to Kay's table. For the first time she could see exactly how small the man was. Maybe an inch taller than her, if that, and her a petite example of womanhood. He was no copper, that was for sure.

Kay admitted to herself that the prospect of being approached by a policeman had been her biggest dread. Every now and then Strathclyde Police cracked down on the sex industry. Usually their tactics consisted of nothing more subtle than sending carloads of uniform cops out to arrest the street girls working the city centre. But Kay was aware that with her success she had collected some important clients from all walks of life and connections with those at the highest level in the sex industry. To catch the likes of her and her punters they would have to try a little harder than sending out a load of PC Plods.

But no way was this guy tall enough for the police. 'Ah'm Bud Cumming,' he said, leaning over and offering her hand.

'No way,' Kay laughed before she thought of her response. 'If you're Bud Cumming I'm Madonna.' Lenny had taught Kay a great deal more than how to enjoy sex and drive getaway cars. Once he had revealed the source of his work to her he would chat about the wider scene of organised crime. Bud Cumming was a name that didn't appear in the newspapers for the simple reason that he didn't get caught often and when he did it was for small-fry issues. While the public remained blissfully unaware of who or what Bud Cumming was, the street folk knew him as one of the leading players in Glasgow, controlling an increasing slice of the city's drugs trade, protection rackets, hit contracts, money laundering and whatever else. Bud Cumming was new school, running his empire with the usual currency of terror but also dealing with teams in London, Liverpool, Newcastle and abroad. Kay looked at the small, bank manager-like figure standing in front of her and simply could not tally it with what she had heard of Bud Cumming.

'I don't think so,' she responded dryly, 'in either case.'

'Gen up,' he replied, smoothing his glasses up the bridge of his nose.

Kay just shook her head and stared right into his watery eyes, 'Look, just leave me alone to have a quiet lunch, okay?' He was standing near her shaking his head impertinently. 'Gonnae just fuck off?' she spat, her descent to the vernacular and the foul language being a deliberate ploy to maximise impact.

'Okay,' he said with a smile, holding those hands up again and backing off. 'Should try the pasta, it's real good.' And he walked away to a table at the other end of the bar.

All through lunch, Kay bridled her annoyance which threatened to bubble up into an angry fury she was capable of and didn't like. What was the wee bloke's game? Easy to say that he was Bud Cumming since no one except his close associates knew what he looked like. Kay was used to men pretending they were something they were obviously not. Almost every punter she had ever had invented something for himself. Mostly it was just another first name. Sometimes a type of work they considered made them seem more exciting, interesting. Sometimes it was outrageous. Claims to be top professional footballers when they had thighs skinnier than a pre-pubescent boy. Or members of successful rock groups – not the front man who was always too well known, but the bass guitarist or whatever. And crime – now there was a strange twist. During the longest trial in Scottish criminal history in 1992 – Paul Ferris, charged with the murder of the son of Arthur Thompson, the Godfather of crime in Glasgow, as well as a stack of other allegations – every second punter claimed to be the cousin or friend of Ferris. Like the time some TV channel ran a series of documentaries about the Kray twins – suddenly the johns had London connections. All lies, of course. The real street players who used working girls – they never revealed what they did. Something they had in common with the police and the lawyers. So with punters, crime suffered a sort of reverse principle and that was what Kay reckoned Joe 90 was applying. What had always intrigued her was why her customers lied to her and other working girls. Why lie? If they paid their money they would get the services. Working girls didn't need to be impressed. Couldn't be impressed – they didn't care enough. Now the small guy in the corner of the bar, what was he after? Was it a simple line to try and pull her? Bum up his credentials to something he considered exciting and invite her to lunch. Was that all it was?

Kay paid for her lunch – a meal she had still managed to enjoy in spite of the acid burn of annoyance caused by the wee man's approach. If she could be sure he didn't go to The Dovecote every day she would certainly make it a regular haunt. She relaxed too soon.

'Look, Ah know ye dinnae believe me.' He was standing right

beside her at the cash desk. 'But here's ma mobile and pager numbers.' He handed her a slip of paper with the two phone numbers written clearly under the name BUD CUMMING in bold capitals. 'Any time ye need me . . . jist phone.' With a smile he turned and headed for the door.

This was going too far. A try-on for some quick sex was one thing but to persist was madness. Wee Joe 90 was certainly off his nut and Kay reckoned The Dovecote was off her list. Dull men looking for pretend excitement – those she could and did deal with on a daily basis. Deluded individuals working a game up into a full-blown fantasy – no, that was too much grief and she was having none of it. Absent-mindedly she slipped the paper with the phone numbers into her purse along with her change and headed to the door. That would be the last time she visited The Dovecote, she was thinking. Now she would have to find another place to take Lenny's sister. Couldn't go back on a promise.

Out in the car park, she paused to unlock her motor when a car horn's friendly peep-peeing made her turn. It was Joe 90 driving slowly past at the wheel of a top-of-the-range, silver Mercedes, smiling and waving in a gentle, cheery manner.

'Fucking nerve,' thought Kay. 'Guy is well off his head for sure,' and she watched the Merc head smoothly towards the exit. The guy obviously had money. If she was smart she would have turned his approach into a little bit of business. Put up with his fantasy of being Bud Cumming for a while in return for him paying the highest rates. Other call girls would have done that in a flash and gone along with his delusions. She was more careful, always making sure that the venue was neutral, the john found out nothing about her personal life and someone she trusted was always close by. She could have done that with Joe 90 but not that day. That was her time, for her, Kay the person. Not for Kay, the working girl. Besides, rich or not rich, he was certainly unstable trying to pass off as Bud Cumming. The Merc hummed as it waited to exit the car park and head into the fast flow of traffic on the dual carriageway. Kay liked cars and she stood and admired the cut of the vehicle from the rear. And there it was. To this day she can't remember the numbers but the letters on the personalised number plate reached out and slapped her awake.

BC . . .

BC for Bud Cumming. Unless his name was something similar like Billy Cunningham or Bobby Clarke or whatever. Maybe that was why he was pretending to be Bud Cumming – simple convenience of sharing the same initials. Then again, the big sleek Merc was the kind of car she expected the real Bud Cumming to drive. As it slid effortlessly out on to the main road and accelerated into the rush of traffic, Kay watched the car disappear into the distance. Kay's experience of Lenny Lovat had been enough for her. What she regarded then as exciting, edgy, living with her heart she now considered reckless and immature.

'Bud Cumming or no Bud Cumming,' she thought, 'thank God I'll not be meeting him again.' Kay was through with crime and criminals once and for all.

Knock Knock . . .

'What the . . . ?'

'Did I catch you at a bad time?' asked Joe 90.

'No . . . eh, I'm going . . .' Kay was stunned to see him standing there on her doorstep just a few days after they met at The Dovecote. 'It'll always be a bad time for you,' she spat, recovering her grasp of what was happening.

'Now, please . . .'

'I was just going out.'

'Right, work of course. Should've thought. Well, Ah'll no . . .'

'Wait a minute. What do you know about my work?'

'Ah know a . . .'

'And how the hell did you know where I live? What are you, a bloody stalker?' Kay kept the wee pest on the doorstep. Furious that he'd simply turned up at her home uninvited only a few days after they'd met and she'd told him to go away.

'Told you, Kay, Ah know a lot about you and Ah want tae know more.'

'Who's that in the motor? You come team-handed?' The sight of another man sitting in the driver's seat of the silver Mercedes parked at the kerb outside her house was even more alarming to Kay than Joe 90 turning up at her door. She considered slamming the door and phoning . . . who? She couldn't phone the police. Cops were just like johns, somehow sensing she sold her favours, and weren't slow to move on in expecting free fun or information on her punters and bosses, bartered against the privilege of being left alone to get on with her work. If she didn't cooperate she'd never work in the city again. That was just one instalment of the total price she paid for being a working girl. Staying anonymous from the authorities was absolutely essential. Kay had never fallen for that one and wasn't about to now.

'He's my driver,' Joe 90 said, pushing his glasses up his nose and turning to wave at the man in the car who gave a curt nod back. 'But listen, Ah come bearing gifts.' He held up two bottles of wine. Kay weighed up her options. The police were out of the question. Slamming the door on this guy's face wasn't going to put him off – she could see that much. Besides, how did he know where she lived? And if he knew that did he also know all the other things about her he'd already suggested – such as her work?

'Shit,' she cursed inside herself, 'it's just another lean-on. Fucker probably works for the Inland Revenue or the council or some debt-collecting agency. My number's come up and instead of doing his job he probably wants a freebie for himself and that big bruiser of a pal of his in his car as well no doubt.' Kay had been here before, numerous times. It was regrettable but she could handle it. Shagging a stranger was much easier and quicker than being investigated for not paying tax or whatever. Sooner started sooner done.

'You'd better come in.' She swung the door open and he stepped carefully over the threshold, following her into the lounge.

'Nice place. Real nice.' He looked around at the room where everything was neat and tidy and fastidiously clean.

'Yeah, thanks.' He nodded in an approving manner. What did he think, that a prostitute kept her house as a hovel? Probably, since that's what most people believed.

'Seriously, nice flat you have, Kay. Like the way it's decorated – real tasty.'

'Thanks, I like it.'

'Especially for this neighbourhood.' Kay knew it, this was where he started to run her down and start climbing onto her back.

'What's wrong with Arden?' she snapped.

'Woah!' He raised both hands in the air and went as if to back off. 'No offence to you. Seriously. Arden is not the worst.'

'I know that,' Kay growled, ready for a row. She'd give him a freebie okay but she wouldn't let him run her down.

'And it's not the best either. In fact it's close to being the worst.'

'And where the fuck are you from? Buckingham fucking Palace?'

'Naw, naw. Heh, heh . . . Buckingham Palace. Good one that.' He had a pleasant face when he smiled and didn't look so fretful. Pleasant, like an eleven-year-old boy's face. 'Naw, Ah grew up in Bawrrheid though Ah don't stay there now.'

'Where?' She hadn't heard of that one.

'Bawrrheid. Ye know?'

'No, never heard of it.'

'Whit, ye've no heard of Barrhead?'

'Oh, B-A-R-R-H-E-A-D. Right, thought you were saying something else.'

'Naw, Bawrrheid.'

'Christ, a council slum at the end of a country road.' It was three miles out of the city, heading south. In urban terms they had practically been childhood neighbours.

'Well, it's no the best either.'

'No and it's a damn sight worse than Arden. At least we're in the city.'

'Aye, jist in the city an' smack bang in the middle o the Badlands.' He laid the two bottles of wine down on the table. 'Have ye time for a wee swally?'

'Not really. Got to go any minute.'

'Right, what about a line then?' He patted his breast pocket and lowered his eyes, staring at her over the top of his thick glasses.

'A wee line of what?' The bastard was forcing his way into her life and then trying to trick her into a drugs rap. Did he think she was soft?

'Come oan, it's just a wee bit Charlie.'

'Charlie who?' Kay hoped she wasn't blushing with the embarrassment of playing such a naive role.

'Ha, good one that. Ha, maybe we should gie it a surname, eh? Like Charlie Cumming – guaranteed tae make ye feel good.' Kay looked at him with mock contempt. 'Or Charlie Chalk . . . honest polis, it is Charlie CHALK. Ha.'

'You ARE mental,' but for the first time Kay couldn't help but smile at his absurd and prompt sense of humour.

'Ah'm mental? It was your suggestion.'

'No it wasn't . . . oh, never mind.'

'You're right leery o me aren't ye, Kay?'

'Leery? What's that?'

'Christ, no that line again.'

'No, seriously. I don't know what you mean.'

'Suspicious. Wary. You're worried I'm the filth trying to trick yese intae something. Aren't ye, eh?'

'Aye, well. Aye. What can you expect when you just turn up like this knowing my name, where I live and . . . ?'

'Fair comment.' There he was again with palms in the air and backing off – the actions of a conman rather than one of the city's most feared gangsters. Or was it? 'Don't suppose it would help if you went out and asked my driver who Ah was? Naw, cos ye'd suspect Ah'd put him up tae it in advance. Right?' Kay was nodding her head vigorously. 'When d'yese have tae go?'

'Any minute. A colleague's coming round for me.' In fact it was a neighbour who said she'd pop round for a coffee and a chat. A woman who was the least likely candidate for being a call girl in the whole scheme. Kay hoped she would turn up pronto. Not just to get rid of the wee pest but because she was booked for a house call later, a lucrative two hours' work she couldn't afford to miss.

'Right, Ah'll back off.' Hands up in the air again. 'Give ye peace. But how's about we see each other again?' Kay checked her watch and out of the window spotted her strait-laced neighbour walking quickly towards her house. The only neighbour she trusted enough to be friends with. It would be really awkward if she walked in in the middle of this scene.

'Okay. When?' She spoke to Joe 90 while her eyes watched her neighbour's approach.

'Tomorrow night? Ah'll bring more wine.'

'Okay, you're on. Tomorrow night here, on one condition.'

'Name it.'

'You don't bring your minder there,' nodding in the direction of the silver Mercedes.

'Harry? Ha, he's a harmless soul, so he is. But if ye insist.'

'I do and you've got to go now.' The neighbour was crossing the street.

'Pleased to meet you, Kay Petrie.' The wee pest held out his hand and Kay took it once again, still worrying about how he knew her whole name. She used her actual first name at work but only her first name. Gently but firmly, he held on to her hand rather than shaking it, forcing her to look him in the face. 'I'm really pleased tae meet you, Kay Petrie. How do you do? My name IS Bud Cumming.' For the first time Kay was beginning to believe the small man. She had a feeling of awe, respect and fear growing in her chest. The kind of range of sensations she remembered from school when some teacher was giving her a bad time. Bud Cumming turned and moved towards the door where he stopped. 'When you leave this house, Kay, you leave with your head held high.'

'What?' He had lost her now.

'Never be ashamed of what you do.' Now he had her attention. 'Always be proud to be what and who you are, Kay Petrie.' With that he was gone. But not for long.

Civil War

Kay's time with Lenny had taught her a few things and she was a quick learner. But tie-up merchants like Lenny are loners, sole traders who work on their own most of the time. They are connected to the wider crime scene, of course, since how else are they to dispose of the goods they have stolen or launder the dough they have blagged? But it is not the same for a tie-up merchant as it is, say, for a bank robber and very different again for those involved in essential group-driven activities such as protection rackets, stolen motors, drugs trafficking. Lenny, therefore, had a fair idea of what was going on in organised crime in Glasgow but didn't share it all with Kay. Why should he have? Tie-up merchants don't talk a lot. Besides, it just wasn't that important for his speciality, for his work, his life.

So Kay didn't know it but civil war was threatening to break out on the streets and Bud Cumming thought he could grab a major slice of the action. The state of unrest had started when the man traditionally thought to be the kingpin of crime in Glasgow, Arthur Thompson, had broken all of the cardinal rules by cooperating with the police in bringing various charges against Paul Ferris, the man who would be king, according to the pundits. Thompson's son, Fat Boy, had been shot dead on the street and Ferris faced the charge of killing him. Not only that but the Godfather had brought charges against Ferris of trying to murder him by running him over near his own home. Add to that knee-capping and a dozen other charges, and Ferris was up against it. Not for the first time, the bar-room philosophers declared that Ferris was a dead man. Not for the first time, the press printed the words as headlines.

When Paul Ferris was found not guilty on all charges in 1992, the media predicted bloody retribution. In fact, what they got was Paul Ferris acting more as a peacekeeper and expanding successfully into legitimate enterprises. Ferris was never a man to do the expected and so it proved once again. He had personal wounds to carry. His two best friends – Bobby Glover and Joe Hanlon – had been summarily executed and dumped in a vehicle on the day of Fat Boy's funeral. He had been tormented by prison wardens as he was held in solitary confinement during the longest trial in the history of Scottish criminal law. His own elderly father had been tormented and beaten up by the Thompsons while his son was held in jail. Ferris dealt with it all and did what he thought best. He started business connections that linked Glasgow to Manchester to London. He was successful. Now old Arthur Thompson had died in his bed of a heart attack. Back in Glasgow trouble was brewing.

There were a stack of main players in the city as, indeed, there had always been. Life on Glasgow's streets is far too complex and changing to make for easy headlines so the press, as always, had taken the line of least resistance and made ogres out of individuals, emperors out of also-rans. While they were still predicting that Paul Ferris was behind everything including plans for World War Three, the others were edging round each other looking for the chance to take over. There was quiet Bobby Dempster, in many people's eyes the real king of crime in Glasgow – the man Arthur Thompson wouldn't cross. There was the McGovern family in the north of the city. And in the east, Thomas McGraw, The Licensee.

McGraw was a most unlikely king of crime. Ask those who grew up with him in the street gangs and graduated through borstal and prison at the same time. He was a mediocre fighter, not very bright and with an exaggerated sense of his own derring-do. In short he gabbed a lot and much of it was lies. Everybody who knew him knew that. But they also learned of his most sinister characteristic through hard years of watching their friends, relatives and associates sacrificed for the greater good of McGraw.

The first signs emerged in the 1970s when he was part of the Bar-L team, a successful gang of post office robbers. The regular team members began to notice that, in spite of great care and precautions, every second job or so one member would be mysteriously lifted by the police. At first they thought it bad luck or merely a matter of the odds in their precarious activities but it came to be too common, too regular. Then McGraw started boasting about how he could have charges dropped, guarantee bail, arrange for troublesome individuals to be arrested in possession of heroin they didn't know they had. When the police started hanging around his home and drinking at his pub, The Caravel, it was finally out in the open. McGraw traded with the police, and the most common exchange currency was human. In return, he received certain favours – a blind eye here, information there – till eventually the bizzies were driving him away to safety from scenes of crimes where he had been caught red-handed. McGraw had none of the attributes or an ounce of the respect held by Bobby Dempster and the McGoverns but he did have something they did not have and would never seek: a licence from the police to commit crimes without prosecution. His was the modern way. No street code, no friends, no scruples. He was The Licensee.

The man we are calling Bud Cumming saw an opening. He was a thinker – capable of running his illegitimate business like a corporate enterprise. Bud Cumming wasn't satisfied with his slice of the city. He ran legitimate businesses such as security firms, owned pubs, bought land, built houses. He was ambitious and already traded with teams from Liverpool, Newcastle, Manchester and London. Bud Cumming reckoned he had little to fear from other teams, being in charge as he was of one of the most lethal mobs in the city. But McGraw had something he could use – influence over the police. Such a facility was particularly useful for an ambitious man with one boot planted in the cut-throat world of crime and the other shoe planted on the terra firma of lawful commerce.

Bud Cumming crossed the city and shook hands with the devil. In Glasgow McGraw was the senior partner but Bud Cumming was the player. As for the future, Bud Cumming believed that belonged to him. Not just Glasgow but the whole of the UK. He was a man with brains, a vicious team and now he was licensed to commit crime. Civil war was right up Bud Cumming's street. The night he shook Kay's hand he knew that bad times were coming down. But he also believed he was going to be the winner. Who would doubt it?

The Talkative Insomniac

Bud Cumming returned to her home the next night and the next and the night following that. Weeks turned into months with him calling on her like an old-fashioned suitor trying to win her favours. None of this was strange to Kay. She was used to the attentions of men. What threw her was his politeness and overriding need to talk. Just talk. Oh, she'd had a few punters like that but they were lonely and sad for all too flagrant and sometimes fragrant reasons. But Bud Cumming wanted to talk with her not at her. Was choosing to spend his time with her. And it wasn't all one way. He'd ask her something then shut up and listen. Kay struggled hard to think of the people who had listened to her in her life. You don't pay a call girl a lot of money to hear what she thinks. He got to her all right, that Bud Cumming. Made her feel important. Made her think about what her views were about this and that and shock herself by discovering they were already lying there, all well formed and ready to share. The longer they spent together, the better she felt about herself. For the first time in a long time she began to relax, feel safe with a man. And not just any man but Bud Cumming, one of the most powerful, feared and lethal gangsters in the city. Of that much she was now totally convinced.

Bud Cumming always knew where she would be even when she hadn't told him. He'd turn up in the most unexpected places like the supermarket, her mother's house, when she was going out for the night. Kay had stopped wondering and fretting about this knowledge he had over her whereabouts. Quickly he had convinced her of two things – he was THE Bud Cumming and

145

he was a remarkable man. She'd never met anyone who seemed to know so much about so much. Not general knowledge. 'Ah'd be absolute crap in a quiz,' he'd once admitted.

'Aye, unless it was about street life,' Kay countered, much to his amusement. That worried Kay to begin with – how he'd talk openly of this gang, a gunman, drug deals, scores to settle.

'That Big G's mob huv ripped us aff again. Too big for their own bloody boots,' he'd muse, much as a straight Joe would talk about last night's football results. 'Gonnae put in big Paul, he'll see tae them.' Kay felt that she didn't want to know about all this, but at the same time her curiosity and sense of awe drove her crazy. It was the same attraction as driving for Lenny, pulling her into the dark at the edge of the light. A place where she didn't know what to expect. An exciting place. A dangerous place. 'The Big G thinks he's untouchable jist cos he did a bit o work wi old Thompson. Fucking Godfather, that was a movie, eh? In real life the old cunt's deid.' Cumming spoke in a kind of code that left Kay feeling her way around his sentences, deciphering the meaning through touch and concentrating very hard. Kay was hooked. She wanted to know all about that underworld that existed in her very street. Real but invisible. Who didn't want to know about crime? Bud Cumming was an expert, a fully fledged member and he had stories to tell. Kay listened and learned.

'Ye need tae take care, Kay,' he warned her one night. 'This's a dangerous fucking place we live in.' Her stomach flipped with nerves at his words of caution. If anyone would know of a threat to her it would be Bud Cumming. What did he know? Where was she in danger? At work? Probably, but from who? So many people to think about. Other girls, punters, bosses. Guys who'd tried to pimp her and she'd told to get stuffed? She'd worked for the Welsh family. Well known for their history of violence. Once they were close to taking over the city from old Arthur Thompson. Then there was Spot Henry. Not the same league but she knew he was connected. But she'd always got on well with them. A good earner for them and that's all they cared about when they ran brothels or call girl services – money. But she was well aware that in her work people seemed to line up to do others down – reason or no reason. Why was that? Did some of the women feel so bad about their daily humiliation they needed to fuck someone else? Like the poor folk in the past turning out in their droves to watch a public hanging. Come to think of it, the wretched sod getting hanged was most likely to be one of them.

'Christ, Bud, tell me who's after me?' she blurted out, taking an enormous swig of her drink.

'Whit? Aw, sorry, hen. Didnae mean tae frighten yese. Naebody.'

'What? WHAT?'

'Naw, naw,' Cumming smirked. 'They widnae dare, eh? No now.' He was right. She realised for the first time that just knowing this man served a useful purpose. Already he was protecting her just by associating with her. Not a bad advantage to have in her line of work.

'So, what the fuck did you mean?'

'Ah was talking about life. Life in general. Well, people more like.'

'Going to explain what you mean . . . please.'

'People are oan the make, Kay. All people. Accept that?'

'Aye, well a lot of folk.'

'Naw, every bloody person on the planet.'

'What about doctors and nurses and . . .'

'Money and status and, besides, tae most o them ye're jist a lump o flesh.'

'Like in my business.'

'Precisely ma meaning,' Bud Cumming replied. Kay thought of all the johns who had sworn allegiance, love and everlasting fidelity to her only to dump her for some fresh young talent or cheaper rates round the corner. She thought of her mother who only ever thought of her own sexual needs. Of her grandmother who had terrified her and used her child's body. Of her older sister, Amabel, who had bugged her for ages to introduce her to the game. When Kay had eventually agreed, with grave reluctance, Amabel took to it like a natural in every respect. Within days she was partying with her dyke colleagues for free drugs and, probably, sexual pleasure. Kay didn't care about that at all but got miffed when, almost immediately, Amabel started trying to steal her clients and bad mouthing her behind her back. Kay thought of all her punters who were lawyers, doctors, social workers, politicians – cleaner than clean in their public face, paying to abuse her in private.

'You're right. People are selfish shitholes.'

'Good girl. Now as long as you know that the rest is easy-peasy. Forewarned is forearmed annat.'

'Still not with you, Bud.'

'When you speak to someone where do you look?'

'Eh?'

'Having a conversation where do our eyes focus?'

'On their eyes.'

'Right. An whit dae ye see?' Bud Cumming was losing her.

'That they've got blue or brown eyes?'

'Is that it?'

'Aye, could you just explain . . . please.' The polite request seemed to be a regular mantra in Kay's chats with Bud Cumming but he never objected, always answering with patience.

'Ye have tae watch for the signs . . .'

'Like their eyes not meeting yours or shifting about a lot when they're telling you something?'

'Aye, that's the ticket. And if they keep rubbing their nose.'

'They're lying.'

'Spot oan.' Kay hadn't realised but she was a past master at judging people's body language for trustworthiness. It was one of the reasons she had prospered and survived so well as a working girl while other women had perished. 'Ah'm impressed, Kay. Knew ye werenae a mug.' But if Kay was skilled at judging body language, Bud Cumming had extended the art. He gave her long detailed lessons on when sentences didn't mean what they said literally. How relationships were often covers. 'Guy makes a big fuss o being best mates wi this other bloke while totally cold shouldering a third party. Ye have tae question that. Tae yersel like.'

'Why? People take to people. Have best friends, don't they?'

'Aw aye, sure 'n' most o the time it's true 'n' harmless. But yese have tae be prepared for the odd occasion it's jist shite. A decoy. Then it could be lethal. Like Big G, eh? He put it aboot that he hated McGraw, The Licensee, right?'

'If you say so.'

'Naw, he did. Come oot wi palaver aboot them being at war ower taxi territories. Mind?'

'Eh, no don't think so.'

'It was in aw the papers. They even shot a few up for good measure. Firebombed some boys. Couple o their guys got seriously damaged.'

'Oh, right I remember that. Awful.' Kay recalled feeling revulsion that taxi drivers had been burned and shot. A working girl's best friend was often her regular taxi driver. Discreet, friendly and unquestioning. If you got the right one they'd hang around outside your house, call to be sure you were safe. They were always rogues but often caring rogues.

'Well, dae ye mind that The Licensee was getting investigated by the tax people for laundering bent notes and drug money through his cabs?' Kay shook her head. 'Well he was. I mean laundering the dough AND being investigated while he and Big G were at war. Polis did fuck all about the hostilities – well, they widnae as far as McGraw's concerned. Jist left the two squads tae kill each other thinking that The Licensee was gonnae win. Dae their job for them. Thing is, it was aw shite. Just a cover. Big G and The Licensee were in cahoots.'

'But they were killing each other.' Kay couldn't get the image of a burned-out taxi out of her mind.

'Naw they werenae. They were damaging each other's drivers. Just foot soldiers. Dispensable. In the meantime Big G's motors were handling The Licensee's bent dosh. For a cut, of course.' Bud Cumming stopped and drew a couple of lines of cocaine on the hard smooth surface of the coffee table. 'Pair o them was thick as thieves. Ha, thick as thieves.' He rolled a fifty-pound note into a thick perfect straw. 'Thieves, aye, but fuck all thick about them.' Leaning over, he expertly hoovered the white powder up first one nostril then the other. Holding the end of his nose, he inhaled and snorted, his eyes watering, pupils narrowing to pins as the coke kicked home. 'Christ, it's rare stuff that.' He repeated the spiel he always spouted after every line of coke. But Kay knew he was right. Bud Cumming only consumed the highest quality Colombian snow, unlike the talcum powder and chalk-cut crap his men sold on the street.

They became lovers that night, many months after they had met, much like young friends become lovers – talking themselves into exhaustion and falling into bed since it was the only place left to go. Kay expected Cumming to be a skilled, creative, experienced lover, reflecting his talk, his knowledge, his power. What she found instead was a man with a small penis and an impotence problem. Talking in the lounge he had been in control. In bed it was her turn. She applied all her skills and every trick but his cock remained a flaccid contradiction to what she knew to be the power of the man. He wanted to kiss a lot and cuddle – always the acid test for her, distinguishing as it did between a paying punter and a lover. Kay was relieved to find she didn't mind Cumming's need to be held close, be comforted. With his limp dick his kisses seemed almost platonic, childlike and unthreatening. Naked and wrapped round each other they lay and talked and he talked dirty.

'Aye, that school doon the road frae me. Ye should see the lassies. Thirteen or fourteen years old, man, and they've got their kilts up round their arses. Often thought o getting one o the boys tae pick me up one. Jist so Ah can see if they've goat a hairy fanny tae go wi the tits an the legs.'

Kay joined in, drawing the attention back to herself, 'You like hairy pussy?'

'Naw, jist tae see like.'

'Or nice smooth ones like this.' She pulled his hand gently towards her cleanly shaven pubes. 'Feels silky, eh? Just like a wee girl's.'

'Aye, one o they wee schoolgirls.'

'Want me to dress up for you sometime?'

'Oh, aye. Aye.'

'My hair in pigtails. Wear a short gym slip and navy blue bloomers.' Kay had the outfit already, it being a common request in floor shows for stag nights.

'That wid be good.'

'And you can lift up my skirt and treat me like a bad girl.'

'Dirty wee lassie.'

'And punish me for being rude.'

'Play doctors and nurses.'

'And would I be the nurse?'

'Naw ye'd be a dirty wee fucking cunt like they schoolgirls. Just asking for it. Tempting a man. So he has tae ride yese. Ride yer dirty cunt . . .'

Cumming rolled over between Kay's legs and started pushing his half-hard hard-on into her, mumbling obscenities into her ear. It was rough, frantic and over in seconds. As he lay panting, Kay stroked his head, smoothed his cheek and thought. Bud Cumming's ranting had been a sexual fantasy reserved only for bed. Hadn't it? The type of thinking that would horrify and disgust him at all other times. Of course it would. This was Bud Cumming, a top player on the streets. These people hated paedophiles. All of them. Didn't they?

Bud Cumming lay on his side and told her that he couldn't sleep. Hadn't slept for years. But he didn't mind if she did.

'It's really late. Jist you relax and drop aff,' he said. 'Ah'll jist lie here. Ah like it here.' Kay mentally worked through what she had to do the next day, from early morning practical arrangements to a shift in her latest sauna workplace, Oasis, in the afternoon. She was going to need some sleep or she'd be struggling.

Bud Cumming did what he did best and talked. 'They cunts in Govan are straying on to our patch. Greedy fuckers. There's enough for everybody. But naw, naw. They huv tae huv the lot.' Kay snuggled down in the bed and prepared to catch a couple of hours' sleep. Happy at the soft, monotonous tone of his chat, as lulling, soporific, meaningless as listening to some boring chat show on the radio broadcast in the middle of the night. Just soft noise to shut out the world. 'Gonnae send in that Paul. Scare the shit oot o them. That Paul, man, he's a killing machine. Put him in a room an tell him tae start killing he'd fill a skip so he would.' She'd already worked out that Paul was his equaliser. A young man of formidable reputation who had been running drugs gangs in the city since he was thirteen years old. Now he worked for Bud Cumming.

'What's Paul's second name?' she asked.

'Sim. Paul Sim, a killing machine that . . . a real . . . fucking . . .' Cumming snored for what was remaining of the night. He slept well for an insomniac. Kay would have to wait for her answers on Paul Sim, but not for too long.

Kissing the Goat

'Want ye tae meet me,' Cumming's voice on the phone sounded relaxed, matter of fact.

'Sure, where we going?' Kay replied without hesitation. They had recently moved beyond their routine of meeting at her place and visited some of the best restaurants and clubs in town. Places Kay had heard of but rarely dared to enter. Now she felt confident and at ease in his company as they swanned into The Buttery with its Victorian-dressed waiters and antiques or hung out at the Ubiquitous Chip surrounded by la-di-das from the BBC headquarters just up the road.

'Jist a wee place Ah go to now and then.'

'Right, wherever you want.'

'Nothing fancy, it's business, but we'll move oan somewhere later if yese like. Anyway, The Old Chestnut bar. Know it?' It was a pub she had driven past many times but never stopped at. It looked rough and ready for all comers. As if above the door there was an extra sign saying 'ENTER AT YOUR PERIL'. But then maybe her suspicions were based on its location in one of the worst schemes in Glasgow, a veritable no-go area for the police, never mind the public.

'Aye, I know it well.'

'Right, see yese there in about an hour.'

'An hour? In the afternoon? I thought you meant tonight.'

'Naw, there's some folk Ah want yese tae meet. Can ye make it?' Cumming asked a question but his tone laid an expectation – be there.

'Eh, aye. Yeah, of course. All I need to . . .'

'Right see ye here in a hour.' The phone went dead.

Cumming had sounded terse, demanding, which was unusual. Kay concluded that he must be worried about these friends he was meeting or that other business was weighing on his mind, intruding on his usual gentle manner with her. A quick call to the sauna confirmed that she wasn't needed and the rest of her spare time was spent getting ready. Not that she wasn't always dressed in a glamorous way, meeting each day as if it was the most important day in her life. But this sounded important so she chose her outfit with care. She wished she knew more about these friends of Cumming's. Men and women? Young or old? Business or just friends? In the absence of any information she chose a little black number – sexy but serious. Could be worn at a funeral or a party. She checked herself in the mirror and concluded with satisfaction that, whoever these friends were, she wouldn't show Bud up or let him down.

Mishtakes
Ah've made a few
Then ahgaaain
Too few to menshuuun
Hum, hum
Tae hum tae hum
Tae hum tae hum
Tae tae hum hum HUUM huUuuUuuum
An throoough it all
Tae hum tae hum
Ah did it Myyyyyyyyy
Wayyyyyyyyyy

The singer stood in the middle of the crowded bar, a space cleared around him to avoid his swinging arms thrusting backwards and forwards at every new line. He was as free of teeth as he was of lyrics. His old-fashioned black suit looked worn and grey, with a yellow, sinister stain streaking down one accordion-crumpled leg. His grimy shirt collar was unbuttoned, open to halfway down a pimple-scarred, hairless chest, and a quarter of its tail hung free. Every time he threw his arms out his trouser zipper opened a little further. He was a big man and no one was going to shut him up. Instead they all turned and gaped at Kay.

She could take as much attention from the mainly male drinkers as they cared to show her. Her already straight back tightened even more but she smiled, warm and open. From somewhere a wolf whistle moaned low and long.

'See you, ye wee cunt, yer lost so yese are.' The cackle came from an old woman with breast-length white hair huddled in the corner. Kay thought she was bending forward but then noticed the hunchback.

'Leave her alane, Maggie. Come oan, darling, let me buy yese a wee shandy.' Her knight in silver armour was well past retirement age and supported himself on legs bowed to the shape of a rugby ball, leaning heavily on a dull, metallic grey NHS walking stick.

'Naw, naw, Andy. She's wi me. Hello therrr, sexy. Voddie and Coke is it? Or maybe a wee smoke?' The guy was young, too young to be in the pub, yet he stood there with a half-finished pint of lager and a shorter glass full of a ruby-coloured liquid she guessed to be cheap, fortified wine. Ceremoniously, he took a long drag from a fat joint, holding in the smoke as he offered it to Kay.

'Away tae fuck, ya hoor. Get oot o here. This is ma patch.' Old Maggie was on the warpath again.

'Haw, Maggie, you're retired now, hen.' Bud Cumming's voice came from behind Kay, who turned and smiled at him more with relief than pleasure.

'Retired? Who? Me? Away an fuck yersel. C'moan here an Ah'll show yese a good time.' Maggie demonstrated her good faith in her offer to Cumming by lifting her skirt and opening her withered, wrinkled legs, flashing her puckered, almost hairless sex to the entire pub.

'Aw, for God's sake, Maggie, ye'll put us aff wer bevvy,' roared the under-age drinker-cum-dope smoker.

'Aw? Yese didnae say that last time did yese?' The pub roared in anticipation, laughing at the young guy.

'Aye, away an fuck . . .'

'Did yese . . .' Old Maggie stuck out one withered hand, bending her index finger in a curve for all to see, '. . . banana knob?' The other drinkers howled with laughter as the young man blushed furiously, looking around him, fit to fight. 'Mind, Ah have tae say,' Kay cringed at what old Maggie was going to come out with next, 'it's a big tasty banana so it is.' Maggie's tobacco-brown-stained tongue lolled over her chin then around her upper lip. 'YUM . . .YUM.'

Bud Cumming took Kay by the elbow and led her gently away from the rising fracas.

'Everybody knows the wee man has been nipping Maggie,' he said, raising his eyes. 'Sneaks in her back door at night thinking he'll no be spotted. But this scheme disnae sleep.' Cumming had led her to the far edge of the bar to a table around which a group of men sat. 'Guys, this is Kay,' he announced.

The group of men raised hairy fists in salute. Nodded scarred faces or greeted her with a curt 'Aye'.

'Hello, pleased to meet you,' said Kay politely while she wondered what the hell Cumming had dragged her into. She sat down on the one spare seat Cumming had pointed at before he took up his own chair in the middle of the group.

'Right, where was we? Aye, Big G's mob. So what's the full score?'

To his left side a man stirred and cleared his throat, 'Seems like they've got local troubles. Couple o rogue dealers that'll no behave.' The guy was one of the least fearsome looking of the group but Kay could still tell just by looking at him that he was not be messed with or trusted. Later she was to find out that he was George Lennon, Cumming's second-in-command. 'Trouble is, if Big G intervenes, he'll get a bad press locally,' Lennon continued. 'The guys they're up against carry some support. Locals annat.'

'So,' said Cumming, 'question is do we help Big G?'

'They're a bit o a handful.' It was a small-built man, handsome but for a scar running the full length of his face. 'Known tae carry.' It was Jas O'Reilly, well known as the team's driver. Calm and almost slow in his day-to-day manner, he turned into a speed king behind the wheel.

Violence wasn't Jas's business but it was his brother, Iain's, who butted in, 'Christ sakes, if we cannae match a couple of single players. Mean it's only a fucking handful o amateurs and jist doon the road and wide open, man. No exactly Pitt Street fucking polis station.'

'But can we trust Big G?' This was from Shuggie Patterson, a well-known player from the local scheme. Kay watched his hands fidget and his eyes flit about every corner of the room. When his eyeballs stayed still for long enough she could see that his pupils were tiny sharp pinheads. Shuggie was stoned. 'It's no like we've been oan the best o terms with that big bastard,' he reasoned.

'That's shifted now,' said Cumming. 'We've come to an agreement. An arrangement.'

'You sure?' Shuggie's eyelashes fluttered in Cumming's direction as he spoke. For his pains he received a sour glower as an answer.

'Usual drill, right. Paul. Okay?' Cumming glanced round the group and the heads nodded one by one. Kay looked to see if the Paul mentioned was there. Was that the Paul Sim Cumming had mentioned before? The killing machine? He wasn't there.

'Aye right,' replied George Lennon on behalf of the group, 'Ah'll get young Paul oan tae it right away.'

The discussion moved on to address supplies from Liverpool. 'There's a bundle due by car at the end o the week,' Cumming started. 'Can we arrange the handover at the usual place, Iain?'

'Aye, sure.'

'Think he should go wi extra weight.' It was Shuggie again. 'Ah'm no sure o that guy that was here last time.'

'Fuck sakes, Shuggie, you're gonnae have tae leave off that wacky baccy stuff, it's making ye para.' It was George Lennon. A bluff man, he could never see the problem with the troops doing any job.

'Naw, Ah know whit Shuggie means,' Cumming interrupted. 'The Manchester guy that works wi them, right?'

'Aye, cunt wanted tae know too much aboot oor business last time he was up.' Shuggie looked relieved that Cumming was supporting him.

'Aye, a nosy shit right enough,' Jas agreed.

'Never did trust that Manchester crew,' Cumming said. 'Too many Glesga guys in their ranks.'

'Aye, an fuck knows their agenda,' Shuggie added.

'Okay, done. We'll get Paul tae join in,' Cumming decided.

'Fuck's sake, man, ye want tae frighten them aff entirely?' Jas the joker of the group cracked and the others laughed. 'Tell that Paul tae behave himself, eh?'

Kay realised she was at a meeting, a business meeting of one of Glasgow's top gangs. Why she was there she did not know. No one seemed to avoid the agenda – quite the reverse as they worked through a whole list of concerns. The conference covered drugs supplies, drugs sales, two hit jobs and a local difficulty with the sale of stolen cars.

'They're no fucking ringing them right,' Jas ranted. Cars were his business. 'Lazy fuckers are being dead sloppy, man.' It was the closest they came to revealing the specific subject matter of any discussion. Everyone knew that ringing a car was disguising a stolen vehicle by changing its plates, its colour and its chassis number. But at no time had they actually mentioned heroin, or killing, or dealing, in spite of discussing these matters at length. Still, Kay was amazed that they were having that conversation at all in a public house – even though they monopolised one corner and all the patrons knew well enough to stay away.

'Well, have a word then,' Cumming said, and his meaning was clear.

'See you, ye fat bastard, Ah'm gonnae slice you good.' The young dope smoker was in the middle of the pub, a sharp-pointed, short kitchen knife gripped in one fist and a small, domestic butcher's cleaver in the other.

'C'moan, pal, was only joking yese.' The pub singer was clearly the target of the young man's wrath and didn't like it one bit.

'Yer patter stinks, ye cunt.'

'Aye, well, Ah didnae . . .' Too late. The blade sliced down his cheek, setting a crimson blush to add to the other stains on his shirt. A second later the young man brought down the cleaver into the fat man's arms, stretched up over his head. Then the knife was stuck into his stomach low down, just above his gaping fly. Pandemonium broke out in the pub with men circling the pair, pleading with the young man to drop his weapons. The only patron who seemed pleased with the turn of events was old Maggie, sitting in the corner, flapping her skirt up and down, cackling like a demented hen.

'That does it,' said Cumming. 'Cannae get peace in this fuckin' place.' Kay couldn't believe how unfazed he and the other men were. Murder was happening yards away and no one had batted an eyelid. 'New venue for Thursday.'

'Fucking good idea,' said George Lennon, looking at the scuffle with distaste.

'Me an Kay tried that Dovecote the other week,' Cumming said.

'Aye, and how was it?' She couldn't believe they were

discussing the merits of pubs amid all that violence and noise.

'It was good, eh, Kay?'

'Yeah. Aye, it was . . . quiet.'

'Dovecote it is guys. Okay?'

'Thursday at one o'clock, Bud?' asked Jas.

'Aye, one sharp. Dinnae be late, eh?'

Cumming took Kay's arm and led her out of The Old Chestnut, followed by the other men. In the car park, he passed a handful of coins to two scruffy young boys for guarding his car. As Kay opened the passenger door she wondered again why she had been there.

'See you on Thursday, Kay.' It was George Lennon.

'Nice meeting ye, Kay. See ye in the Dovecote,' said Jas the driver.

'Aye, maybe we'll get a chance tae chat there, Kay, quieter like,' yelled Shuggie, pulling his collar up and skipping off the kerb with a grin, avoiding the bodies spilling out of the pub and rolling bloodily on the pavement.

'What dae ye think o them?' asked Cumming as he steered his car out into the stream of traffic.

'Aye, nice guys I'd say.'

'Nice? Dinnae let them hear ye say that,' Cumming chuckled. 'But they like you.' Kay wondered how the hell he knew that. For most of the time she'd just sat there and listened. 'And oan Thursday ye'll meet the entire team,' he added. 'Christ there's more of them,' thought Kay. 'Including young Paul,' Cumming chuckled. 'That'll be an experience.' Kay felt a shiver of fear run up her back. She wasn't looking forward to meeting Paul Sim.

Love on a Knife Edge

Who is it?' The rumble on her door so late at night had startled Kay, taking her breath away and setting her heart thumping in her chest.

'It's Bud.' Cumming's voice whispered harshly, a stage whisper on broken glass. 'Let's in, hen, quick, eh?' Kay didn't hesitate but even as she undid her locks and chains she sensed that something had to be wrong. It wasn't extraordinary for Cumming to call on her late at night, he kept topsy-turvy hours, but he usually knocked a quiet but distinctive rap-a-rap-rap. That rattling woodwork and the tone of his voice spelled trouble. When she edged the door open a great weight pushed it wide and in staggered a giant of a man, panting loudly and splattered in blood. The young man hurried straight past her into the living room without stopping to say a word. For a second Kay thought she was being raided. Ever since that first meeting with the team in The Old Chestnut she had held a secret dread that she was going to suffer a fall. It manifested itself as a dull pain at the top of her stomach, near her breadbasket. Like indigestion, but it was fear. These guys had enemies in droves, so maybe, likely, she had inherited their enmity and it had just barged through into her home. Then Cumming ambled into the vestibule, his face white and drawn but his expression as calm as ever.

'Sorry about this, doll,' he said, as if he had returned late from the pub having imbibed one drink too many. 'Wee bit o trouble and ye were the closest safe hoose.'

'Safe for what? What's happened? That guy looks wild . . .'

'Sheesh, calm down. Looks worse than it is.'

'I'm very bloody relieved to hear that. What's happened to him?'

'Him? Happen tae HIM? Haaaa, good one that, hen.'

'Look, Joe 90, Ah'm no in the mood for laughing.' Kay was angry and her accent showed it as well as her use of a nickname that some gave Bud Cumming but seldom in his hearing. She'd always thought of him kindly, jokingly, as Joe 90 but never before used it to his face. Cumming had that edgy look, stepping from foot to foot, holding her gaze with his own eyes, begging understanding without explanation. The look of a humbled lover, a misunderstood child, an unusual look for him. In short, he knew he'd overstepped the mark.

'It'll be fine, honest, Kay. It's jist Paul, he needs cleaning up.'

'Paul? Paul Sim?'

'Aye.' Cumming threw a glance, part embarrassment part plea to keep her voice down.

'You've brought Paul Sim into my home?' Kay's voice dropped to an urgent murmur.

'Aye, eh . . .'

'Covered in blood?' she demanded. The answer was so obvious that Cumming hesitated, not being used to being put on the defensive. The silence surrounded them, deafening them in the still of the night till she could hear the blood pumping in her temples.

'Well?' she blurted at Cumming, impatient and still scared.

'Excuse me, Kay, could I wash up in the kitchen?' Paul Sim's voice jolted through her, an aberration that didn't exist till it spoke, till he spoke, till now in her living-room. What should she say – get out? Go away? I'm terrified of you?

'Sure, eh, aye. Wait though, I'll get you some towels,' and she was off to the linen cupboard but not before seeing Cumming smile and mouth at her, 'Good girl.' For tuppence she'd have let him have it. A right good slap in the chops. That's what she felt like doing but what she did was fetch towels, old dark ones she could throw out if the blood didn't come out in the wash. She cleared away the dishes from the drainer, switched on the immersion for hot water and fetched Paul Sim a new cake of soap.

'Sorry about this,' Paul Sim muttered to her when they were alone in the kitchen. He'd stripped off the blood-soaked shirt that she noticed belonged to Cumming. Why was he wearing Cumming's shirt?

'No matter. You look in a right mess,' she offered, conceding that the guy needed help and she was stuck with him now. Besides, it hadn't been his decision to come to her house. 'Are you hurt? Will I fetch . . .' Paul Sim looked up from the sink where he was bending over splashing his face and heavily muscled torso with warm, soapy water.

He looked up and smiled. 'Naw, hen, naw naw. Ah'm just fine. No a scratch.' His expression was calm, contented, with a sly smirk at the side of his mouth. The joke was on Kay and she didn't like it.

'I'll leave you to it, Paul. If you want anything, just shout.' In the lounge she cornered Cumming, 'What's going on? I want to know.' In spite of the intrusion and the possibility she was going to be implicated in some violent crime, Kay still held Bud Cumming in too much awe to stay angry and hostile for long.

'Best ye know nuthin.' He turned away to stare at the TV screen still flickering with the volume turned off.

'No, Bud, I'm due an explanation.' He turned and looked at her, his jaw working at the dilemma. 'Please,' she insisted.

'He was doing a favour for somebody, that's all.'

'There has to be more to it than that.' She stood in the middle of the room, her hands straight down by her side, her chin slightly jutting forward and a thin-lipped expression on her face spelling determination. It was a stance he was familiar with and knew she would not be easily appeased.

'Ye heard o Ronnie Neeson?'

'No, should I have?' Ronnie Neeson was serving life with many years added on for jailhouse troubles. He'd participated in the riots that raged through Scotland's prisons in the 1980s and wouldn't lie down to anyone – screws or cons. To some, Ronnie Neeson was a hero fighting the system. To others, he was a wee man too big for his boots. Whatever they thought, everyone respected him.

'Aye, if ye read the papers. He gave a bit o grief tae this certain party in the jail. Big Paul did his brother the night tae even the score. A wee threatener wid no have worked wi Ronnie.'

'Fucking hell, Bud, what did he do to him?'

'Aw a cracker, man.' For the first time that night Cumming seemed to relax. 'Slashed him a beauty right down the back o his lug hole. From here tae here.' Cumming illustrated, drawing his finger slowly down from his skull at the back of one ear, along his jaw bone, under his chin to the soft flesh of his throat. 'A rasper. Bled like a stuck pig.'

'So I can see.'

'Have I left a spare shirt here, Kay? For the boy like?'

'I don't like this, Bud. Don't like this at all.'

'Ah know, Ah know. There wisnae anywhere else to go, but.'

'What if I hadn't been in?' He started backing off again, palms in the air in that awkward expression of conceding. 'Or I'd people in?'

'Aye, yer right . . .'

'Or I was out and some of my family or friends were here?'

'Point taken.'

'I'll fetch that shirt . . .' Kay knew when to back off. She had been angry and had come to believe that Bud Cumming would respect that – wouldn't need to be told again and again like some people.

'So Ah'll phone in future,' Cumming muttered quietly but distinctly. Kay stopped in her tracks at the lounge door and turned back to him.

'You'll wha . . .' She was interrupted by Paul Sim emerging from the kitchen scrubbed and clean. Now he looked what he was, a strong young man hardly more than a child. But powerful – standing well over six foot, with the triangular torso of an American footballer, thick biceps and wrists as broad as Kay's neck. A strong chin that always looked set, determined, and a broad forehead. Sim was a picture of health and well-being that didn't fit his occupation or what he'd just done that very night. But he was in the room and was looking at Kay,

'Sorry, Kay, but Ah've messed up these towels,' Paul Sim said.

'No problem. Get us a plastic bag, hen, and we'll dispose o the towels, eh?' Cumming offered. Kay looked at him, her mind still on his comment about phoning first. If she let that pass it meant that she would be accepting that it would happen again. Kay knew that she had to speak out now. Tell him what was and was not acceptable. Draw her lines, her boundaries. Leave him in no doubt that she didn't want to be included in any way with this violence. Put him straight. But there were two sets of eyes on her – the myopic scowl of Cumming and the clear gaze of young Paul Sim. This was a matter between her and Cumming. A private matter. To speak out in front of one of his team wasn't right, she knew that. To let rip the anger she felt would have run a risk of Cumming losing face. Kay already knew that the world he inhabited depended so much on reputation. It was as important as power, as the potential for violence. She wouldn't do that to Cumming – he may have upset her but she still thought the world of him. It was a matter between the pair of them, not for other ears. Besides, Paul Sim unnerved her and what she had learned tonight had added to her fear. She'd hold her tongue for another time,

'I'll get the shirt and the bag,' she replied and left the room. From inside the linen cupboard she could hear the muffled voices of the men talking happily, joking, in the lounge. She hoped they were reliving the success of their work that night. Taking pleasure in the hit. Sucking all the joy out of that poor man's suffering. Anything as long as they weren't laughing at her. She'd learned Cumming's lesson well. Watch what people do and say then work out what they don't want you to know. What they are hiding.

As she saw Cumming and Paul Sim to the door, the farewells were more appropriate to the end of a pleasant social visit.

'See yese the morrow, hen,' bellowed Cumming with a warm wave as he headed towards his car.

'Thanks for yer help, Kay,' said Paul Sim, the carrier bag full of blood-soaked shirt and towels dangling from one of his big fists.

'Aye, nice to see you both,' replied Kay politely for the benefit of any eavesdropping neighbours. 'Can we meet for a wee chat tomorrow, Bud?'

'Sure. Lunch at The Dovecote?'

'Aye, just you and me?'

'Of course. Round about one o'clock?'

'Yeah, that's fine. See ye there.'

'Night, hen.'

'Good night,' Kay called pleasantly, shutting the door. Tomorrow she would tell Joe 90 Cumming exactly where to get off. Seeing him was fine but she didn't want a repeat of that night's scene. Kay Petrie wasn't going to get involved in any violence and she'd tell him that straight the very next day.

Shot the Craw

Y ou're where?' Kay spluttered into her mobile phone, confused and bewildered at Cumming's message.

'Wee place in the country. Ye'll no know it,' he answered in the matter-of-fact tones of a husband calling home from the train to tell his wife when to expect his arrival so she could have his dinner on the table.

'But we were meant to be meeting.' Kay had been practising her speech all morning. She was going to tell him that the events of the night before were unacceptable but the rest was still okay. She had worried that she wouldn't carry it off and he'd dump her from his life entirely. Now this.

'Yer in or yer oot,' she'd heard George Lennon tell a pale-faced, young team member one day and the other men nodded and glowered. She hadn't seen the young guy since. Maybe the same rules applied to her? All that worrying and he had disappeared overnight.

'Ah know, Ah know. Sorry but.'

'We agreed at only two o'clock this morning. What could've . . .'

'Kay, I'm sorry, hen, but it's serious. Unavoidable . . .'

'Business, I assume,' she butted in, bitterness glimmering in her voice. She'd become used to business always coming first with Bud Cumming but she'd built herself up all night to clearing the air between them and now she was being thwarted.

'Aye, ye could say that. Listen, I don't have long . . .'

'Meeting about to start, is it?'

'Eh? Naw, naw, Ah've got tae drive a bit further. Cannae hang aboot.'

'Obviously . . .'

'Kay, believe me this is serious. Go and see the boys today. Usual place. Lennon will explain. Ye'll understand then.' Cumming sounded unusually tense, almost frightened. Not that a casual acquaintance would notice but Kay knew him well enough to catch a faint quiver in the timbre of his voice.

'Okay, Bud. Sure. Listen, are you all right?' she relented, never being able to feel anger towards Bud Cumming for any length of time.

'Me, fine, hen, never better. Just a bit tired frae the driving.' She hated the need for secrecy and his overriding concern with security. Cumming refused to have a straightforward conversation on the telephone, either speaking in code or saying nothing meaningful, not even where they were going to meet for a social drink. He and his crew had taps set up on a number of rivals' phones and assumed they had reciprocated. When she once asked him if it was the police he was worried about he just burst out laughing and reassured her that they had been taken care of and were no threat whatsoever.

'Phone me when you get there, eh? Wherever that is, please?' she asked, now worry for his well-being replacing her pique.

'Course Ah will. Jist keep yer moby oan. Got tae split. Talk later.'

'Yeah, you take . . .' He'd already hung up, leaving her none the wiser other than she wasn't going to be seeing Bud Cumming for a while.

George Lennon was standing alone outside The Old Chestnut as she drove past on her way to The Dovecote. Much as Kay hated The Chestnut and the area, she couldn't wait to find out what was so important to drag Cumming away in the middle of the night. Slamming on the brakes she quickly steered into a U-turn at traffic lights, ignoring the blasts of car horns and a swerving corporation bus. She was taking a diversion to have a chat with Lennon.

'How ye doin, Stirling Moss?' Lennon was a wry man not much given to smiling. This was the closest he got to cracking a joke.

'Cumming told me to see you.' Kay wasn't much in the mood for pleasantries either.

'Aye, he said annat.' Lennon looked around him, watching the uneasy welfare queue outside the sub-post office across the street, bored young men walking the walk, kids looking for something else to explore. This was his home turf and he watched it closely, seeing significance where others saw none. 'Let's take a dander,' he said, jerking his head in the direction he wanted them to move. Kay had had maybe three or four one-to-one conversations with Lennon before and wasn't sure how to take him. As Cumming would say, it wasn't so much what he told her but more what he didn't convey that worried Kay. He was an absolutely loyal lieutenant to Bud Cumming but business was their bond and nothing else.

'A guy's been killed,' he started, his eyes still scanning around him. 'They're blaming Bud.' Lennon stopped as if that was adequate explanation. First the blood-soaked Paul Sim scrubbing up in her house, now her lover accused of murder. Kay felt dizzy, displaced, not there.

'Who?' she gulped in air. 'Who has been killed?' Lennon kept walking slowly, not answering, not turning round. Two men were approaching along the pavement. As one spotted Lennon he abruptly turned, took hold of his friend's arm and led him across the road, dodging fast-moving cars as they went. Kay watched Lennon's eyes steadily following the men, silently telling them that they had been marked.

'Jist a guy. Fucking waster that works for a rival firm. Small fry. As if Cumming wid bother wi him,' Lennon spat through clenched teeth, sending a fine stream of spittle streaking the ground with a splat. 'But somebody's fingered oor friend, right?'

'He didn't do it, did he?' The words were out before Kay

could think. It was a natural question, reaching out for reassurance, but one that earned her a scowl from Lennon.

'Naw, fuck's sakes, Kay, ye know the score. He gies orders, no does the dirty.'

'Aye, but I just need to know . . . to know what we're up against.' She surprised herself at how calm her voice sounded and Lennon was obviously impressed.

'Yer right. Spot oan, of course. But wee Bud's clean.' She noticed that when he spoke Lennon's lips and jaw hardly moved. Even if an expert lip reader had been focused on his face through binoculars from across the way they would still be clueless as to what he was saying. That was the whole point, of course. 'Jist has tae keep oot o the way for a while an it'll be sorted.'

'Who grassed him, George? Dirty bastard.'

'Aye, dirty fucking bastard right enough. But it's been coming for a while. No unexpected like.'

'I take it it's a secure issue,' said Kay, using the team's shorthand for the security business. Lennon stopped in his tracks and turned to stare at Kay, then he smiled, a thin-lipped mockery of joy but it was his smile right enough. He was impressed by her language.

'Dead right,' he nodded vigorously. 'Fucker disnae like oor angels guarding the toon. Imagine that, eh?' And he laughed a dry chuckle that sounded as if he was going to cough. His little word play amused him no end. Bud Cumming was an unofficial director of a security firm we'll call Guardian Angels, one of the largest and most lucrative in the country. Guardian Angels was run by a guy we'll call Ally Jolson, an ex-cop and convicted fraudster backed up by The Licensee and the likes of Cumming. The company employed some heavy players – officially and unofficially. But then so did many of the security firms. What could not be disputed is that they did a reasonable job and were much better than the firms staffed entirely by retired policemen who, after all, only knew how to detect crime after the deed. The firms run by ex-cons were experts on how crimes are committed, a knowledge easily applied to the task of stopping it happening in the first instance. But there was a down side. Some, not all but certainly some Guardian Angels, had other business interests of a strictly illegal nature and used the world of security to cover up these dubious enterprises. For people like Joe 90 and The Licensee, the legitimate was always tainted by the crooked in the chase for power and money, so others treated them in that way. In the case of Guardian Angels the pundits were absolutely right. Guys like Cumming gave the security business a bad name.

'Where has Bud gone?' Kay asked, already knowing the answer she was to receive.

'Can't tell yese. Ah mean Ah don't know masel. Expect he's moving around wee country hotels down south – that's his usual routine.'

'How did the guy die?' asked Kay, resisting the urge to ask the victim's name.

'Shot,' Lennon shrugged and spat again. He had some filthy habits for a man with so much money.

'Witnesses?'

'Naw, but they're saying there was. The usual routine.'

'Do we know who the grass is?'

'Aye, aw aye.' Lennon stopped and guided Kay round, turning back towards her car. 'And we know where he is.'

On a patch of wasteground across the street two young boys were rolling around on the ground screaming and slapping at each other. Goaded on by a group of boys and girls their own age as well as a few bored men and women drawn away from their usual station hanging around outside the off-sales – the fight seemed pathetic and sad.

'Gie him a fucking doing,' howled one of the men.

'C'moan, Tommy, stamp oan the cunt's heid.' A teenager was standing close to the pair, kicking whichever body was closest.

'Ye'd better sort him, Tommy, or yer da'll gie ye worse,' screeched a woman, a can of super lager in one hand and a lit cigarette in the other. Tommy was getting the upper hand and climbed on top of his opponent, straddling his chest and kneeling on his shoulders.

'Say yer wrang,' he shouted.

'Nuh,' replied the prone child, prompting the other to let loose a hail of punches into his face.

'Go oan, ye wee prick.'

'Nuh,' through tears. More punches drawing blood from his mouth and nose.

'Ah'll finish yese aff if ye dinnae admit it.'

'Fuck off, ye fanny. Yer team's shite.' The repeat of the dispute which had started with football and ended up on religion brought fury to the winning combatant who grabbed the other by the hair and started bashing his skull into the concrete ground again and again. Behind his back a grown man with a lit fag in his mouth, dressed in layers of coats, had removed the losing fighter's shoes and in two fierce movements yanked off the boy's trousers and underwear. His white, skinny legs flapped in the grey city light as the crowd laughed and pointed. The teenage boy, bored with kicking the fighters, kneeled down beside the pair and grabbed the boy's tiny, curved penis.

'Chinese burn,' screamed a tot of a girl. 'Gie him a cracker.'

'Naw, you dae it,' dared the teenager.

'Ma ma wid kill me,' replied the girl.

'Well she's no here,' butted in one of the male drinkers, 'an Ah'll no tell.'

'Leave the lassie alane,' ordered a woman old enough to be the loser's grandmother. 'Hud ma can, eh?' She handed her drink to a watcher and knelt down beside the boy who was no longer struggling, his face deathly pale, eyes closed and his mouth gaping. 'Let's see whit they Proddies are made o,' she said and started to masturbate the small boy to the noises of encouragement from the onlookers. Then she grabbed his penis and twisted hard again and again to the sound of the boy's frantic wails.

Kay turned away sick and disgusted, haunted by her own childhood nightmares. That was real life across the way. People queuing up to abuse the weak. To use them sexually. To laugh at their pain. People were like that. All these years she had been so naive. Time and time again she had been the scapegoat but still she chose to think the best, always convinced that her life would improve. But it wasn't her life, just life in general. That's the way it was and always would be.

'Who are you going to be, Kay?' she asked herself. 'That poor kid across the road? You going to be like that forever?' Opening the driver's door of her car, she turned to Lennon, 'Tell Bud, if he phones you first, whatever he wants I'm up for it.'

'Aye, course Ah will,' he replied. 'An if he phones you first tell him that it's going to take a couple o weeks tae sort.'

'Just that?'

'Aye, he'll know.' Lennon checked his watch and spat on the ground. 'Ye'll be coming tae the pow-wow at The Dovecote later, eh?' Behind her Kay heard a howl of glee rising up from the small boy's tormentors and decided not to turn round.

'Course I will. Business as usual, eh?'

'Aye,' replied Lennon, spitting one more time, 'life goes on.'

'As of now it does,' Kay thought to herself, putting her car in gear and racing out into the stream of traffic. 'I'm not going to be a victim ever again.' Kay had decided to put herself right behind Bud Cumming. Wherever he was going that was okay with her. From now on other people could be the suckers. Not her, not Kay, no way.

Busman's Holiday

When Bud Cumming called she didn't hesitate. A few hours to pack, she checked the road map and headed south. It was a long drive but worth it. Her promise to herself had been spot on, she knew that now. Not only was she going be a player rather than a victim, she was Bud Cumming's woman. So he based his life on crime. So what? She had earned a living for a number of years from activities that the state considered illegal and polite society considered immoral. Well, publicly they did, while secretly she listed journalists, lawyers, Church of Scotland ministers, politicians, at least one priest, a rabbi and tens of policemen among her johns. One colleague she knew did tricks for an outspoken feminist pundit who was always on the TV riling against the exploitation of women. Hypocrites the lot of them. It all added up to her, Kay Petrie, being placed beyond the edge. Not that she wanted to be there – it was where they put her. So what was the big difference in her man being a crime overlord? At least he wasn't two-faced about what he did.

By the time she saw the signs for Oxford she was weary and sweaty. Skirting through Aylesbury, she thought she was lost. When she finally turned in to the driveway of the designated country club she wondered if Bud Cumming was playing a practical joke. According to George Lennon, Cumming hid out in 'wee country hotels'. Well, it was certainly in the country but small it was not. The manicured lawns and rows of poplar trees lined the private road for what seemed like miles. Through a gap in the trees she spotted a golf course, lush and green with two brightly clad men marching smartly down a fairway followed by two caddies lugging golf bags of impressive girth. The building appeared suddenly round a gentle bend – more palatial than a country hotel. When she parked, a liveried doorman appeared at her side window before she had stepped out of the car. For a minute she thought he was there to turn her away, tell her that scruffs like her were not allowed.

'Good evening and welcome, madam,' he said, standing smartly at attention. 'Your journey was pleasant I trust.' He smiled at her warmly.

'Yeah . . . oh yeah,' Kay muttered, her fluency lost in the long silent hours of the journey.

'Travel far, madam?'

'Yeah . . . eh, no,' she caught herself in time as she was about to say where she had come from. Golden rule: reveal nothing to anyone, not even the most innocuous-seeming bystander. 'Not too far.' As the doorman carried Kay's cases into the hotel, she turned to watch a group of men and women playing croquet on a nearby lawn. They were dressed in summer togs – baggy linen suits for the men and flouncy, floral dresses for the women. The colours and the noises of their cheery banter reminded Kay of some film about the privileged upper classes, a million miles from her place in Arden, Glasgow.

'Good evening, madam,' the male receptionist smiled, his voice purring like a smooth, expensive limousine. 'How can I help you?'

'I'm here to join my husband, Mr Black,' replied Kay, cursing Bud Cumming under her breath for not choosing a more original pseudonym.

'Certainly, madam, we have been expecting you.' The receptionist's smile stayed constant on his face, as if his lips were stuck. Kay looked at his pale blue eyes and thought she saw disinterest and boredom that didn't match his pleasant expression. Without further ado, the receptionist rang a bell and a man in dark trousers and a crisp white jacket lifted Kay's case and asked her to follow him. In the lift – one of those old-fashioned jobs full of brass fittings and gates which had to be closed manually – Kay started ranting to fill up the silence.

'Lovely hotel you have. Reminds me of one I stayed in last year. It looked the same but didn't have the facilities – you know, the golf course and croquet and so on. It was down by the sea, mind. Like the sea. But the country's nice as well. My husband prefers the country. He likes his feet to be on firm ground . . .' The bell-boy looked straight ahead and said nothing as the lift climbed slowly. Kay twittered on, '. . . my husband is that type of person. Always likes to be sure of where he is. I guess that's why he chose this place . . . my husband . . . my husband . . .'

As they walked down the thickly carpeted corridor, Kay didn't let up. She wasn't sure why she was so nervous. Was it meeting Bud Cumming away from their hunting ground in Glasgow? Or was it the manners of the staff in the hotel? Or just the pretence? As they reached the door she was still spouting. 'My husband has been talking about taking up golf for so long now. Maybe he'll try the game now that he's here . . .'

'Likes 'is sport yer man does.' The porter's first words in the refined, muffled setting of the luxuriously appointed corridor shook Kay. Unlike the others she had spoken to since her arrival, his accent was olde worlde, rural with a guttural twang.

'Eh, yes,' she replied. 'Yes, he does.' Wondering what Bud Cumming had been playing during his stay. The porter murmured something she couldn't make out and stopped abruptly, knocking on a bedroom door marked by a name rather than a number. Kay was still gaping at the porter when the room door was opened.

'Hullo, doll, great tae see yese,' boomed Cumming, grabbing Kay and hoisting her off her feet, if only an inch due to their similarity in height. Behind them the porter shuffled in and laid the cases down neatly. There was plenty of floor space. Cumming had rented a suite of rooms that must have been

bigger than Kay's own flat. 'Thanks, pal,' breathed Bud, letting
go of Kay at last and handing the man a generous tip. 'Ye made
good time, eh?' he said to Kay.

'Aye, not bad,' she replied while watching the porter shuffle
out. Did she imagine the man looking up momentarily and
staring her straight in the eyes? Did she imagine that look was
one of 'I know what you're up to', looking down his nose at her?
Was it that obvious, she wondered.

Bud had booked dinner at eight and they just had enough
time to shower and change. The rule was formal dress and Kay
was relieved she had packed heavy and come well prepared. One
of the things she loved about Bud was that he didn't grab her
immediately and use her sexually. She knew that was because he
had a low sex drive, a tiny penis and a recurring impotence
problem. But that was okay by her – a welcome relief from the
johns who paid their money and stuck their cocks into her
without as much as a by your leave.

Down in the bar, they sat drinking a few vodka martinis
before dinner.

'Ah've got someone Ah have tae see, hen,' Bud suddenly
offered.

'When?' Kay asked, expecting the answer to be the following
day or even later that night.

'The now.' Bud lifted his drink and looked straight at her
through those thick lenses. 'He's staying here the night but is
going first thing,' he explained. 'Don't want us tae have tae get
up early in the morning, eh?' Kay wondered what the fuss was
since Bud rarely slept, although he was increasingly sleeping
when he was with her. Called her his saviour, saving him from the
insanity of the unhappy insomniac.

'Yeah, no problem,' replied Kay and managed a smile, though
in truth feeling a little miffed that he should be planning to leave
her so soon after her arrival.

'Good girl, in fact here he is now.' Bud was on his feet and crossing the room, holding out his hand in welcome. The man was in his fifties, white-haired, with a suntan and suavely dressed. One of those men who looked good regardless of how old they were. 'Won't be long, hen,' Bud called over his shoulder, leading his associate out of the room. 'Order whatever ye fancy.' Kay didn't know why but she hoped that the porter with the sly look wouldn't come into the bar while Bud was gone.

Bud was true to his word and was only away for half an hour. Over dinner and several bottles of champagne they chatted about inconsequential matters – what was happening in the news, members of their respective families, trivia – though back in the room they relaxed.

'One of the things Ah like about you, Kay, is that Ah can trust yese,' said Bud, now worse the wear for the drink.

'I hope so,' she replied, 'because I'd never betray you.' It was a more emotional statement than Kay was used to giving but she had only the day before decided to throw her lot in with Cumming. Besides, she had matched him glass for glass. 'But do you really trust me or are you just saying that?' Cumming looked at her from the other end of the sofa, shoved his glasses up on to the bridge of his nose and smiled.

'See the guy that Ah met doonstairs?' he asked with a smirk.

'How could I forget,' Kay laughed, 'I haven't had that much to drink.'

'Wannae know who he is?' Cumming looked at her with a certain impertinent, small-boy expression he often used when about to be generous with a secret.

'Eh . . . aye.' Kay was thinking carefully, unwilling to risk too much. Asking for information was not an attribute that street players admired. 'Mean, I'm curious but only if you want to tell me.' Cumming smiled wide, enjoying the moment.

'He's the father of a soap star an he's just been charged oan a multi-million pound drug-trafficking deal.' His smile turned to a conspiratorial wink. 'That lassie, blonde-haired Ah think. Good looker.' Kay wasn't surprised that Cumming couldn't be more specific. She had never seen him watching anything on TV, let alone a soap series.

'Haaa,' she laughed, 'you're useless when it comes to the telly.' Cumming shrugged in acceptance of the criticism. 'Is she on *EastEnders* or *Coronation Street*?'

'She's no.'

'I thought you said . . .'

'She left the show,' he laughed, enjoying the tease.

'Okay, but which?' Kay punched him on the shoulder playfully.

'Ah'll tell yese if . . .'

'What?' Kay was beginning to feel tense. The tease had worked and now she needed to know more about the mysterious stranger.

'. . . ye'll come tae bed.'

'Oh, let me think.' Finger on her lips, puzzled expression wrinkling her brow. 'Mmm . . . eh . . . oh, all right then.' He knew he didn't have to negotiate.

Two sweaty hours later, they had sniffed several lines of coke, helped along with some speed and still Bud Cumming had failed to reach an orgasm. It was a pattern Kay was getting used to in their lovemaking. With her, he would gain an erection after some skilled foreplay, oral stimulation, lots of massage and dirty talk. Once hard he would enter her and ride like fury, refusing to take his time or relax in case his cock withered. For most men the approach would result in premature ejaculation but Bud Cumming was different – he simply couldn't come most of the time. They lay in bed silently, their limbs wrapped round each other, Kay stroking his cheek gently, sensing his unarticulated disappointment.

'*EastEnders* – I think,' he said, breaking the quiet.

She kissed his cheek, 'Thank you.'

'Do one more thing for me?' his voice sounded hoarse.

'Anything,' and right there and then she meant it.

'I've always wanted tae try something . . .' Then he fell asleep.

The next night the hooker arrived on time. She looked about fourteen years old, skinny, with acne on her cheeks. But for her dyed blonde-red hair and dark, dusky skin Kay could have imagined she was looking at her own mirror image of a few years earlier. They didn't make dinner that night. Just made a mess of the sheets.

The three-in-a-bed didn't happen again that trip but Cumming would ask, 'Who will we have the night?' every afternoon, as if Kay had asked for the experience in cahoots with him. But he was only joking. A little dirty thought to spice up their days. They were lovers who trusted each other enough to push the boundaries out. And that's what saw her through, helping her to distinguish between their little games and the expectations placed on her as a working girl. That and the fact that the other woman was sent packing in the early hours of the morning while she stayed on. Prostitutes didn't stay on.

They moved around the south of England, flitting from one luxury hotel to another, always in the country and using different names. Bud Cumming had an impressive stash of money, credit cards in a range of names and different signature styles to go with them. The cards were genuine and paid out so the hotels never complained, never suspected. He treated her well – buying her whatever she wanted and, more importantly, telling her secrets about his business. Kay had already learned a lot from her inclusion in the team's business meetings but was keen to learn more. She never asked, but he told her. The London connection that was about trading illegal weapons and how, through him, half the teams in Glasgow were doing business. The drugs connection with one Liverpool team and their direct link to Dublin. How he had instigated contacts directly with the suppliers in the Middle East and South America with plans to cut out the many middle-men who took a slice of the drugs trade. Exporting ringed cars into Kenya, Tenerife, Tunisia. The growing link with teams in Eastern Europe in smuggling tobacco back into the UK, augmented with some booze and the occasional bundle of heroin. How the international scene was the future but, right now, it could only be kept open if his base in Glasgow was secure, and that's what Cumming was worried about.

'If the foreign mobs get a whiff o weakness back in ma home patch they'll drop me pronto,' he explained.

'How would they find out?' asked Kay.

'These are no amateurs,' he explained with an exasperated sigh. 'These guys have been working on an international basis for generations. Some o them used to be in the secret service or the army in their homelands. Tell ye, Kay, there's already Russians and Iraqis and Colombians back in Glasgow – no that they declare themselves, like.'

By the time she was driving away back home, Kay's view of the whole crime scene had changed, expanded. She had thought that the gang scene in Glasgow was complex enough but that was only where it started. Kay couldn't see the difference between crime and commerce when it came to organisation. In fact, Bud Cumming had listed some well-known, international legitimate companies – names that everyone knew – who were his partners in ploys such as smuggling tobacco and laundering money. It got so she wondered if there were any differences between legitimate and illegitimate business. Add to that the bent politicians in various countries and alliances with the forces of law and order and she understood why Bud Cumming didn't sleep. The whole show was a perplexing labyrinth.

'Poor Bud,' she thought as she raced up the motorway home. Home to Glasgow, where soon she was to meet the real reason Bud Cumming didn't sleep.

Fee-Fi-Fo-Fum . . .

His massive frame blotted out the light as he stood in her doorway. Once seen, it was a shape and a look she could never forget.

'Oh . . . hello,' she muttered, trying to raise a pleasant tone and doubting that she had succeeded.

'Hi, Kay,' answered Paul Sim in a booming voice that matched his barrel chest, 'wee Bud asked me tae look in on you.'

'That's . . . eh, nice,' she replied, craning her neck back to look him in the face. She applied her rule – see beyond their words and suss what they are trying not to tell you – and drew a blank. He was six-foot-six, broad as the doorway, handsome, fresh-faced with a strong jaw that jutted like concrete. A living cartoon caricature of a powerful man. And he terrified her.

Kay knew that she had to invite Paul Sim in. Serving coffee and biscuits, she thought about what Cumming had told her about the young man sitting quietly and politely at her table. He was twenty-one years of age and the gang's equaliser. The one they called on to dish out extra violence, terror and pain when it was needed. Bud Cumming would threaten other teams with years of experience and fierce reputations by sending young Paul to see them. It always made them think and usually concede to his demands. With the young guy, it didn't matter what odds he was up against and he cared not a whit for the infamy of his opposition. He simply hurt them. Paul Sim had his own business dealing coke, Ecstasy, jellies and blues throughout some of the most heavily populated housing schemes in Britain. His customers always paid up and other dealers never considered moving in on his patch. Aside from that Bud Cumming paid him for his work with a blade or a gun or a hammer. Aged twenty-one, Paul Sim was well on his way to becoming a major player on the streets of Glasgow. Cumming had admitted to Kay that he was scared of Paul Sim and she had asked why he kept him on.

'Nobody tells Paul whit tae dae,' he had explained. 'Nobody. Besides, Ah cannae sack ma ain cousin, eh?'

Kay looked at the man mountain and shivered. She could imagine those hulking fists grasping a cleaver or a gun. But the face was dour but sweet. His age, she supposed. Angel-faced killer, the schemes were full of them, just usually not so large, so menacing.

'Good coffee, Kay, cheers,' Paul Sim said and she felt her insides jump.

'No problem, can I get you anything else?'

'Ha, Ah was gonnae ask you the same question,' he grinned a great wide smile, full of even white teeth.

'Eh . . .'

'Bud asked me tae check up ye were safe but Ah reckon ye can take care o yersel, eh?'

'Ah'd like to think so.'

'Aye.' He drummed his fingers on the table and looked around the room as if he were unsure of himself, nervous and ill at ease. 'But if there's anything Ah can get for you . . .'

'Like . . . eh, what?' He sucked air noisily through his lips and considered the question carefully.

'Money or drugs, or if ye need a lift anywhere we could take yese.' Paul nodded sideways at the door and Kay moved over to the window. There was Cumming's silver Mercedes parked outside her house with the chauffeur at the wheel.

'Aw, I didn't know you had Harry with you.'

'Aye,' Paul shrugged.

'You should've brought him in.'

'Naaa, don't want tae spoil the bastard, eh? He'll get ideas above his station.' Paul Sim sneered and for the first time Kay could see the cruelty in his young face.

'That's a shame,' she persisted.

'Och, dinnae worry aboot Harry. Cunt thinks he's Bud's lieutenant.' Paul was nodding his head gravely, seriously. 'An he's no even a good driver,' he said, smiling again.

'Still, it's a . . .'

'Ah heard you were a bit o a dab hand behind the wheel yersel.'

'Aye, not bad, but who told you that?'

'Aw, Bud did. Says you used tae drive for Lenny Lovat.'

'Did he now?' Kay thought that her escapades with Lenny had been a secret between the two of them. She had learned that tie-up merchants were singularly secretive about their modus operandi and she had expected Lenny to be no different. What had happened? Had her legal husband turned talkative in jail, languishing in his drug-induced stupor? How else would Bud Cumming know?

'Said ye were better than Lenny, which is a big compliment.'

'Mmm . . .' Kay was for giving nothing back. How did she know that Bud had told Paul Sim anything at all? If Bud was frightened of the young man maybe it was for other reasons as well as his potential for violence.

'Ah'm shite at it masel,' he continued, 'especially wi the lights oot in the dark. Cannae see a fucking thing.' Kay nodded and looked away, praying that the team's muscle wasn't about to ask her a direct question. He didn't. 'Listen though, Ah'll have tae shift. Got some guys tae see aboot a wee financial transaction.' The smile on his face seemed pleasant enough but Kay wondered what the 'financial transaction' entailed and shivered again. 'Sure Ah cannae get yese anything?'

Kay watched the silver Mercedes pull away from the kerb before she sighed with relief. She had been told to use the number sparingly, only in an emergency, but she didn't care.

ARMED CANDY

Snatching her mobile phone she dialled the number she had
memorised to prevent it being written down anywhere and
discovered by the police should they ever raid her home.

'I've just had a visit,' she said to Cumming, rather than hello.

'Who?' he replied. 'The bizzies? Christ sakes, Kay, ye know ye
shouldnae phone me if the polis are aboot.'

'No, no the fucking police, your mental cousin.'

'Whit? Paul?'

'Aye, Paul.'

'Was Harry wi him?'

'Aye, in the motor but that's not . . .'

'In the motor? Harry stayed in the motor?'

'Yeah but . . .'

'Ah asked Harry tae visit yese. Make sure ye were aw right.
No Paul. Whit's he up tae?'

'I don't know and I don't care. Just tell him to back off,'
snapped Kay.

'Back off? Tell Paul tae back off,' Bud Cumming was laughing
at the other end of the phone line.

'Bud, it's no funny,' Kay pleaded. 'He scares me.'

'Naw, yer right, hen. It's no funny, he scares me too.'

'But . . .'

'Look, Ah told ye afore, no one can tell Paul tae dae anything.
Nobody. Yer stuck wi him.'

A few blocks away in the driver's seat of the silver Mercedes,
Harry was not happy. He had been promised and now he felt let
down. That big Paul Sim had got in the way and he wasn't for
arguing with him. Harry sat on his temper and accepted that he
was stuck with big Paul. Nobody told him what to do. Nobody.

Winner Takes All

Kay sat in the familiar surroundings of The Old Chestnut and watched the men. They were all there, apart from Bud. George Lennon held the chair, working through items as if it was a well-oiled board meeting. Jas O'Reilly and his brother Iain contributed seriously, steadily. Shuggie Patterson was his usual jumble of nerve-induced outbursts, his eyes small black pinheads staring through the bodies around him. Vinnie Mallon, another regular, had left his usual post at the pub's door where he set up local deals and watched the turf to listen to latest developments. With Bud away all hands were needed, even Vinnie, who was a minor player. Harry the driver sat wedged next to Lennon, nodding his head in a self-important way at every pronouncement. Paul Sim was there, sitting on the edge of the group, slouching back on his chair with one ankle resting on his other knee, watching the proceedings through slits of eyes. Anyone who didn't know better would have thought he was about to fall asleep. Kay knew better.

'So it's the night . . . agreed?' said George Lennon, more as a decision than a question. Heads nodded around him. 'Get it sorted, Paul, and we can get wee Bud up the road, eh? Taken a month already – too long.' Paul Sim's answer was the slightest raising of his eyes and a narrow grin. 'Good. Next thing,' continued George Lennon, 'what about this cunt frae Manchester? What's it's name, Danny James?'

'He's bad news, George,' butted in Shuggie Patterson, 'if we dinnae sort him. Man, he's gonnae bring us grief big style.' Heads moved in agreement.

'We should get big Paul tae see tae him then,' offered Harry the driver.

'Have tae agree,' said Iain O'Reilly. 'In fact, if yese want, Ah'll see tae it.' His brother Jas, known as a driver and a pair of safe hands, shook his head, disappointed at Iain's readiness to go for a gun but saw better than to say anything lest he look out of alignment with the rest of the team.

'Whit dae you think, Kay?' asked George Lennon. The men all looked up towards her, except Paul Sim, who stayed exactly as he was.

'Well,' she started, 'seems he is a problem.'

'Aye . . .'

'Fucking right he is . . .'

'Bad cunt an no doubt . . .'

George Lennon glowered at the men who fell silent immediately.

'So if he wasn't around,' continued Kay, 'we would feel easier.' Shuggie Patterson went to speak but caught Lennon's eye and thought better of it. 'But what will his team think?'

'Who gives a fuck?'

'Sort they wankers oot as well . . .'

'Bunch a tubes . . .'

'Mm, tubes that we need,' said Kay. 'Wankers that can survive the heat of Manchester – Mach 10 City no less. A team that'll no take kindly to us terminating a contract. A contract we need to earn . . . well, how much, George?' George Lennon looked at Kay and frowned. Money wasn't spoken about in such situations, ever. Kay raised her hand at him and smiled, 'I know, but if I said a great deal would that be fair?'

'Aye, fair comment,' he replied gruffly.

'And we are willing to lose that because of what? This one guy makes some of you nervous.' Kay's turn to shake her head. 'Don't think Bud would approve of a loss of income, do you? And who'll deal with us then? Once we get the reputation for taking care of

their members. And once that happens we're out in the cold . . .
if we're still around to feel it.'

As she had been talking, Kay watched the men watching her.
George Lennon had started stock still then gradually,
imperceptibly, began to nod his head. Seconds later, Harry the
driver joined in but more vigorously, keen for Lennon to see he
agreed with his view.

'Spot on,' declared George Lennon, 'and it's no up for debate.
RIGHT. We'll ask Bud tae come up the road via Liverpool and
have a wee word wi the team boss. See if they'll, eh, put in a
substitute for that Danny James cunt.' Lennon's football analogy
missed most of his colleagues but pleased him no end, causing
him to raise one of his rare, wry grins. 'Right, is it back here for
the meetings or dae we go tae The Dovecote?' demanded Lennon,
signalling that the serious business was over.

'Ah like it here so Ah dae . . .'

'Maybe better tae vary it so's folk cannae guess where . . .'

Kay said her goodbyes and left them to their chat. As she
pulled at the heavy swing doors, the effort made her turn and she
spotted Paul Sim, eyes wide open, watching her. She had been in
the bar for over two hours and he hadn't said a word. Not like his
now frequent visits to her home. He would arrive at all times of
day and night, sling off his jacket and sometimes his shirt and
talk and yap about the streets, how you deal with certain moves
and police tactics while smoking a joint and washing down
handfuls of blues or whatever he had at hand that night. Kay had
grown more at ease in his company but was still troubled by why
he was visiting her. She knew that Paul Sim had a woman, an ex-
topless model, tall, black, vivacious. Gorgeous by anyone's
standards. As far as she could ascertain from the other men, Paul
was not a fanny chaser like some. Business, drugs and
particularly violence was what Paul was known to get his rocks
off on. Women came far down the list. But Kay had grown fond
of him in an unusual sort of way. Like zoo keepers must get fond

ARMED CANDY

of their captive bears, knowing that they would never understand the beasts and at any time they might just choose to rip their guardians limb from limb. Whatever could be said about Paul Sim, he could never be seen as safe.

She had just arrived home and had time to start the shower running, strip off her clothes and pour herself a glass of wine when the doorbell went. She cursed, threw on her dressing gown and headed to the door. Harry the driver was standing there looking pale, drawn and terrified.

'Harry, what's up?' Kay asked a second before he fell through the doorway. But he hadn't fallen but had been pushed by Paul Sim, who came sauntering calmly in behind in that long stride of his. 'What the fuck's going on?' screeched Kay, wrapping her gown round her throat.

'Tell her,' demanded Paul, poking Harry sharply in the ribs with one beefy finger. Harry, usually a pert and dapper man, stood with stooped shoulders, teeth nervously nibbling his upper lip and kneading his fingers together. 'GET OAN WI IT,' roared Paul, thumping the smaller man between the shoulder blades, sending him staggering forward and almost into Kay.

'Kay, Ah'm sorry,' muttered Harry, the strain of tears close to breaking his voice.

'What?' said Kay. 'What's this nonsense? Paul, stop bullying him for Christ's sake.' Kay stepped round Harry and squared up to Paul. Since childhood she had hated bullying and wasn't going to stand for it now, not even from the team's killer. Paul looked down at her and grinned.

'Ye need tae hear whit the wee shite has tae say, Kay,' Paul said quietly, reasonably. 'It's important.' Maybe it was the hours they had spent together at the table drinking coffee and talking on all his impromptu visits but Kay connected with that sombre tone in a way she would have found impossible weeks before. She knew Paul Sim was being sincere.

'Come on, Harry,' Kay turned to look at the driver. 'Just tell

189

me. You'll be okay . . . promise.' Tears of terror ran slowly down Harry the driver's cheeks. The man shook, quivering in his boots. He was just too scared to speak. 'Paul,' Kay ordered, 'tell Harry that you'll no hurt him.'

'Aw, Kay, but . . .' Paul protested.

'Just tell him or he'll not say a word. Tell him and mean it.'

'You sure cause . . .'

'AYE, just bloody well promise. Not a hair on his head. RIGHT?' Paul Sim crossed the room and took hold of Harry the driver by the point of his chin, tilting his head back till they looked each other in the face.

'Ah'll no hurt ye, promise.' Still holding on to his chin. 'This time, ye wee fucking waster.' Minutes later, Harry the driver had either believed what he heard or, more likely, worked out that if he didn't say anything he was going to get hurt badly anyway. The only choice he had now was to speak up, keep his end of the bargain and hope that big Paul Sim would keep his promise to Kay.

'He said Ah could shag yese,' Harry muttered, hanging his head.

'What?' gasped Kay, glaring up at Paul, assuming Harry meant him.

'Said that while he was away Ah could come roon here any time an . . . well, and fuck ye.'

'While he was away . . .' Kay wasn't grasping the point.

'Aye, 'cept Ah telt big Paul an well, ye know . . . he wanted yese for himself, eh?'

'Bud told you that you could . . .?'

'Aye,' nodded Harry, still keeping his eyes on the floor waiting any minute for a blow either from Paul or increasingly from Kay herself. 'Said ye widnae mind oan account o yese being . . . ye know?'

'No, I don't know,' said Kay, her voice gone quiet and cold the way it always did when she was shocked or furious.

'A working lassie annat.' Harry wasn't enjoying this conversation at all. If only Bud Cumming had been back in Glasgow he would have protected his driver. 'Bud said it, Kay, no me. Ah didnae know.'

Paul held on to Harry by the scruff of his neck and led him to the door.

'You sure?' asked Paul, swivelling round to face Kay.

'Wh . . . what?' Kay was still trying to come to terms with the new information.

'You sure ye dinnae want me tae gie this wee dickheid a right good doing?'

'Eh, no. No, not his fault . . . is it?'

'Naw,' replied Paul. 'Suppose no.' He pushed the small man out through the doorway then turned. 'That business will be sorted the night.' Kay looked at him with puzzlement written across her face. She was too deep in her thoughts to make sense of code. 'Bud will be back in a couple o days – there'll be no reason for him no tae be after the night.' Kay nodded vaguely. 'And Kay,' she looked up, 'Ah'm sorry.' He marched Harry out of the flat, leaving Kay alone to her thoughts.

For a year she had been part of Bud Cumming's life. From the start when she didn't believe who he was, through the cautious months she had watched and waited for the hook hidden in the tempting worm, she could have walked away at any time. But slowly he had invaded her. Slowly and thoroughly getting inside her head till she felt that he was part of her and she part of him. How could she have been so blind? Was it the fact that he was the only man she had ever met who hadn't instantly treated her like a sex slave? That made her lower her guard. Was it something to do with the way he confided in her? Surely. To do with his power? Undoubtedly. Included her in the inner core of his team? It was an honour. Asked her opinion? For sure. And listened to her? Even more important. His complexity as a human being? That beat any of the straightforward johns she had known. She was even soft on how he looked – that short-sighted, watery-eyed, little-boy-lost look – exactly the opposite of who she was normally attracted to. Why was that? Was it because she engaged with him, with how he thought and felt first and as a man second? Well she had thought that was how it had been between them but maybe she had been wrong. What she did know was that he gave her the self-esteem back that she had lost many years ago in the nightmare of her childhood. What was it he had said? 'Never be ashamed of who you are. When you walk out of here hold your head high.' That was what had sealed it, that and comments of a similar sentiment. She had believed that he meant it. Felt he had when it was spoken. Little magic slices that no one could take away – not even her – and would forever remain true no matter how much she tried to tell herself she should now know that he was just like the rest, the abusers and the users. No, she could feel how he had conned her but she couldn't shake those moments. Not now, not ever – she sensed that already. Whoever Bud Cumming was, whatever his game, Kay knew she was hooked and that was that.

'SEE YOU, YA BITCH . . . AH WAS STUCK IN SHITTY HOTELS FOR WEEKS OAN MA AIN AN NO THANKS TAE YOU, YA SELFISH COW.' Bud Cumming was sitting at the back of The Old Chestnut, his team standing all around him, howling into his mobile phone. 'WELL, AH'LL TELL YOU, YE COW, AH HAD TAE SLEEP WI HOOKERS COS YE WIDNAE COME DOON TAE ME . . . AYE, AH SAID HOOKERS.' Kay had walked in for the meeting, the first since Bud's arrival back in Glasgow that day, only a few days after Harry the driver's revelations. Cumming hadn't noticed her standing at the edge of his men but she could hear him all right. 'OH YESE WILL, WILL YESE? WELL LISTEN UP, TART, IF YE DINNAE BUCK THE FUCK UP AH'M GONNAE SEND BIG PAUL ROON TAE GIE YOU A RIGHT SORTING . . . MIND YOU YER UGLY ENOUGH ALREADY, YA CUNT.'

Kay looked at the man next to her, Shuggie Patterson, and chanced a question, 'Bud got women trouble, eh?'

Shuggie looked round and shrugged, 'Aye, it's the dame he lives wi. Gives him grief aw the time.'

'Ye'd think he'd speak to her more privately,' Kay added.

'Och, he's forever telling them off in public – oan the phone like.' Kay liked Shuggie. When he wasn't too doped up or stressed out he was sweet, naive, not like his colleagues. The two of them had established some sort of bond but poor Shuggie had failed to realise how important Bud had become for Kay. Or maybe he had and was doing her a favour, telling her the truth.

'All of them?' Kay smiled. 'What is he, a glutton for punishment?'

'That's whit Ah was thinking,' replied Shuggie. 'Last Ah counted there was five o them and each as bad as the other. Right fucking harpies the lot o them.' Kay nodded in response. 'Apart frae you, Kay, you're different.'

'AH'LL TELL HIM TAE SLICE YE RIGHT OPEN, YA BITCH, SO YOUSE BETTER GET YER ACT THEGETHER,' Bud Cumming hung up and sat smirking at his men.

Kay had heard him issue threats before, to men, and always by phone. She wondered if this was yet another aspect of his personality she was learning. Was Bud Cumming a coward that couldn't hold his own in a face-to-face? Even with women? Or those men he would have killed? When the men all took their seats Kay joined them and was immediately grabbed by Cumming.

'Hello, doll, God, Ah've missed you.' Before she could stop him he was smooching all over her face.

Kay wanted to be sick. Instead she wrapped her arms around him and whispered in his ear, 'Sort your domestic problems out then?' Silence from Cumming, just a stiffening of his shoulders as he realised she had heard all. 'You lying bastard.'

After the meeting, Cumming followed her home. The two sat in easy-chairs facing each other and spoke.

'Surely you knew,' Cumming pleaded.

'No,' was the only response Kay had and that said it all.

'Well, it's no big deal, is it? Mean, you and I we've got our heads screwed oan right? We're no going tae fall intae aw they wee petty jealousies annat. Are we?'

'No.'

'Look, Ah dinnae want tae lose you, right? Ah mean in any way.'

'Think you've lost a wee bit of me already.'

'Och, Kay . . .'

'But it doesn't matter, does it . . .'

'Course it does,' Cumming interrupted.

'. . . since I'm just a prostitute.'

'Is that what's eating yese?' Cumming's pale eyes now zoomed right in on her face.

'You know how I hate . . .'

'Whit did Ah tell ye? Fuck all wrong wi whit ye dae.'

'. . . used to do.'

'Whatever. Ye think that's any worse than most other things?'

'Aye, course it is. It's no good. No fucking good.'

'An being a copper is? Or a lazy teacher? Or a fucking wank o a doctor? Or an ambitious fucking gangster?' Bud Cumming held out his hands, bringing them forward to his chest, unnecessarily signifying that he meant himself. It was the old statement and all it did for Kay was emphasise what she already felt – that Bud Cumming truly meant what he was saying. He was saying the two of them were the same, did things that didn't make them feel good and others judged badly. But so what? Who were these judges to judge? Kay wasn't going to hover on that issue, didn't need to, she was going to change the subject back to the important point.

'I just wish you had told me all about the other women. About all the others.'

Cumming shrugged, 'Jist thought that it didnae need explaining.'

'Would've been useful to know. Leaves me wondering what else I don't know about you.' Bud rubbed his face, suddenly drawn and weary. He took off his spectacles, misted them with his breath and wiped them with his silk tie.

'Look, Ah know yer in a tizzy, Kay, but listen, eh?' Kay nodded and drew on the thick joint she had rolled herself in the hope it would calm her, make her mellow. 'Ah would like us tae stay pals.' Kay rolled her eyes upwards. 'Naw, listen. No jist pals. You're good for me, Kay. You're good in the team. Ah can trust you. Ah want ye tae stay a part o the organisation.' She had thought about that already. As much as she had contemplated throwing Bud Cumming over while knowing she couldn't, she also knew that she enjoyed the work in the gang. Was excited by it, felt important, didn't want it to end. Kay didn't understand any of this – she only knew that was how she felt.

'Of course I'll stay on, Bud. Did I suggest otherwise?' She managed a smirk.

'Keys – Ah gie up.' He held up his hands in mock surrender and smiled. 'People that win, Kay, they're above aw that shite. Need tae stand above it.'

'And what if when they end up standing alone . . . what good's that?'

'Naw, naw, ye've got it wrong there, Kay,' Cumming sighed. 'See the winners, they're never on their own. The winner takes all, Kay. The winner takes all.'

For the next few weeks Kay licked her wounds in the privacy of her home, only interrupted by the visits of Paul Sim. Big Paul never mentioned Harry the driver or any of the business with Bud Cumming. He just stuck to his normal routine of being there, downing handfuls of pills and gabbing till they wore off. In between Kay threw herself into work. So Bud Cumming knew she was a good driver – she'd drive all right. And she started to appear as the fast controls at exchange deals and meetings between gangs. Her face was being clocked being the only woman in the vicinity of such business. Then she fronted the deals herself, walking into hostile territory with two minders and a bag full of money to be exchanged for drugs, goods, services. She was tiny, female, drop-dead gorgeous and brooked no shit from any heavyweight. They noticed her all right and the word spread.

Some weeks later, Paul Sim called at her home late one night. She didn't know what he had been up to and didn't care. What she did know was that he was hot, sweaty and needed a wash. He splashed himself down at the kitchen sink as he had months before, except this time no one else's blood stained the water. Returning to the front room he sat at the table, bare-chested.

'Got something for ye,' he said and his face looked so young, almost innocent.

'I've heard that one before, Paul,' grinned Kay, winking in an exaggerated, obscene manner. It was a mark of how things had changed that she felt safe enough with the giant equaliser to crack jokes, double entendres.

He laughed and continued, 'Naw, serious like. These jobs ye've been oan . . .'

'Yeah . . .'

'. . . dangerous like, so Ah think ye should have this.' He rustled in his jacket pocket and pulled out a package hidden entirely by one of his great fists. He turned his hand over and pushed it forward. Was that a blush she noticed on his cheeks? There in his hand was a tiny black pistol wrapped in its cloth holster and soft, satin ties. It was so small it looked like a young child's toy and Kay laughed. Was it a joke? A hurt look came over Paul Sim's face. 'It's a Derringer, Kay. Ah suggest ye wear it roon yer thigh.' She didn't know what to say. 'Better safe than sorry, eh? Don't want ye taking any risks.'

Kay had been wined and dined at the most expensive places. She had been given gifts of gold. Holidays abroad. The list went on and on. Every time the giver was a man and he wanted something in return. Not gifts really, just another way of buying her. The small black pistol was the first time she could remember receiving a present so that she would be all right. She had no intention of wearing the gun but that was beside the point. It signified care. That SHE would be all right. Not THEM, not the men. It was a first.

Later that night she took Paul Sim by the hand and led him to bed because she wanted to. Between the sheets she discovered that all along she had been looking for a man like him. A big man, furious, angry and scary. But an honest man. All man. Her man. Life on the streets of Glasgow was about to change – big style.

Finishing School

'Men, they always reckon they can get my knickers off. Always ogling as if they sense what I used to do.' Kay was explaining some of her reservations about fronting deals.

'So use it,' replied Paul, edging closer to her on the couch in what used to be her living-room. Now it was their living-room.

'What?' That wasn't like her man. Over the first few months of their relationship he had established beyond all doubt that she was his and his alone. Mind you it was reciprocal, with him giving her a hundred per cent back. They were consumed by each other and now he was advising her to flaunt her sexuality, or was he?

'Let them ogle,' said Paul. 'Let their minds drift. Men can be right slavering idiots when they're trying tae impress a doll, right? Ye know all aboot that, eh?'

'Yeah, but they're supposed to take me seriously,' she replied. 'How am I going to do that if they're standing there with fuck-me-now eyes?'

'Ye dinnae realise yer power, dae ye?' Kay threw him a sceptical look. There she was, five foot one in her heels, dealing with some of the most vicious mobs in the country, and he's telling her she has power.

'Paul, when I was a working girl I wanted men to feel that way. It put my fee up. It put me in control. Good for business that fat blokes with fatter wallets are looking at me seeing SEX in big bold capitals. But now . . .'

'If their mind's on yer pussy they're no gonnae be thinking too clearly about the deal, are they?'

'No, but . . .'

'So use it. Let them think what they think. Prancing aboot wi their beer bellies pulled in and their chests stuck oot. Let them and you just get oan wi the business and seal the deal.'

'And what if they get the wrong message and try something on?'

'Has anybody done that yet?'

'No, but . . .'

'Ye don't know, dae yese?'

'Know what?'

'How much we scare folk.'

'Noooo, do you think . . .'

For months now Kay and Paul had teamed up to cover his business of drugs, protection and clearing dirty money through other people's legitimate businesses. And they were still part of Bud Cumming's inner core. Cumming, like most of the crime leaders in the 1990s, organised his crew on alliances. People with their own businesses, troops and territories coming together to form a stronger group, much as nations do when signing a treaty. They worked together to take care of each other and had joint enterprises of such a scale they were only achievable if several serious players worked together. Bud Cumming had been true to his word in that his fall-out with Kay did not affect her involvement in his team. But, on a personal front, another pattern was emerging. From time to time when they were alone Cumming would try his hand with Kay, being reduced now to the crudest of overtures.

'Can Ah fuck yese up the arse?'

'You and me, Kay, we're two o a kind – c'moan in the bogs an gie's a blow job.'

'You still shaving yer pussy – let's feel.'

If Paul had known of these approaches, Bud Cumming would be a dead man. Kay rejected Cumming every time and kept his clumsy suggestions secret from Paul. It was her only secret from Paul and a decision she made to keep the peace, knowing her big man would react with violence and the whole house of cards would come tumbling down.

Business was good for Paul and Kay. Life together was even better. No way was she going to risk all that because of the obscene mutterings of an impotent wee man. In her past career as a call girl she had served an apprenticeship in dealing with sexual approaches of every hue. Kay had a PhD in disposing of them without offence if possible. She was still trying to work out why Bud Cumming was playing that game. The best she could come up with was that he was jealous. Not in the usual sense of the bitter, green-eyed monster crawling up his back thinking of her being with someone else. Not sexual jealousy but power jealousy.

Bud Cumming was the boss. The boss should have what he wants and who he wants. He wanted Kay like he wanted to drive around in brand-new, top-of-the-range Mercedes. He needed to show the world that he could have her like he displayed how with one phone call he could have someone killed if he wanted. Bud Cumming had to be the winner, it was the force that drove him on. The winner took all and, so far, Kay's rejection of his advances told him that he hadn't won. Even if he pretended otherwise. Worse than all that, Kay was now in a life partnership with Paul Sim, the one man Bud Cumming and his whole team were terrified of and with good reason. When Cumming cornered Kay and suggested some sexual activity, he was smart enough to know that she would never tell Paul. Kay would work out the repercussions of warfare in the team and choose to keep quiet. Whatever Bud Cumming was, he didn't lack intelligence or tactical nous. Now Kay and Paul Sim getting together – that was a problem.

'Ye should learn tae use every bit o experience,' continued Paul, rubbing the back of Kay's neck.

'Yeah, I know,' she replied, ' I try to. But the sex just gets in the way.'

'That's in yer head, Kay,' Paul went on. 'That's how you feel in the situation but ye should be thinking o how THEY are seeing things.'

'Explain . . .'

'They look at you and they want tae shag yese and are terrified shitless at the same time. Now if aw they're feeling is fear ye'll get whit ye want aw right. That's how I do business.' He paused and smiled long enough for Kay to punch him playfully on the shoulder. 'But that has its limits. Fear makes these guys sharp, alert. They're used tae fear. Sex oan the other hand melts their brain cells so they dribble doon tae their hard-ons. You have them like putty and we score big time.'

Paul had been training Kay for life on the streets. She already knew a great deal but Paul Sim was her finishing school. In the process he worked her hard. Mainly as a driver and co-negotiator. Twelve-hour shifts and work to do when they got home. But they were together and she didn't mind. Sometimes she would look at her sweet-faced giant and wonder how he had arrived there at that point in time with her and his reputation in Glasgow's schemes. She knew better than to ask directly. Such information is best received as a gift, when the teller is ready to tell, and she wouldn't have long.

'Even the worst times – ye can learn frae,' Paul muttered. 'Especially the worst times if yer strong enough and smart enough.' Kay held his hand. 'You don't know aboot ma childhood, dae yese?' Kay shook her head and cuddled into one of his massive shoulders, all ears and attention as Paul Sim told her the story of growing up in Glasgow. 'Ah've got a past tae . . .'

In 1974, Paul Sim was born into a family in the same council-house estate he now ruled. His was an unremarkable working-class family at the time when work had long since run out. The 'underclass', the sociologists were calling them. No work for generations, no prospect of work, no hope, no future. They couldn't even aspire to be working unless something or someone radically changed. In spite of media hype to the contrary, most of these good folk didn't abuse their kids, turn to crime or fester in some heroin-induced stupor. Most just got by as best they could.

From an early age just surviving wasn't good enough for Paul Sim. By the age of six his family were struggling to deal with his energy. That was one way of putting it. If he had been born into a privileged home no doubt he would have prospered on the rugby pitch or the cricket field or both. Given the space, the means and the resources, his energy and thrust would have proven to be assets, that and his size.

Always big and muscular for his age, his primary school teachers struggled to cope with him. The older guys on the street corners felt he was fair game for a square go. His father reckoned that what he needed was discipline in the form of a right good kicking, which he frequently administered. He was only six years old and he was having none of it. He fought back.

By the age of eight he was taken from the family and put into a children's home. No doubt the official reason for the care order was to protect Paul's care and well-being. He didn't see it that way. The residential staff were just another group of adults telling him what to do and when he did what he wanted they quickly resorted to other methods.

Paul had to fit in, it was as simple as that. When he didn't they had to encourage him – that was their job.

Stripped and put in his pyjamas during the day to stop him running away, he was locked in his bedroom with no TV, no books, no games, no place for his energy to go. When they opened the door to give him meals they were dismayed that he kicked out and headed for the street. Surely he had to be a disturbed child? So they locked him up more and more, for longer and longer periods of time. When that didn't work some of the older, male care staff knew what they had to do. Closing the door behind them, the two men squared up. The first grabbed Paul by the front of his pyjama top and pulled him close. It didn't bother the guy that Paul was not far short of his height – he was just a child after all.

After Paul had been beaten he plotted. Three days later, having agreed to go to school, he was driven there by a member of staff. Before the staff member was back at the home drinking his tea, Paul had run away. Now started the pattern of his childhood.

For five years Paul Sim was constantly on the run from the authorities, sleeping out in the area where his family lived. He didn't so much return to his roots but created new ones for himself. For Paul, life on the streets was his schooling and his apprenticeship. Every time he was caught by the police and returned to the children's home he learned a lesson – getting better and better at staying free. At first he sought out warmth and shelter in the heating ducts of high flats. There were plenty high-rise blocks in the schemes and he reasoned that if he kept changing his location every night he would never be caught. He hadn't known that the place was alive with people running away from something – jail, psychiatric care, families – and their favourite sleeping place was the heating ducts. He soon learned and took to the ruins of an old castle based in a preserved woodland slap bang in the middle of one of Britain's most deprived areas. It was a cold, damp, spooky place and even adults were reluctant to go there during the day. Paul Sim spent five years of nights there.

By the age of twelve he was running a protection racket, strictly small scale and basic but effective nevertheless. Individuals were given a stark choice between paying up or losing their front teeth. Usually they paid up – Paul Sim was getting to be known. By the time he was fourteen the child-care authorities simply ignored him. Paul had learned how to survive in the wild and on the streets. He stole everything he needed. If short of money he would wander into a street he knew a local gang considered their patch. When they came for him he'd stand his ground and beat them to a pulp, using any improvised weapon at hand. Scattering the group, he'd grab the slowest and rob him of his money, his weapons, sometimes his clothes. Many times he made errors and big brothers or fathers of his victims would come hunting him. Many times he got caught and suffered the consequences. But each time he tried to work out the signals he had failed to spot. Became expert at reading situations. If that didn't work, he was always prepared for the unexpected and devised tactical strategies of escape to recoup and return, this time wreaking a vengeance so severe that fear blunted his opponents' leading edge.

It wasn't such a big step then when at fourteen years old he decided to become a drug dealer. There was good money to be made from drugs. Survival money. Paul knew all the local drug dealers so decided to start at the top. He waited till the two men, a long-term partnership, had taken up their usual stance of an evening. Marching up to them he demanded their money and their stash. They laughed at the kid and told him to fuck off. They thought it was a joke. Before the chortle died in their mouths, Paul had stabbed one in the throat and was gouging the other in the breadbasket. The two men survived, but only just, and went on to turn their backs on crime. Well, there was now no room for their trade in their own area and, besides, it's difficult to be a drug dealer when you suffer from the long-term disabilities that Paul Sim inflicted.

So, by the late 1980s Paul Sim was an established drug dealer in one of the biggest markets in Britain at an age when he was still a child and should have been in care. But it wasn't all plain sailing. Constantly threatened by others with well-established reputations who tried to take the boy's business off him, his existence was one of constant alert, frequent violence, occasional defeats and revenge. Every time and every day Paul Sim learned and learned. He took to carrying a pistol all the time and using it when the odds were stacked against him. When you were a team of one you needed all the equalisers you could muster. Besides, everybody else on the scheme was carrying weapons by then.

Occasionally he ventured into partnerships. Usually the other party approached Paul, attracted by his capacity for violence and his obvious intelligence, well proven by his capacity to survive in such shark-infested waters at an early age. Paul tried his hand at bank robberies, protection rackets on pubs and shops, more than one hit contract and proved capable at them all. But he didn't like partnerships. Trusting in someone else introduced new factors to be wary of. Paul had survived on his own on the streets from the age of eight. He wasn't going to trust others easily, if ever.

When a well-known gangster approached Paul, the young drug dealer was still only fifteen. The gangster we'll call Zed was in his mid-twenties, had already done a four stretch and carried a fierce reputation as a hard man and skilled heist merchant. Most young players would have felt honoured to be approached by Zed. Not Paul Sim. He was wary of the guy, having been let down too often before. But he was tempted by the size of the promised booty and agreed.

The robbery went like clockwork with no one getting hurt or caught. As part of the usual precautions, it had been agreed that the money would be stored in a safe place for three weeks till some of the police heat died down. Also, the two men would not be seen together during that period so that no one could suspect that they might answer the witnesses' description of two tall, heavily built robbers. It was a standard precaution – nothing to worry about.

When the time for sharing out the cash came there was no sign of Zed. Paul went hunting for him and found him on the other side of the city with a girlfriend, the daughter of a well-known drug dealer in the city. Paul had no truck with the woman – just Zed. At gunpoint he led his erstwhile partner out of that flat, drove him across the city and back to one of the countless abandoned flats in the scheme, except this one he had prepared in advance. Once there, Paul beat Zed up – just enough to assure acquiescence – then set about boarding the flat up from the inside. Boards were secured to the windows with six-inch nails. A corrugated sheet was secured to the inside of the house's only door. Zed had arrived in hell.

He was systematically beaten up. Burning cigarettes pushed into the flesh on his back, under his arms, the soles of his feet. He told Paul about the money after two days. Zed thought that was the end of the matter. Paul tied Zed up, gagged him and left the flat, boarding the door up with the corrugated iron from the outside. To get the dough he had to raid a house where three experienced players hung out. He did so carrying a pistol and a shotgun. They didn't resist – they had heard of Paul Sim. With the money safely hidden elsewhere Paul returned to his old friend Zed.

The money was only part of the point. Making an example of the guy for others to see was the main task at hand. The torture continued for three more days. Not so much physical punishment but fear. For as long as Zed was there and in the company of Paul he expected anything to happen, to die at any second. Paul let him think that and just hung around like a silent prison guard while Zed sweated. When the man fell asleep, Paul yanked him to his feet and beat him mercilessly. Zed was beginning to crack up.

On the fourth day, Paul stripped off Zed's clothes, rolled him over on his front and buggered him. Twenty minutes later he buggered him again. By this time Zed's spirit was broken, shattered. No restraints were necessary – he wouldn't have left if Paul had opened the door. The sexual humiliation went on all night and into the next day. Rape is power. Power is the very fuel of the streets. Paul used it coldly, deliberately to full effect. Finally, he urinated over the man and walked out of the flat, leaving the door ajar. At the bottom of the close mouth he went to the nearest public call box and phoned Zed's friends, telling them where to find the man. A short while later Paul phoned the police. The friends had just enough time to take in the full horror of Zed's ordeal before the bizzies turned up. It was a message they never forgot.

A year later Zed was released from psychiatric care. Within a fortnight he had knifed a young man to death in the street in an argument over a bag of chips. He remains in jail. No one ever grassed up Paul Sim. All the money was his though he was originally happy to settle for half. Zed was ruined, his friends weakened and everyone on the street was more terrified of Paul Sim than ever before. It was a lesson he learned as a child. If someone was going to abuse you a little – abuse them a great deal.

When Paul signed up with Bud Cumming he did so carefully and cautiously. Cumming had approached him on the basis of family ties as his cousin and a mutual interest in business. Paul never mentioned to Kay if he had any thoughts about Bud's collusion with his childhood abuse. Cumming was older, a cousin who lived nearby, and it is likely that he and his own parents knew all about the treatment of young Paul at the hands of his father. Knew all about it and did nothing. Maybe it wasn't that important to Paul Sim anymore. But he was never happy with an alliance – not even with his cousin.

When Paul and Kay got together they were lovers first and work partners later. Given the man's childhood it is remarkable that he was able to be involved in a relationship at all – never mind one so full of passion. But Paul didn't choose the relationship. Kay didn't choose it either. It just happened and they loved one another – something else Paul Sim never told Kay. But he didn't have to. She knew.

Bud Cumming knew all about Paul's background of course. That was part of Cumming's approach. Just as he had been watching Kay for a number of years ever since she had accidentally hooked up with Lenny Lovat. What Cumming lacked in brawn and bravery he made up for in intelligence, information and a fine grasp of psychology. He knew all about the pair of new lovers and it worried him back into insomnia. Bud Cumming was going to have to do something about Paul and Kay and do something soon.

Counting Sheep

As usual, Bud Cumming couldn't sleep. He had a problem. Not that he was a stranger to difficulties but this one needed some careful handling. It had started with complaints from some dealers in Govan and the Gorbals, guys he supplied through his links with the Liverpool mob for a sizeable share of their profits, of course. It was one of many deals he didn't tell his whole team about. Why should he? He was the only one who knew the complete picture and, besides, they'd only expect part of the earnings. There was an unspoken rule that Cumming made sure that no one moved in on the dealers' patches and they were now calling for help. Trouble was it was two of his people they were complaining about – Paul Sim and Kay.

Usually that type of local issue was no problem. Cumming had dealt with so many of these that he could have written the handbook. The usual routine was to call the parties together under his stewardship. No guns, no grief, just discussion. If they couldn't reach some compromise he'd suggest one – all the while making sure he continued to earn the same cut, if not more. If that didn't work he had a choice – let them sort each other out or take sides himself. More than once he had sent his boys in to waste guys they had been in cahoots with for years. Then he would allocate the territory to the other side – for a cut of course. Trouble was, it was usually Paul Sim he sent in to dole out the grief.

The next problem was coming from his own boys. They had been grumbling on and on for months. Normally he and Lennon would have told them to shut up and toe the line. This time

Lennon agreed with the team and privately so did Bud Cumming. The issue was that Paul and Kay had become too big, too powerful in the eighteen months or so they had been together. Cumming had always tried to keep his team on par with each other. Not with him, of course, or Lennon who was given a lieutenant's enhancement. But Paul and Kay had proven to be too energetic, too successful, too good a partnership and the boys didn't like it. They had never taken to big Paul. Okay when it was him that was put in to deal with some hellish violent situation. Or when it was him that ran the risk of a long jail term for the murder and mayhem he delivered on their behalf. But at other times the whole crew got edgy at associating with a man they considered to be a wild animal with brains and Cumming knew what they meant. Paul's trouble was that he never relaxed, never let his guard down, never made friends till now – till Kay.

Paul and Kay were taking over a whole expanse of the drug trade. They were supplied in the main through Cumming's sources: primarily Liverpool for heroin and dope but also London for cocaine as well as acid and Ecstasy factories near Oxford and Birmingham. The lovers had been so successful that they had increased the output markedly, making Cumming's suppliers happy at the rise in their profits. The dealers Paul and Kay sold to were equally satisfied with their increased orders. The supplies were regular, good quality and security was sound – who was going to mess with Paul Sim?

The businessman in Cumming approved of developments that expanded the market. Even the politician in him was pleased – through Paul and Kay his own power base was expanding. But the inner strife of the troops needed to be dealt with. An unsettled team is dangerous. Apart from that, the suppliers from down south were beginning to mention Paul Sim a mite too frequently for Bud Cumming's liking. Young Paul was getting too powerful. Too powerful by far.

As if that wasn't bad enough, Bud Cumming had to go and

meet with The Licensee and hear more bad news. Cumming and The Licensee had an agreement but the small myopic one knew fine well he was not the senior partner – yet. Through The Licensee's contacts abroad, Cumming hoped to expand his empire into a truly multinational concern. It was the modern way of organised crime. Cumming knew that and wanted to be a big league player worldwide.

The Licensee had well-established links all over the place. Ireland – pubs, counterfeit money, guns. Germany – building contracts, property, illegal immigrants, long firms. Spain – property, holiday complexes, tobacco smuggling. France – drug smuggling routes from the Middle East. Eastern Europe – ringed cars, booze and tobacco. Tenerife – a safe hiding hole. And that was only the start.

Back in Britain the same Licensee had moved dirty money into legitimate businesses through paper companies shielding the real man behind it all. He had manoeuvred his way into social contact with big-time masters of commerce through long-standing arrangements he had with bent policemen and association with a particular freemasons' lodge full of members who were well-to-do in the world of banking and investments.

On security he was sure-footed. Not only had he spent most of his adult life in alliance with the police in Scotland trading arms and people for immunity from prosecution – now he was expanding that insurance certificate. Lately he had taken up with a Liverpool guy, a former gangster, who had a special relationship with the police in a variety of forces, Customs and Excise all over the UK and had somehow managed to deal out strife for the security forces in Belfast. The strategy was clear and one which Bud Cumming subscribed to wholeheartedly. Keep your home base secure and expand abroad. If the home base cracked your foreign partners would run a mile.

Bud Cumming had his own links down south and in Europe. What he knew was that if he could stand alongside someone as rich and connected as The Licensee then his own empire would grow bigger, faster. That's what Cumming wanted and nothing was going to stand in his way. Nothing and no one.

Now The Licensee was unhappy with him. Cumming never failed to be amazed at how petty-minded his partner was for a man with so much money, so much power. He had expected to find someone calm and clear-headed, only interested in serious talk of strategy and human chess moves. To be blunt, The Licensee preferred gossip and never tired of passing heartfelt comments on individuals' characters. He was more like a sweetie-wifie than a crime lord. But he was powerful and Cumming needed him. When they had met at The Licensee's insistence, Cumming had expected a bit of business. Instead he got a story all about The Licensee's brother, Frank, being stabbed in prison a few years before. Stabbed so badly he was in hospital for two days simply to reconstruct the wounds. And the man who stabbed him had gone unpunished. An affront that could not be allowed. No, no, that man would have to be seen to. Bud Cumming was probably sitting there listening, planning to get big Paul Sim to see to the bloke, whoever he was. Who was he anyway? Paul Sim, that's who it was. Paul Sim would have to be punished in jeopardy or the deal between The Licensee and Bud Cumming was. All agreements null and void.

No wonder Bud Cumming couldn't sleep. Having someone killed would not have bothered him for a second. But he had decided to kill Paul. Not Paul his cousin. Not Paul who had taken chance after chance on his behalf. Not Paul who had risked a lifetime in jail to do work for Cumming. None of that bothered Bud Cumming a whit. What concerned him was that it was Paul Sim, the perfect killing machine. Paul Sim who they were all terrified of. Who would try and kill Paul Sim?

Lesser minds would have hired a team of well-known hitmen and stood back. But Bud Cumming knew better than that. Paul Sim's cunning and ruthlessness had survived many a similar attack before. Paul Sim wounded and angry with him was just too much to contemplate. No, that was not Bud Cumming's style. He thought things through. Big Paul was going to have to be weakened till he was easy meat. It was going to take a while and cost Cumming money but not to act would cost him everything, all his plans. He lifted the mobile phone and dialled the number of the supplier in Liverpool.

A local problem, he explained, suspecting that his Liverpool contact had more scruples than he did. The gear that was delivered directly to Big P would go to another name from now on. Cumming would pay over the odds for the supplier's inconvenience. Till further notice. It would be sorted out soon. Within an hour all the suppliers had received the same message and agreed. They didn't ask too many questions. Bud Cumming was big business and local troubles were none of their concern.

Now that was first strike to Cumming. Next he would have to work out a way of breaking that partnership. Of creating a rift between Paul and Kay.

Deadly Letters of Love

'We've got problems, Kay.' Big Paul swallowed a handful of pills and washed them down with Irn Bru straight from the bottle. 'Serious fucking problems.' The first statement hadn't worried Kay at all but the second unnerved her. The two of them had been used to problems – it went with the territory. But Paul was always on top of them, plotting a way through and planning to come out even stronger than before. So far he had always won out. But serious? That's not a word he used often. 'Some cunt's cut off oor supplies and worse.' What could be worse than no supplies to someone who distributed drugs? Surely that was the life force of the enterprise. No drugs, no business, no money, nothing. 'Ah'm owed money – a lot o money an none o the fuckers are coughing up.' Paul swallowed more pills. Kay worried that he was taking too many drugs himself these past few weeks and now she reckoned she knew why. He had obviously been worrying about the situation, trying to resolve it on his own and failing. That was why he was sharing his concerns now. Paul wouldn't lumber Kay with a problem just to have her worrying too. No, he'd sort it and tell her what had happened, how he had fixed it. The big man had obviously tried and failed. 'Ah think there's a plot tae do us in.' Kay's puzzled expression said it all. The words did not equate with what she knew of Paul. Who would be brave enough or stupid enough to tackle him? 'Kill us, hen,' he spelled it out. 'Some bastard is trying to finish us off. This is just the start.'

'Who is, Paul?' asked Kay, fretting over who exactly was powerful enough to make her man frightened. She was imagining outside teams, big firms from London, or the Yardies who were trying to set up a crack cocaine link into the city. Maybe the Triad groups usually content with their monopoly of certain parts of Glasgow had grown more ambitious. Her list of possibilities seemed to ring false like some plot from a B movie. She knew of these gangs' links in the city but didn't know enough about them to rule them out.

'Fucked if Ah know,' Paul rubbed his face wearily. 'The guys that owe me dough – it's no them. Big Malky Mackie, he's due us fifty grand. He's no got the balls to take me oan, though. But he's hiding frae me – ducking an' diving some place else.'

Kay knew all about Malky. A local drug dealer in the scheme Paul was from who worked for Paul, under his direction, a semi-independent franchise that would collapse without Paul. Malky's father had a reputation in the city. Street players reckoned he was responsible for the rape and disfigurement of a number of prostitutes, though he was never caught. Add to that a proven record for torturing opponents no matter what sex, age or lack of proof of their activities and he well earned the nickname of The Animal. Like a poor doctor's receptionist Malky assumed the influence of his father just through association. The son had inherited the same sadistic streak but none of the bottle. No way would he take on Paul Sim on his own unless he had been consuming too many of his own goods. Besides, his father had taken a sort of retirement and moved into the taxi business.

'There's another few – owe me five tae ten grand each,' continued Paul, 'but they're even less likely to take me oan.' He slipped in another handful of pills. This time Kay noticed they were blues, Valium, though God knows what else he had been taking. Paul's weakness was cocktails of pills and that night he was hitting them hard. 'Some bastard has tae be behind them – ordering them tae keep ma money back. Same bastard that's cut off ma supplies.'

'Can't we go speak to them?' Kay asked, feeling a bit foolish knowing that Paul would have thought of that a long time before. It was just that she didn't know what else to say.

'Ah thought so . . . always thought that no cunt could hide frae me.' He was now sucking the blues into his mouth one by one between words. 'But they must be oot o the city, the fucking country.'

'I meant our suppliers, Paul.'

'Fuck sakes, you think Ah'm bloody stupid?' The colour rose to his cheeks, his big fists clenching tight. 'No cunt's taking ma calls. No cunt.'

'We should maybe go see Bud,' suggested Kay.

'Aye, we're gonnae have tae though . . .' Paul Sim never finished his sentence. Instead he had a shower, changed his clothes and tucked his pistol into his waistband before declaring, 'There's some guys that owe me smaller amounts – hundreds here and there. How's about you and me going tae collect? If some cunt is behind this they'll maybe no know aboot they fuckers.' It was the old preparing-for-war routine. Don't sit and fret. Get ready and money was always necessary.

'Aye, good idea,' replied Kay, going to fetch her coat.

'One thing, Kay,' said Paul, 'you're driving. Just driving – right.'

'Eh . . . yeah, sure,' she replied, getting a sense of how worried her man was. They had always been careful but now she could tell that he didn't want her around at all.

As if he was reading her mind he continued, 'Ah'm only taking you cos that's whit we dae – drive aboot the gether. Need tae look as normal as possible. As if fuck all's wrong, eh?'

'But nothing is wrong, is it?' she declared. He frowned. 'Between us, ye big idiot. Between us.' For the first time that night he smiled and leaned over to kiss her, reaching a big hand down to cover her buttocks and pull her in close.

'One thing,' he murmured in her ear, 'that wee present. Mind? Ah think ye should wear it.'

The first night she wore the Derringer tucked inside her panties till she found out that it had no safety catch. After that it was strapped to her thigh and from then on her outfits were chosen more to cover its small bulk and allow quick access rather than to match her mood or the occasion. For weeks they cruised the city like that. Paul loaded with three guns including the sneaky spare tucked in his boot. Kay at the wheel of the car, windows closed, doors locked, feeling the metal shape of the pistol against her thigh. No one refused them what they were owed. In a few days they had raised enough money to continue some of their business but nowhere near the scale they were used to. All of Paul's established outlets bought from him when he appeared. They never grumbled about the poor quality of the gear he was now flogging due to his reduced choice of supplier. What he didn't know was that as soon as he had left they made a call to Bud Cumming. Cumming was watching and waiting. Biding his time, which would come any minute now.

Kay knew she should never have let Paul out on his own that night. He was down, very down. It was clear that their efforts were insufficient to rescue their trade. She had suggested again that they speak to Bud Cumming about their troubles. Paul had flown off the handle and grown muddled and hazy in his rage. The pills were being hammered consistently and at times he was losing his grip – the very state that Paul always lectured her against. 'Stay alert and in control' was his motto and now here he was sacrificing his wits to handfuls of blues and jellies. The row ended with him accusing Kay of wanting to go back with Bud Cumming, of planning to finish with him because they were in trouble. Nothing could have been further from the truth. Kay had realised that somehow she loved her big man even more during their difficulties than when life was straightforward.

She was accustomed to them having heated rows and passionate reconciliations so she thought little of it when he stormed out, saying he was going to a local social club to meet someone. If Paul behaved to form he would be back in a few hours, grinning and apologetic, sweeping her up in his arms and making love through the night. Kay ran a bath and poured herself some white wine, making herself ready for her man's return.

The fellow Paul was meant to be meeting never turned up – Bud Cumming had seen to that. He hung around for a couple of hours, drinking booze and swallowing great fistfuls of pills while getting angrier and angrier. But Paul was known in the place and an associate stood and chatted with him at the bar.

'See the old guy over there?' the associate whispered, nodding in the man's direction. 'He's the father of so-and-so, the cunt that owes you money.' Paul was so out of it he didn't need much encouragement. Over he went to confront the old guy who was no relation to the man who was in debt to Paul. None whatsoever. But he was a proud man and didn't take kindly to the youngster calling him out in front of his friends. He knew who Paul was, of course, by reputation only. But even so – pride is pride, especially on your home patch.

Paul Sim was good at violence, of that there was no doubt. But he was also careful, using his muscle productively. The same Paul Sim despised the young teams who fought for the sake of fighting. But that night he was convinced the old bloke owed him money and times were bad. When the grey-haired man denied the claim Paul persisted. When the accused told Paul to fuck off it only took a second for the long-bladed knife to be whisked from Paul's waistband and stuck into the side of the objector's head.

The old boy hit the deck, the knife still embedded in his skull. Paul stood and gaped as around him pandemonium broke out. The victim had lived in the scheme all his life, was thought of as a decent guy and well liked. An innocent. Paul Sim had gone too far. Behind the bar one of the staff called the police. Over by the door, the man who had passed the information to Paul about the old man's son owing him money hovered and waited. He didn't budge till he heard the siren of the police car and then stepped out sharply, taking up position across the road. When he saw Paul handcuffed and being hustled into the back of a coppers' meat wagon he pulled out his mobile phone and dialled.

Bud Cumming was delighted with the news. He had had the boys put out word around the scheme that anyone who could get Paul Sim lifted was up for a generous payment. Sure he would pay the young guy and also offer him work. Paul Sim had just paid the price of being a loner with no friends. Bud Cumming's plan was progressing well.

It was three days before Kay found out that Paul was in jail charged with attempted murder. Paul had refused to speak to them at all – not even giving them an address. So they checked his record and went to his last known address – the home of his former partner, the tall, vivacious black woman. Kay was frantic. He had never gone missing for days before. She thought he had been killed as he predicted. Leaving the house was something she didn't want to do. Surely if he had been hurt or arrested the police would come to tell her. A few times before he had been injured in some fracas but made his way back home in need of care and attention. Eventually she left the house for short flurries, checking out his usual haunts and visiting an aunt and an uncle he had lately formed a relationship with. No luck and no information. When on the third day there was a knock at the door she rushed to answer it, praying it was Paul who had lost his key and not a policeman. It was neither, it was Bud Cumming.

'Why did ye no come and see me, Kay?' Cumming asked after he had told her that Paul was unhurt but in police custody.

'Didn't want to bother you, Bud,' she replied. 'Things haven't been too good recently.'

'More the point ye should have,' he reasoned, reaching out and holding her hand. She told him about the suppliers drying up, the unpaid debts and went on to say how worried she had been by Paul's increased drug-taking. Cumming oozed sympathy and shock.

'Looks like he's gonnae do some time,' Cumming offered eventually. 'The old guy he stuck was well respected – stacks o witnesses. Straight guys that cannae be bought.' Cumming didn't mention that The Licensee had a special relationship with a load of cops at the arresting police station and Kay didn't know. If Cumming had been playing the game by the rules, a call to The Licensee would have eased Paul's way. If he couldn't have the charges dropped, at least they would be reduced to minimal impact. Of course, neither The Licensee nor Cumming were going to help Paul Sim in any way at all. Instead Cumming just told Kay that she could rely on him for any help she needed – any help at all. Then left the house without giving her a bean.

Paul was sentenced to two years on reduced charges of serious assault. Deducting the time he had spent on remand he would be out in seven months.

'No time at all,' he reassured Kay during early visits in Barlinnie, just before he passed her coded messages on what drugs he wanted smuggled in. So Kay supported her man the prisoner, going back to her old tricks of crushed pills hidden in the folds of greeting cards. In the meantime, she returned to her seat at Cumming's inner circle, though things had changed. She thought it was because her head was so full of worries about Paul – about how vulnerable to attack he would be in jail, about how he would be when released, about how he would cope with being cooped up and ordered around. But that was only half the story. Cumming and his troops were now using her. Seeing her as someone who had made a move which failed and now deserved to be ostracised. As someone who remained loyal to the one man they saw as their biggest enemy, Paul Sim. As someone who had chosen the wrong side, even though she didn't know there was a war. As someone they could use. Would use.

On the surface, Bud Cumming continued treating Kay as

someone special. He returned to visiting her at all sorts of times and she was a little disgusted with herself at how easily receptive she was to the little man's attention. If she had only admitted to herself she was lonely maybe she would have been able to break away. But the past few years she had been content in her devotion to big Paul. He was her work and her life. Now she didn't even have other working girls to get along with. So, she enjoyed Bud Cumming's attention and returned to her former role of best friend and confidante. Only this time she was telling him everything while he just pretended to tell her anything worth while.

When her older sister Amabel turned up on the scene after several years of no contact it did not surprise Kay at all. Amabel was like that. But this time her timing was perfect and the two women started spending more time together. Privately, Kay admitted to herself that Amabel was the most selfish person she had ever met. Whatever Amabel did, she always had a hidden agenda. She was after something. But Kay couldn't see what she had for Amabel to take away anymore, so she relaxed. One night over a drink she explained to Amabel how money was a little tight. Paul's business had been ruined and would stay that way while he was in prison. Kay was getting sparse sporadic money from Cumming's team and knew that probably reflected her lacklustre contribution. In the meantime, she was smuggling increasing quantities of drugs to her Paul. Now she was a customer rather than a dealer the drugs didn't come cheap. Amabel promptly suggested that Kay returned to being a working girl. Offered to get her a job in the sauna where she was working. No need to tell Paul – it would only worry him. No need to tell Paul! Kay knew he would go stark raving mental if he even suspected she had returned to being a working girl. He didn't mind her having done that in the past but now they were together – that was different. It was one of the many small reasons why she loved him. But money was tight and she had to keep the house going and support her man through his jail time. Reluctantly Kay agreed to carry out a few shifts. Her decision pleased Amabel much more than Kay could realise.

Paul was under pressure in jail. One day at recreation time three cons jumped him, two holding on to his arms while the other repeatedly stuck a makeshift blade into his stomach. But it took more than that to put Paul Sim down. Strength was his main attribute and he survived well enough to get his own back on his attackers with trumps. Barehanded he put all three of them in the hospital wing. Attacks on Paul Sim were few and far between and he concluded correctly that someone had paid the men well for the knife attack. The paymaster was Bud Cumming, something that Paul suspected but never shared with Kay. He didn't like to worry her. But assaults were the least of his problems. Kay was too proficient at smuggling drugs into Paul. Several times he was caught out on random drugs tests and had months added on to his sentence. Kay understood why prisoners took to moon-walking to ease their jail time but still felt hurt and let down that his actions meant they were apart for longer than necessary. When he was two months from release and she could count down in days he phoned one night at his usual time.

'Going out later?' he asked after their usual hellos.

'Aye, I thought I would,' she replied, knowing she was going to do a shift at the sauna.

'Where?' He was never that curious, possessive or seldom so monosyllabic. Something was wrong. 'WHERE?' he repeated.

'Just going to see Amabel,' she replied in a little girl's voice that appeared from nowhere.

'SURE?'

'Aye.'

'One more chance, Kay,' he warned. Kay's face was burning in a deep, crimson blush.

'Yes, I'm going out with Ama . . .'

'Yer a lying little bitch and you and me are finished. Fucking DONE.' Then he hung up.

When she went to Barlinnie the next day for her usual visit, she was told that Paul did not want to see her. And the next time and the next. Kay cornered Amabel at the first opportunity.

'Did you tell anybody about me working in the sauna?' Kay demanded.

'Naw!'

'You fucking sure?'

'No way, man, whit wid Ah tell anybody for?'

Amabel may have been telling the truth, nobody knows but her. What we do know is that Bud Cumming knew about Kay's work and arranged for some extra business for her. Bit-part players from the other side of the city – faces she did not know – had the pleasure of her services. When they visited friends and relatives in Barlinnie they let it slip, man-to-man, that they had been to the sauna and guess who served them? Paul didn't believe the first whisper. Nor the second. But within weeks the word was coming from too many disparate quarters. It felt as if every man in Glasgow had been shagging his woman, his Kay. Prison is one of the worst places in the world to hear such news.

Kay was down, that was for sure. Her depression was made worse by giving up work, running out of money and still Paul wouldn't see her. She was so low she felt she needed something, some help to get her by. Maybe one Valium would do. She went to Paul's bedside drawer. It was his private space where he kept money, notes and a ready supply of drugs for his own consumption. There was sure to be a Valium there. And there was, but that wasn't all. As Kay washed the pill down, she caught the sight of notepaper with unfamiliar handwriting. Seconds later she smelled flowery women's perfume. She hated herself for being in that drawer at all but now it was too late. She picked up the notepaper. It was a love letter to Paul from someone called Samantha. He had never mentioned a Samantha from his past but even a quick read of the neatly written lines convinced Kay that Paul and Samantha knew each other intimately. Another time, another place she would have laughed it off, blamed herself for being where she shouldn't have been and confessed all to her man. But right then it plunged her to the depths of despair.

When two nights later Bud Cumming called by she really wasn't in the mood for company. As usual he gibbered on and on about the developments on the streets, business and asked the usual questions about Paul. Cumming revealed he had been to see Paul that week and reported that he was a very angry man.

'Says you and him are finished, Kay, that cannae be right, eh?' Cumming asked. Hearing the words come from another somehow made it feel all the more real and Kay burst into tears, something she was not prone to do. She cried herself sore. Cumming put his arm round her and made comforting noises. He convinced her that she was depressed and what she needed was a wee pick-me-up. She swallowed the first of the pills he offered.

'Naw, ye'll need tae take them aw,' he insisted gently, 'they're low dosage.' Kay sniffed and swallowed more pills. 'Ah didnae like tae tell ye this, Kay, but . . .'

'What,' her voice sounded hoarse, broken. 'Tell me what?'

'Well, Ah dinnae think it's ma place.'

'No, please . . . go on.' Anything to ease the pain she felt.

'Big Paul . . . well, Ah'm telt he's been seeing somebody else for a good long while.' Kay turned and looked straight at Bud Cumming. 'Some dame called Samantha apparently – that's aw Ah know.'

When Cumming left a couple of hours later, he slipped a bottle of pills into her hand to help her through her troubled times. Kay felt woozy, unsteady and sick, as you do when you discover the love of your life has been seeing someone else. She returned to her childhood brainwashing and started blaming herself for not being good enough, for expecting too much, for being too small, for being a whore. She took some more of Bud Cumming's pills and hoped the magic would work.

In the early hours of the morning she discovered herself in the bedroom going through the large wardrobe. Most of the space was occupied by her outfits but she wasn't interested in those. She wanted to get a sense of her Paul, feel his smell and touch something that was his. All she had access to were some clothes hanging on his side of the closet. She buried her face in a shirt, inhaling deeply. She felt the zip of a pair of trousers and remembered one happy night. She reached down to pick up a pair of shoes. Then she spotted the box. An ordinary looking shoebox but it stood out because she couldn't remember seeing it before. Staggering with the pills, she hoisted the box and plumped down on the bed. Lifting the lid, there it was – that same flowery scent. Thirty or forty letters, no dates, no addresses but all signed Samantha.

Kay remembered pulling open the drawer at Paul's side of the bed. She couldn't read the small print on the first strip of tablets but then she didn't much care. Little brown plastic bottles with childproof seals were opened and emptied down her throat. Feeling along the base of the drawer she found different pills of varied shapes, sizes and colours. She swallowed what she found. Then she picked the phone up and dialled. Kay couldn't remember who she phoned or what she said. She just had a vague idea of telling someone how she felt about her Paul.

When her old friend from her call girl days found her, Kay was lying on Paul's pillow and was already in a coma. By the time she was rushed into the Victoria Infirmary her family were alerted. Amabel was first on the scene. She listened to the doctors tell her that Kay had taken a weight of pills and they hadn't quite worked out what. That Kay was in a coma and they couldn't predict her prognosis.

'Her whit?'

'Her chances of survival.'

'Aw, right. Ye mean she might die?'

'I'm afraid that's a possibility.'

'Aw, shame.'

'Or maybe some brain damage or disability – in truth we simply don't know because we don't know what she has taken.'

'Right . . . shame.'

Out in the car park of the Victoria Infirmary Amabel stopped and lit a cigarette. Then she picked her mobile phone out of her handbag and dialled. On the other end of the line the lips speaking into the mouthpiece arched in an irresistible smile before thanking her for her trouble. Amabel hung up, sprayed some perfume down her front and hailed a taxi. She was going out for the night, to the dancing. Bud Cumming liked Amabel. She was the type of woman he could work with, being devoid of any scruples whatsoever. He pondered on the phone call and decided he would visit Paul soon. It was important that he heard the bad news about Kay from someone close.

Auld Acquaintances (1997)

'S top it, ya cunt, leave her alone.' The young female doctor ignored her. 'You. I'm speaking to you . . . hey, BITCH.' Still no reaction from the medic who continued working on the patient in the next bed. 'If you don't stop I'll . . . I'll . . .' The spittle flew through the air in an arc, landing on the white-coated back. And again. And again. The medic ignored Kay and went about her business.

Why wouldn't they listen to her? If only Kay could move she'd sort the bastards for messing about with her and the other women. Why wouldn't they listen? If only she could move, she would leave. They must have her tied to the bed. Why do that? She couldn't move her arms or her legs. Did they have her in a straitjacket? Was she in some madhouse? Was that it? She'd finally cracked. They must have drugged her as well. Some dope, man. She slept a lot of the time – nightmares, terrible nightmares about being naked in the street and everybody laughing at her. Everybody except her Paul. He was angry and cried. Wept like a little boy while the others just mocked. Strangers she had never seen before – pointing and giggling while her Paul cried and cried. Must be dreams, eh? Some dope they had given her.

Sometimes she couldn't speak. Her lips wouldn't move. And other times when she could – shouting and screaming – the other folk just pretended they couldn't hear her. Those others in the white coats, always coming and going and sticking needles into her and turning her in the bed, but never answering any of her questions. Just ignoring her. But she saw them all right. Saw them through a grey mist, like an old black and white TV with fuzzy reception. Some poison they must have given her all right. And sometimes she couldn't see but she could hear. Heard everything. Heard what they said about her, all of them. Even that family of hers, that mother and Amabel. Sitting there talking about how much they had to drink the night before and whatever waster Amabel was seeing and whether they preferred *Brookside* or *EastEnders*. She tried to tell them that they were both shite but they just ignored her like everyone else did. Then there was the time she came. The old wicked witch. Kay couldn't see that time but she could smell. And that was a smell she would never forget. Flabby tits pushed up against her, wiry pubes jagging her leg, stale breath panting quicker and quicker and that sweat mixing with that dirty fanny stink. She knew that her granny was sitting there. Couldn't see her. Didn't need to. She'd smell her at a hundred yards.

'Hey, you. I'm fucking telling you . . . she doesn't want you to do that, leave her alone or I'll . . . I'll . . . fucking gob on you again . . .' The doctor turned that time. Grey face but nice face – Oriental, wide smile, little cleft on the end of a wee pointed chin, large oval eyes. Kind eyes. Couldn't fool Kay. She knew a con merchant when she saw one. So she spat again, aiming at the doctor's face.

When Kay woke up she didn't know where she was or realise that she had been in a coma for over a week. They greeted her awakening with warm smiles, welcoming her back from the dead then wrapped her in cotton wool. For three days they would tell her nothing, kept her sedated and soothed her route to eating solids, sitting up, moving her limbs. She just wished they would answer her constant question, 'What the fuck am I doing here?'

On the third day, the female doctor with the smiley face and large, oval eyes sat down at her bedside. At first Kay heard nothing. She was too busy remembering the embarrassment of spitting on the young woman. Then the words began to seep through. Not only had Kay been in a coma but she was left with a twist to her face, blindness in one eye, a weakened leg and arm and slurred, slow speech. With time and care – in hospital, of course – these ailments would improve but they couldn't guarantee a full recovery. To sweeten the bad news they sedated her again and left her to dreams – nightmares of grey faces and a voice they couldn't hear.

The world had continued to revolve while Kay was in her nowhere land. Amabel's circumstances had improved thanks to a generous payment from Bud Cumming. Well, he might have considered his philanthropy to be lavish but Amabel had a way with money. Most of the dosh had found its way onto her back, up her nose or down her gullet double-quick. Cumming had been to see Paul to tell him about Kay. We don't know what was said between the two men but we do know that Paul wasn't left feeling any more sympathetic towards his lover. In fact his anger increased. It would have been Cumming's style to alter the basic facts to Kay having taken an overdose of heroin – something that Paul did not approve of – and being found out of it lying naked in some guy's flat. That would have been his style but we don't know what he said. Big Paul Sim was hurt and angry. Angrier than before. So bloody furious he made sure that he stayed off the drugs to guarantee his release at the earliest possible time.

Bud Cumming reported back to McGraw that his wishes were close to realisation. He didn't bother explaining his strategy, which he reckoned was too sophisticated by far for The Licensee. All that mattered was that Cumming believed he was right and his plans with The Licensee were progressing very well. So much so that now he sat with his team and regularly discussed how Paul Sim could be killed. All sorts of suggestions were put forward by the gang. Cumming accepted them all and told them that it was too early to decide. Certain events had to unfold, especially since, against the odds, Kay had wakened out of her coma. Whatever Cumming was about he had a real admiration for Kay. He wouldn't be surprised by what she was capable of next. Mind you, he had a couple of surprises lined up for her too.

Three weeks after Kay awakened from the coma she somehow managed to leave the hospital. Not that the doctors knew till it was too late. The nightmares of the coma had been supplanted by the terrors of her real life. She had a man in prison, a man who she loved. A man who had fallen out with her and she must go back to him now. A man who people were trying to kill. A man who would be released from jail any week. Kay had to leave and knew that the doctors wouldn't understand. Her leg was trailing, one eye was half-blind and constantly streaming, her mouth drooling and twisted and her speech slow. But she had to get out. So, she watched the routine of the staff and clambered to the wardrobe, leaning on anything at hand, when they were least likely to appear. Slowly she dressed and headed out, clinging to walls till, by arrangement, she was met by Amabel and they headed for fresh air. Amabel should have known better if she was concerned for Kay. But Amabel had her orders – to keep an eye on her younger sister. That's why she visited her every night for five minutes before she headed out to the clubs. But Bud Cumming had been spot on to expect the unexpected from wee Kay. Now he was ready and waiting for her.

'Ye can stay wi us,' offered Amabel in the back of the taxi.

'No thanks,' muttered Kay weakly, 'need to get home but . . .'

'Suit yersel then, ye ungrateful cow.'

'. . . but thanks anyway.' Kay was used to Amabel's coarse ways and made no comment. Besides, her head was dizzy, the natural light flashing in her eyes, and her legs felt numb. She needed peace and quiet. Just to lie down in her own flat and work things out. Amabel helped her to the front door then left for the local shop to fetch some milk for tea. Kay staggered about the flat taking in the familiar smells, the objects that she had grown so used to that she thought she'd never see again. When she made it to the living-room she stopped dead in her tracks.

Something was wrong, very wrong. The three-piece suite was missing. And the TV. Where the sound system should have been there was a square shape indented into the carpet.

'I've been burgled,' was Kay's unsurprising first thought, followed swiftly by a rush of panic and anger that soared above her drug-dulled senses. Holding her arms out for balance she hobbled to the bedroom. No mess and the bed was still there. Kay's relief was short-lived when she opened the wardrobe and discovered the rails empty. Whoever it was had taken every piece of clothing belonging to her and Paul. Good gear, designer labels, expensive and all distinct, unusual, following Kay's very individualistic taste. Who could want such gear and who would be small enough? The drawers had been emptied of tops and T-shirts too, only underwear, socks and stockings remained, though even they were messed up as if someone had been searching for something. Kay slumped to floor and howled. It felt like the last straw, though she was about to learn that it was far from it.

'FUCKING CUNTS,' Amabel screamed on her return. What Kay needed was a calming influence, someone to tell her what to do next. She knew it would be hopeless to look for that from Amabel. 'BASTARDS,' her sister continued, walking about the flat as if the goods might return on each new visit to the rooms. 'Imagine blagging your gear when you're lying in hospital. FUCKERS.' Kay said nothing but slouched on the floor and thought. Thought that Arden was well known for its high burglary rate, as well as every other type of crime. But she also thought that when she and Paul lived there they had the safest house in Glasgow. The locals all knew who they were and were too wise or concerned for their own safety to steal from big Paul. Or even little Kay. But then Paul would be out soon – the local thieves would be well appraised of that from the tom-toms linking street players to every jail in the country. No, it had to be someone desperate. 'Bet it was some fucking junkies,' said

Amabel right on cue. But then, would junkies make such a neat job of the robbery? Kay doubted it. They were more likely to shit on the bed, piss in her drawers, shoot up in the kitchen. None of these signs were there. 'Ye'll never guess whit's happened,' Amabel was speaking to someone at the front door, coming into the hall. 'Some cunt's just robbed the place.'

'Fuck's sake, Kay, you all right?' It was Bud Cumming suddenly appearing in her flat. How did he know she was there? 'The bastards,' he said, looking around him at the cleared living-room. 'Ah'll put the word oot, okay? Get the wee bastards that did this – teach them a lesson.' Cumming fumed and walked, much like Amabel, except stopping every now and then to wrap his arms round Kay and tell her it would be all right. Kay sat on the floor and nodded her head absently. When Cumming left a short while later, offering to give Amabel a lift home, somehow Kay wasn't surprised that he left her nothing in spite of knowing her plight. Someone she didn't work with would have handed her money. If she came across anyone in the same predicament she would have done the same. It was the code. Expected. But Cumming should have gone further for a colleague. He could have replaced everything in the house from his small change. Old-time street players would say that was exactly what he should have done. But he did nothing but talk and Kay wasn't surprised.

Ever since Paul had been jailed a set of events had been leading them on a downward spiral, weaker and weaker, till now here she was sitting in her almost empty flat. If only he hadn't been jailed. None of this would have happened. Why did she let him go out alone that night? True to form, Kay was blaming herself again. If only she had realised that the chain of events had started earlier with a call from Cumming to Paul's suppliers – maybe then events would have evolved differently. But how was she to know?

Kay had no idea of how long she had been sitting on the floor when the phone rang. Long enough for the afternoon to turn into night. She managed to reach the phone before it rang off. It was Paul from Barlinnie. He had been on the phone to Amabel to find out how Kay was doing and had been told of events. He was concerned but gruff. She could hear a little of the warmth of their relationship sneak into his voice. A little feeling but guarded. He would sort it all when he got out, which would be soon. In the meantime, he was going to phone his aunt and uncle – tell them to give Kay something. It was the eleven grand they owed him. Paul had been keeping that aside, feeling that he could trust his family, using them as a deposit account for a rainy day. He realised the monsoons had arrived. Kay was to use the money to take care of herself and the house. There should be enough left over to provide a little cushion for them when he was released from prison. Paul would have work to do then and would get on top again. But it would take a while. Two or three thousand pounds would be helpful – she could have the rest. Aye, he was coming home to her. Where else did she think he was going?

When Paul's prison phone card ran out Kay sat and wept. It was a new habit she was falling into and she didn't like it one bit. But this time she was crying happy tears. Her Paul had come to the rescue and was coming home to her. Life would be good again and soon.

They were full of excuses, that aunt and uncle. So was their grown-up son who also owed Paul the money. Bad deals. Money owed to them. Certain people to see before they could raise the cash. They had planned to pay Paul back when he got out of jail. Honest. Just Kay was asking for the dough a couple of weeks too early. Sorry to hear of her troubles but what could they do? Kay left their house empty-handed. Later that night she was phoned by the aunt. Paul had been on the phone to them and had been most insistent. The money would be paid in full in two days. Guaranteed. Kay put her one and only spare outfit – the one she had borrowed from Amabel and which was too big – into the washing machine. She was reminded of the night she'd left George, her first husband, in a similar state and her mother washed and dried her clothes overnight for her interview at Bubbles. Back then she thought that life couldn't get worse but here she was years later back at the same point. At least she wouldn't have to give Wing a blow job next day. At least Paul was going to make sure that she would be all right.

Two days later, Paul's aunt handed Kay an envelope with six hundred pounds, not eleven thousand. It was all they could raise, she told Kay, and they would pay the balance as soon as they could. The few hundreds would save Kay from serious trouble but it wasn't the same as the full amount due. She knew there had to be something wrong but her mind was still too full of the candyfloss cobwebs of her medication to work it out.

Paul was to be released on Christmas Eve 1997. Two days before he had phoned and arranged for Kay to pick him up outside Barlinnie. They would have Christmas together at least. Maybe it was a positive omen after all their troubles.

The night before Paul's release, Bud Cumming called at her home. 'Change o plan, hen,' he said almost immediately. 'Paul's asked me an the boys to meet him at the gates. Wants tae speak aboot a few things.' Cumming broke the habit of a lifetime and said little more, leaving shortly thereafter with a, 'Dinnae worry – we'll fetch him right back tae yese.'

On the day, Kay had the house prepared as best she could. At least it was clean with well-stacked cupboards and drink supplies, including Christmas dinner with all the trimmings. She was happy, nervous and scared all at the same time. Too much had happened in the months since Paul had been jailed but she was confident that, once they sat down together again, the old magic would appear and wash away the grief. So Kay waited and waited and waited.

Four days later Paul walked through the door, his face like fizz and that big jaw of his jutting out as far as it could. When Kay, worried sick, asked where he had been, 'For a drink wi Cumming an the boys,' was all he would say. Kay knew that many prisoners on release find themselves walking into an unplanned bender for weeks. Some are so enthusiastic that their freedom is short-lived. It is something about not realising the freedom you had lost till you stepped out through the gates. But that wasn't Paul's style. Well, it hadn't been previously. For two days they kept each other company through short, muted conversations and Paul could barely disguise the fury raging inside him. Kay wanted to clear up the issue of the love letters signed Samantha, something they had avoided discussing on the calls from jail. But Paul wasn't in the mood to discuss the time of day let alone a subject likely to raise tempers. Something was eating him big style.

'So who's the guy you've been seeing?' he asked suddenly.

'What guy?'

'Look, Kay, I know.'

'Right – the boys been telling you stories, have they?'

'So stop havering an jist tell me, eh?'

'Bloody fishwives . . .' Kay's anger and frustration was close to boiling over. 'I've been seeing nobody, but who the fuck's Samantha?'

'Whit fucking Samantha?' Paul glowered at her the way he looked at someone who had just crossed his personal line. 'Aye, right . . .' he waved a dismissive arm in the air. 'So why should the boys tell me lies, eh?'

'Good question – why have they . . .'

'An ye lied aboot the other business,' spat Paul, meaning her time back in the sauna but not spelling it out. Kay's face flushed with embarrassment and shame – not at her work but for keeping a secret from him, lying to him. The row went on for two days, getting worse and worse till on 31 December Paul stormed out, saying he was going to see his aunt and uncle. When she pleaded with him not to leave he said he needed to clear his head and eventually, almost calmly, agreed to meet her at a friend's house to bring in the New Year. When he left Kay cried again, cursing herself for the pain she felt, the lie she had told, of not having the words to explain to her man to draw him back where he belonged, together with her.

Paul felt comfortable at his aunt and uncle's house. It was one of the few places he could relax, safe in their hospitality. He even got on well with their son, his cousin. They had done a bit of business for him and done well up till recently. So they owed him over ten grand – so what? They were family and sounded as if they were confronting the same problems that he had. Someone was putting out the word that debts should not be repaid to them. Paul believed them. When he sorted out his problems he would be sorting out their problems. That was what family was all about. In the meantime he would relax.

Paul Sim stretched out on the couch in his aunt and uncle's house. He would have a few hours' catnap before getting ready and going to meet Kay. He knew he had been too stressed for too long. A few hours' kip would help make him feel stronger. A sleep in a house where he could relax, feel safe.

As Paul slept, one of them – his aunt or his uncle – made a phone call in a hushed voice from out in the close. The message passed on, they returned to the tenement flat and sat and waited. Silently waited. When the front door opened and they heard quiet footsteps in the hall they knew who it was. Vinnie Mallon, the guy who normally kept watch for Cumming at the door of The Old Chestnut, and Malky Mackie, the man who wanted to take over Paul's territory. The two men pulled the balaclavas over their faces in case their plans went badly wrong and Paul could identify them. As they stood over his sleeping body, the two householders crept into the kitchen, ashen-faced and shaking but quite determined about what was going to happen. Hadn't they made the offer to Bud Cumming after all? A wee trade-off against certain debts and a way of getting rid of some threats Cumming had lain at their feet. In the living-room Mallon and Mackie drew pistols with silencers out of their waistbands and crouched over the sleeping body of Paul Sim. They had better hurry, the big man might wake up.

Over on the other side of the housing scheme, Kay was dressed up and waiting for her man to join her at the party. She couldn't relax and join in the festive spirit till he was there by her side. She would wait for him all night if need be. It was Hogmanay after all, a time lovers should be together. Besides, he said he would be there, hadn't he? He had promised.

Back in the front room of his aunt and uncle's house, Paul Sim was being shot four times at point-blank range in his skull. He wouldn't be making the party.

Hunting the Dead Man (1998)

Paul Sim was a dead man. Everyone knew that. Four shots into his head at point-blank range were bound to kill him. Okay, he might struggle on a bit – big Paul was strong, everyone knew that. But Paul Sim was a dead man, that was for sure.

Bud Cumming shouldn't have been so cheap. All he had to do was shell out a few grand more and someone with a cool nerve and steady hand would have blasted Paul Sim effectively. But the deal with Paul's aunt and uncle was costing Cumming too much, or so he thought. Vinnie Mallon and Malky Mackie didn't do that badly – for two guys who were petrified by even the sleeping form of Paul Sim. Four shots fired inches from his skull and only two managed to go into his head, one into his brain. They didn't wait to check his pulse. The sight of blood and black matter and shards of his skull splattering the back of the couch were all the evidence they needed. Besides, they had to get out and get out fast. Just in case.

Paul Sim was a remarkable specimen of humanity, of that there can be no doubt. If he had been spotted by a boxing or athletics or football coach when he was eight years old he would have had the potential to be something very special. Instead he survived on the streets as a child, sleeping rough and taking to crime. Judge that as you may, he was still a remarkable man. In spite of the odds, he survived. For a while it looked like he might never walk again but he soon confounded the doctors. Paul Sim was going to live. Everyone knew that. And the first to know was Bud Cumming.

Suddenly relatives came out of the woodwork. Posted absent for years, guilty of cruelty, neglect or merely turning a blind eye during the abuses of his childhood, they all wanted a piece of the fame and maybe some dough from the young man, the newspapers or whoever. Paul was news, minor perhaps, but the papers covered the story of his shooting. If that wasn't enough of an alert to the grasping crew, Bud Cumming made sure they knew the story. After expressing his sympathy and offering help he made sure they knew all about the source of Paul's grief, the one who had brought about this terrible attempt to murder the young man. Swiftly the relatives banned Kay from going near Paul. They now knew she had pushed him into business deals that brought conflict from others. Encouraged him to break away from his team who would have protected him. Taken his money and spent it while he was in jail. Been working as a prostitute behind his back. Seeing another man with better long-term prospects and a fatter wallet. The relatives knew all that now, courtesy of Bud Cumming.

Maybe Paul had confounded the medics by living at all but he still had problems. For many weeks he could not speak or hardly move. With no marriage licence between them Kay had no rights, no say in his treatment or his visitors. Those powers went to the very relatives who had thrown him out when he was eight years of age. It was all too much for Kay. She felt as if she had no fight left.

Bud Cumming was happy to take care of Kay. Back in the bosom of the team, she'd sit there in The Old Chestnut or The Dovecote and listen to their plans and reports, staring blankly into the distance, spaced out, distracted, not caring about anything anymore. Her state of mind was helped along by Bud Cumming's generosity. She needed help now. With her face still twisted, a dull eye and a weak leg she couldn't even go back to being a working girl. Well, she could have, by taking to the streets late at night. Some of the women who worked those streets were in such a state of dissipation, so scabby and ill that all that was left for them was the streets. They were the lowest rung in the trade, charging a fiver for a blow job, a tenner for full unprotected sex. They were finished, sometimes literally, with their HIV blossoming into full-blown AIDS. They were the women most likely to be found battered, broken and dead on some wasteground with rats and stray dogs for company. Kay would rather kill herself than take to the streets.

So, Bud Cumming looked after her. Well, his team thought he did. Cumming gave her enough, but just enough to keep the bailiffs from the door. These payments weren't charity. Cumming owed the young woman. Owed for services rendered now and in the past, for huge profits he had made on the back of her suggestions, her work and, most of all, he owed her for her loyalty. If Kay had gone to another team, the media or even the police and told them all she knew about Cumming she would have been well rewarded and he would be in deep trouble. The thought never crossed Kay's mind. So Cumming gave her enough to get by and as many drugs as he could force into her mouth and up her nose. Kay didn't need much encouragement. She was so depressed by the state of her Paul, her own health and the lack of any future she could see that she was quite content to blast the thoughts from her brain, bury her worries under the thick mattress of narcotics. Kay had lost everything and she simply didn't care about herself anymore. The drugs left her in exactly the docile state Cumming wanted.

Then he was out. Paul Sim totally foxed the doctors by meeting every physical test in double-quick time. The man was lucky to be alive and here he was walking the treadmill, lifting weights, standing on one leg only a smattering of weeks after being shot in the head. The medics tried to tell him that he needed a longer period of recuperation. He sneered and signed himself out. Now there was going to be trouble.

'Fucking bad news, guys.' Bud Cumming had convened an extraordinary meeting of his team. 'Big Paul's back oan the street and he's gunning for us.' The words penetrated the drugs fug that was Kay's head and she looked up, keen and eager. 'Naw, naw, hen.' Cumming looked across at her, shaking his head. 'It's no good news – especially not for you.' Kay didn't understand.

'Paul's got the notion that some o us were behind his grief.' Mumbles of protest rose from the other men gathered at the table. 'Aye, aye, Ah know,' Cumming held up his hand for silence. 'Somebody – Ah dinnae know who – has slipped him the word that some of us actually shot him.'

'Oh, for fuck's sake . . .'

'Whit bastard's telling him they lies?' said Vinnie Mallon.

'It'll be that Big G again – trying tae mix it.'

'Ah think the Govan mob are at it . . .'

'Whatever,' Cumming interrupted the idle speculation of his men. 'He's let it be known that he's back and he's gonnae take everything he can put his mitts oan.'

'CUNT . . .'

'Telt ye we could never trust that big bastard – nae offence, Kay,' said Iain O'Reilly.

'There's worse,' said Cumming quietly, seriously leaning on the table staring across at Kay. 'He's oot tae get you, hen.'

'Get me . . . what . . . get?' Kay wasn't taking all of this in.

'Says you set up the hit oan him. That you were the only person that knew where he was going that night.' Kay was shaking her head in disbelief. 'Says he's gonnae kill ye.'

The room went silent, or so it seemed to Kay. All she could feel was a loud buzzing in her head, flutters in her chest, her stomach heavy and grumbling. Her Paul kill her? No way. Her trying to kill Paul? How could he believe that? Someone must have got it wrong. Kay slipped fingers into her handbag and grasped a handful of blues into her palm. She had had how many that day already? She didn't know and didn't care. Just needed to shut it all out. Blank it out.

'Gonnae need tae protect Kay,' said Shuggie Patterson, slouching forward, wringing his hands together in front of him.

'Oh aye, an are you volunteering like?' gibed Iain O'Reilly sarcastically.

'No, Ah was jist . . .'

'Thought it wid be no, ye wanker,' spat O'Reilly.

'C'moan you,' butted in his brother Jas. 'No need for this – got tae stick thegether, eh?'

'Fucking should've got rid o that big Sim bastard years ago, man. Ah said so . . .' Iain O'Reilly was all for action. Started to propose they got tooled up and went hunting Paul.

Vinnie Mallon suggested they find out where Paul was going to live and hit him there, adding, 'Cunt's tough aw right but he's just had a couple o bullets in his napper. Bound tae be weak, man.'

Even the usually taciturn George Lennon joined in, 'Should prepare and wait for him. Prepare oor ground. Double up for a while. Wait till he comes at us and then take him oot.'

Through it all Kay nodded and listened with an increasing sense of fear. These men were plotting Paul's death and she was listening, colluding. Worse, they were going to kill him to protect themselves and her. Paul was going to be killed to protect her. She had no reason to doubt what was being said but somehow she couldn't quite accept that Paul was out to get her. Finish with her yes, but kill her?

'Kay, you're gonnae have tae move oot o yer flat, hen, and pronto,' said Cumming, rounding up the meeting. His calm reminded Kay of a little scene years before. They had been away in some hotel. He had grabbed her and kissed her, saying how the two of them were similar, special. That two people like them could do anything they wanted and get off with it. They could pick a stranger up off the street and kill them and they would never get caught. 'How's aboot moving in wi Amabel, eh, or even wi me if yese fancy?' Cumming winked at Kay across the table. 'Right, guys, full war cabinet the morrow here. Get everybody present – an Ah mean every fucker.' Cumming was referring to the full complement of local associates. The guys who worked the doors, the protection rackets, who sold drugs to the dealers. Every face in the area was under his control and they were being drawn together to plan a strategy to kill Paul Sim. It was in all their interests after all.

ARMED CANDY

When Kay phoned Amabel to ask if she could move in her older sister already knew about Paul. 'Every cunt in the scheme knows,' Amabel said and Kay didn't waste any time wondering how. Paul was a big name locally. The events of the past month had made him even more of a celebrity. The street grapevine would suck in every morsel of information on everything about him. Kay and Amabel drove to her flat in Arden to pack a few clothes, pick up her medication prescribed by the doctor as well as that prescribed by Cumming.

They had thrown the goods onto the back seat and were about to drive away from Arden when, 'Robbing the flat again, are ye?' Paul Sim leaned in the car window, his big face up close to Kay's.

'Jesus, Paul, God how are ye . . .?' Kay's heart was racing with terror.

'Thought there would be fuck all left tae take after the last time.'

'Paul, I didn't rob the place . . . who told you that?' In fact, Cumming had told her that some of Paul's own relatives had stripped the place bare – something she was willing to believe given they had banned her from visiting him in hospital.

'Ah fucking know ye did.'

'But . . .'

'Shut the fuck up,' he spat, bringing his hand up and into the car. In his fist was a pistol and he pointed it straight at her face. 'Ah know whit ye've been up tae. Ah know everything. If Ah see yese again Ah'm gonnae end ye.' Kay was visibly shaking, wanting to be sick. 'Understand . . . UNDERSTAND?' Paul pulled himself upright and marched off across the road, quickly covering the distance in that long striding gait.

'DRIVE . . . FUCKING DRIVE, MAN,' screamed Amabel and Kay went for it as fast as she knew how, screeching tyres as she rounded a sharp corner, drawing looks and curses from passing pedestrians.

So it was true. Paul was out to kill her. Over the next two

weeks she sat among Cumming's team and listened to their plots to kill Paul. She was there, she didn't say no, she didn't say anything. She half listened while she thought of the image of her Paul's face with the bald patches on his temple and the bandage. He had lost weight, looked pale and drawn. Looked hunted. Was hunted. Why hadn't he killed her right there and then in the car? Was it too public, too broad daylight, too many people about? He would have had to kill Amabel as well. Was that it? She knew Paul and knew he wouldn't hesitate to tackle whoever was necessary. What then – was he giving Kay a chance? Or was it that the issue was personal, between her and him and no one else? Kay wished he had allowed her to speak, to explain that what he had been told wasn't true. Was as far from the truth as it could possibly be. Maybe, if he had given them a chance to talk things through, maybe he would have revealed to her that his recently reconciled relatives had passed on the information about her stealing things from their flat and arranging the hit job. They had been told by a very good source. Someone they trusted. By Bud Cumming. Except Paul Sim didn't know that Cumming was the source of information. That was part of the deal between Cumming and Paul's relatives. If Paul knew it had come from Bud Cumming he would have been suspicious. Cumming explained that he and Kay had had a relationship a long time ago, now well finished, but they knew how jealous Paul could be. They didn't know. They didn't know Paul at all well. But Bud Cumming was a major player, meant well and had been generous with his information and his little bundles of cash. If he said not to tell Paul then that's what the relatives would do. Paul Sim knew none of this.

Paul Sim wasn't out to get Bud Cumming – that was a fabrication made up by Cumming. Paul Sim was just suspicious of everyone. All bets were off and he was back to where he had been – on his own, no friends, no partners, no alliances, no lover. It was the way he worked best, or so Paul Sim thought.

Hot for Winter (1998) - Part Two

Paul couldn't settle in his aunt and uncle's house and paced up and down in front of the window. Some would say he was foolhardy for going back to the same room where a couple of months before he had been shot in the head. Trauma, the doctors had warned him, can be emotional as well as physical. He laughed and sneered. He knew fine well what they meant but dismissed it as weak crap.

The room looked different. The sofa had been replaced, of course. Well, it would have been impossible to get all those bloodstains out. The room had been redecorated and Paul wondered if bits of his skull had gone scattering over the walls. There was some new electrical gear – a big, fancy-looking sound system and a TV that hogged half the room. They had been spending a bit of money all right. Paul just hoped it wasn't his money, the ten grand that they owed him. The aunt had promised to pay him back the very next day. Paul had noticed that when she said that his uncle's face had twisted into a sour look and she had glowered at him – a look that said, 'Shut the fuck up you. Ah'm the boss here.' And she was. Out on the streets they thought it was the uncle who was the hardman and his son the mental blade boy. All that was true, but the real boss was his auntie – hard as steel and she took no prisoners. She also had a good head, a thinker who worked out a plan and stuck to it. Paul liked the woman. When she said that he could get his money the next day or go and collect it himself he reckoned she was trying to help. A guy we'll call Matt Brennan owed them the cash and she offered to phone and set it up. Matt Brennan was known to Paul and the two of them had always got on well. In a world of backstabbers, Paul thought that Brennan was an okay guy who could be trusted as much as anyone could. Paul asked his auntie to set it up and thanked her. She went to make a phone call from the kitchen. But it wasn't Matt Brennan she was phoning.

Paul just couldn't settle in that house. He paced in front of the window and got angry at his uncle for telling him to stand away from it for his own safety. What did he know about safety? Old bastard had lived off of people all his life.

There was some crap daytime TV chat show on. One of those voyeuristic peeks at other folks' underwear affairs that Paul hated. Some bloke in a woman's frock was on speaking in a false-sounding high-pitched voice, talking about men he shagged. His wife sat next to him with the face of a bulldog – no wonder he fucked guys, was Paul's thought. Then he realised he had to get out of that place – he was beginning to watch that shite programme for fuck's sake. His auntie called a taxi for him and he went to leave and still that daft uncle told him not to because it was too cold. What did he take him for? Some fucking wimp? Of course it was cold, it was winter in Glasgow for fuck's sake.

As Paul descended the stairs two at a time and headed for the fresh air, back in the flat his auntie made another phone call. 'He's gone. Naw, that's whit Ah'm sayin'. He's no waiting in here for the taxi. He's oan the street. Aye, that's right. Right. Good,' she said to Bud Cumming before retreating to the kitchen to wipe imaginary crumbs off the work surfaces.

But his uncle had been right – it was freezing. Maybe his time in hospital had thinned his blood because he couldn't seem to get warm now. Paul stood outside and stamped his feet on the frost-covered ground, thinking of his wee Kay. Warm times they had had. Hot to trot. Man, that was a good time. Best time in his life. He used to love going home to her. Just the two of them talking and drinking into the early hours. Huddled up together, hands down each other's clothes. Or naked in bed, how she was so wee but seemed to cover him entirely. Like they were made to fit each other.

Young kids were coming out of school. Made him think of Kay again. Maybe if they had lasted they would have had children together. Paul didn't admit it to anyone else but he wanted children. A wee skinny, scruffy kid was up to tricks with a cap gun that sounded real. He fired it at some pal and it made Paul jump and reach for his own real pistol. Paul grinned. He loved kids like that. Reminded him of himself when he was young. But he would love his boy and make sure they wanted for nothing – especially love. Paul reckoned that he and Kay could have made beautiful babies as long as they had her looks and his height and not the other way around. Aye, Paul and Kay, what could have been?

At first he thought it was the taxi he had been waiting for. Some lazy bloody driver that just pulled up on the dual-lane boulevard that ran through the scheme rather than turning down to his auntie's address.

'Wanker taxi driver doesn't even know the area,' Paul cursed. As he strode closer he noticed that it was no mini-cab but an ordinary motor. 'Yo, Simmy!' a familiar face shouted out of the open driver's window. Behind the wheel sat Jas O'Reilly. Paul had always got on well with Jas even if the man associated with a crew that couldn't be trusted. There was something decent about Jas. Paul smiled and lifted his hand in greeting. Leaning down over the car to speak with Jas, Paul noticed it. The rear passenger window was wound fully down. Paul growled, cursing himself for being so sloppy and at the same time went for his gun in his jacket.

The last thing he would have seen was the barrel emerging through the back window and a smiling face rising up off the back seat – the face of Iain O'Reilly. Paul Sim died three hours later.

As the car sped away, a lone woman watched from her living-room window. She looked sad but unmoved. Steely eyed, hardened, the way farmers are when they put an old favourite dog out of its misery. She turned away and lifted the phone. Paul Sim's auntie called Bud Cumming – he owed her money now, after all.

Crying and Dying (1998)

It was right for trouble and left for home. Kay had a feeling that something had happened. A strange feeling like the few times she had déjà vu or dreaming about the coma dreams long after she was out of hospital. The feelings scared her but she couldn't resist them. They were so strong, compelling, but who was she going to tell about them? Bud Cumming, her evil mother, selfish Amabel? She didn't think so and she wasn't about to share them with her niece either. The teenage girl sat glum-faced, the only other passenger in the car as Kay tried to decide to drive right for Paul's scheme, his hunting ground and trouble. Or left for Arden, Amabel's house and safety. She turned right for trouble but she didn't know why.

The rows of grey, modern tenements scared Kay, where months before she had regarded these same streets as the safest in the world. Well, the safest for her and for Paul. What game was she playing? Chicken? The need to see him in spite of the dangers. Was it the same motivation as back when she had bugged Lenny Lovat into letting her be the getaway driver on his escapades? Being jailed for burglary was one thing but big Paul Sim was going to shoot her. Maybe it was because, terrified as she was, she didn't quite believe her big lover would harm her. Not when it came right down to it. She still believed they were meant for each other.

Kay seemed to know where she was going but had no idea why. When she pulled into the streets and saw the police, the blue flashing lights and the bloodstained grass she realised what all this had been about. Kay knew that Paul Sim was dead. Had

died there on that grass verge in the middle of his home
territory.

'They've goat him. He's fuckin' deid. Stone fuckin' deid. YA
BEAUTY,' screamed Amabel from the window of her Arden flat
as Kay pulled the car up to the verge. All the way across the city
Kay had silently mourned Paul Sim. Now she was going to
celebrate the same death. That day she was kissed and hugged by
strangers, all happy that Paul was gone. Kay did her best to smile
but folk had become used to the sad, mournful look her facial
paralysis had left her with. What she was not about to reveal was
that her muscles had improved a great deal. That she could smile
once again. Instead, she gave a crooked grin when she was
required to and kissed whoever kissed her.

That same night a party was thrown in The Old Chestnut,
hosted by Bud Cumming. He was in great form, buying everyone
drinks and even tolerating the pub singer. His whole team were
there and Kay wondered if Paul had ever stood a chance. Faces
she didn't know were associated with Cumming had come out of
the woodwork and stood alongside him, packing out the pub.
Poor Paul had had nowhere to hide.

'Ah said we should've killed that big cunt years ago,' said a
drunken Vinnie Mallon.

'Ah could've had him killed years ago,' replied Bud Cumming,
one arm wrapped around Kay, the other working up the back of
Amabel's knickers. 'Ah could've had him killed at any time. But
Ah decided it was now.'

Cumming kept Kay full of booze and drugs for weeks on end.
She didn't resist but gobbled everything he supplied and asked
for more. Kay wanted to obliterate her thoughts, wipe them from
her mind. She had colluded in the murder of the very person she
loved. Hadn't she? She had been so out of it on drugs for so long
she wondered if she had actually known of the plans to kill him.
Was that how she had known to go to that street on that day?
She had been so forgetful since the coma and her massive intake

of jellies, blues and constant hash wasn't helping one bit. When she was straight she wanted to kill herself. When Paul's family banned her from his funeral she cut off all of her long hair right to the bone and sat alone in the dark of her living-room for two days, a blade and a bottle of paracetamol by her side.

In one of Bud Cumming's houses one night she had said to him, 'You've got pull with the polis. Arrange for me to see him.'

'See who?' he had asked.

'See my Paul.'

'You fucking daft? Wait a minute.' Cumming had disappeared into another room, returning minutes later with a folder. 'Whit ye think yer gonnae see? Your big pal right as rain?' Cumming pulled the folder open and handed several sheaves to Kay. A man lying flat on his back. A man with a strange look on his face, or rather no expression at all. A dead man. In his chest two bloody round bruises the size of small footballs. The next picture the same man from a different angle and the next and the next. They made Kay feel sick. 'That's whit ye'll see,' said Cumming, 'a stiff lying oan a slab in the morgue.' The body was of a man from Linwood, shot in mistake for a nearby neighbour who was suspected of muscling in on Cumming's business. Kay knew that Cumming had gone on the run at that time and his close friend and namesake, Bud Gibson, had taken the rap for the murder on his behalf. Bud Gibson was sentenced to life and she had never heard Cumming mention his name since. Kay looked at the picture of the corpse on the morgue slab, thought of her Paul and felt sick.

Blot it out was all she could do. Unknown to Kay, she wasn't the only one that the murder of Paul was having a dramatic effect on.

ANGIE BABY

They all called her that, Angie Baby. Maybe it was after the Stones number or maybe it was because

ARMED CANDY

she was so beautiful and so free with her charms.
Who knows? She had grown up in a housing scheme
next to the one Paul and Bud Cumming considered
their territory. By the age of fourteen she was
long-legged, long-haired, with a wide smile and a
body to die for. But Angie had a weakness — hard
men — and slept with them whenever she could.

By the age of sixteen she was acting as a courier
for drug dealers. Angie had weaknesses but heroin
wasn't one of them. She had watched her cousin and
two good friends wasted by smack at an early age
and never touched the gear — except to deliver it.
Reliability made Angie a popular worker. Her
fondness for street players made her popular in
other ways. It was a dynamite combination.

Angie Baby saw fit to take a flat in the city
centre away from the scheme. She reasoned to
friends that if the local junkies knew where she
lived they might wrongly suppose she kept heroin in
her house. That was a dangerous position to be in.

Angie had weaknesses but she wasn't stupid. She
couldn't say no to any known player and most of
them took advantage of her whenever they could.
Even gangsters can fall into pillow talk. When
Paul Sim was killed Bud Cumming's team started
fretting about who might know anything about the
murder. Angie's name came up first, with a handful
of team members admitting they had been with her
lately. Angie Baby maybe had weaknesses but she
belonged to no one. Only one conclusion then —
she'd have to be silenced. But who would do it?

Malky Mackie had been after Paul's territory for
years. Cumming had already decided to give it to
him but there was no harm in making him work for

it. Malky Mackie would kill Angie Baby and, to make sure, Shuggie Patterson was sent along to watch. Shuggie objected, saying that he wasn't cut out for that type of work. Cumming insisted, saying all he had to do was watch. Everyone, including Cumming, knew that Shuggie had been soft on Angie for years.

On the night, Angie let Malky and Shuggie in when they arrived at her door. Why should she worry — she had known these guys for years. Shuggie stood and watched as Malky grabbed the woman, punching her three or four times. Holding her on the ground, he jammed his forearm against her throat. Angie gagged, her mouth open, struggling for breath. Malky pulled a hypodermic needle from his pocket and pushed it under her tongue. One hit the quacks wouldn't find unless they were very particular. It was Angie's first hit of heroin and it gave her stomach cramps, making her sick. She soon settled into a lethargic state, close to sleep. Mackie yanked her by the ankles away from the pool of her vomit. Rolling up her sleeve he gave her another blast, this time in the arm.

The two men stood and watched the beautiful Angie slip away. Mackie knew that the first hit alone would have pole-axed a veteran, never mind a virgin. The second hit simply made sure.

'Ah've always wanted tae dae this,' Mackie said, dropping his trousers. Shuggie Patterson watched as Mackie fucked the prone woman. Watched and cried for better times. Disgust and bile rose in his throat. He tried to stop Mackie, muttering about DNA and such stuff but Mackie wasn't stupid — he had put on a condom.

ARMED CANDY

Mackie wasn't as thick as he looked. When Angie Baby's body was eventually found with her knickers round her ankles and the needle still dangling from her arm they wasted no time concluding that it was just another junky whore who took too much H. Just another one.

Just another one? No way. But Angie Baby wasn't to be the last. Bud Cumming's team had gone paranoid.

Bud Cumming had arranged so many hits he had lost count.

There was that guy Campbell a couple of years before who had hustled their dealers, beating them up and chasing them off his streets, their patch. They had shot him in a pub car park then made anonymous calls to the police and the press claiming it had been political and the assassins were the Red Hand mob from Ulster. Just because the guy was a papist the police bought it.

Then there was that fucker Kelman who had cheated them on a deal. That was bad enough but then he had boasted about it on their own patch. He was beaten to death outside a pub.

That English cunt they killed in the pub next to The Old Chestnut. Stabbed him right there in the fucking pub in front of a pack of drinkers and there wasn't one witness. No, you couldn't beat your own people.

A wee junky lassie, Christ, she was years before. Yapping too much and a couple of straight bogiemen had the grip on her. Doing deals. Saying tell them the beef or she was going to the nick for cold turkey and rough-skinned dykes. Cumming had her beaten to death fist to face in her flat in the scheme.

Then there was that young cunt who tried to muscle in on the boys. Waltzing into the area with a sawn-off and taking the dough from the dealers. Who the fuck did he think he was? Clint fucking Eastwood? Cumming just sent one of the boys to his home. Well – tit for tat, eh? Shot the fucker outside his house. Could hear his wife and weans screaming when they realised what had happened. Too bad. Cost him a good man that job, though. Fucker got caught and went down for life. Be out soon mind. Wonder how he's doing?

The one Cumming liked best was the torch job. Old bastard giving the boys lip. Wising them up in public. A wee bit of that is okay but he just kept on and on. They broke into his house one night. There he was lying pissed drunk, and in a similar state was this dame and another bloke. The boys just covered the target in lighter fuel and struck a match. While he was burning they woke up the woman. Told her that there had been a fight. RIGHT? The two old guys had fought over her. RIGHT? Showed her a pistol and shoved her fifty quid. Said she'd be taken good care of or bad care of – her call. Wee darling gave evidence against the other fucker. Poor bastard had been so pissed he couldn't remember what happened. Alkies, man, they are good for business and cheap – Cumming never did pay the woman any more dough.

So, killing they were used to but this was different. Maybe it was because Paul Sim had been involved in most of the action so far. It was a bad-luck omen to kill the killer. But that's what had happened. They had taken care of the guy that had scared their part of the city. The one who scared them. If they were capable of doing that, then who in the team was safe? No fucker, that's who. Cumming decided that the only way to kill paranoia stone dead was to feed it.

DANNY JAMES

It wasn't Danny James' fault that he was talkative. He was small and had to survive so he developed the patter. Always a wisecracker, never shutting up. His brothers were the same except they were funny. One even made it on to the TV as a professional comic. Danny had been born with no sense of humour so he did what he did – talk, show interest, ask questions. He had no idea it got on people's nerves.

ARMED CANDY

Danny was the Manchester guy that delivered the drugs for Bud Cumming's Liverpool supplier. Bud hadn't bothered to ask the guy in charge to change staff as George Lennon had suggested. Thought it trivial. But a month after Paul's death Bud found himself in The Old Chestnut with Danny asking questions ten to the dozen and the boys going silently mental. Right enough, the wee shite was nosy.

Bud nodded to Vinnie and Jas.

'Listen, Danny, wee bit o stuff tae show yese, man,' said Vinnie.

'Yeah, fancy her over there meself,' said Danny, waiting for a laugh and getting none.

'It's a wee return deal – tae yer boss, like,' offered Jas. 'A little thank you.'

'Yeah? You guys are great, ye know that. I was sayin' to ma mates that us northerners have much more in common with each other than we do wi those London fucks. Eh? Eh?'

Danny emptied his pint glass and followed Vinnie and Jas out of the bar, smiling all the while and never shutting up. Bud waited a second and followed. Behind The Old Chestnut it was pitch dark and hidden from the road. Jas grabbed Danny by the throat and quick as a flash Vinnie pumped a bullet into his temple. The two assassins let him drop to the ground and stood looking down on him.

'Now you shoot him,' Bud Cumming ordered Jas from the edge of the dark.

'Why? He's deid.'

'Aye, maybe, but we want shared responsibility here . . . no grasses.'

Jas pulled his pistol, leaned over, aimed and

fired into the ground inches from Danny James'
head. Jas thought no one would notice in the dark
and they probably didn't. But that was not the
point. Bud Cumming was worried about Jas.

Vinnie and Jas humped Danny James into the boot
of a car and drove him into the country. Not far but
scenic. They pulled into a lay-by and pulled his
corpse over rough terrain till the ground turned
marshy. As they watched Danny James sink into the
ground, Vinnie was trying to remember how many
bodies they had dumped out here in the moor. And if
it was always the same area they chose. Vinnie
couldn't tell - it all looked the same to him.

Iain O'Reilly had been arrested and charged with Paul's murder.
Kay couldn't accept that Iain would have killed Paul. He was the
type of guy who was all talk and only talk – the schemes were
full of them. But the day after the murder he had been reported
as driving the car which someone had described at the shooting.
A lollipop lady of a certain age was the witness. Cumming was
mustering the troops for Iain O'Reilly's defence.

'Ye'll gie evidence, Kay,' he said as a statement rather than a
question.

'Eh . . . sure, aye . . . of course,' she replied, not knowing what
she had to tell. She didn't have to wait long to find out.

'Ye were in The Old Chestnut that day at that time and Iain
was sitting right next tae yese. Sat there for the next three hours
– right?'

'Yeah, of course,' Kay said, happy to give evidence to get an
innocent man off. The police in Glasgow had an unenviable
record of setting the wrong people up for terrible crimes they
hadn't committed. They justified it all on the basis that they
knew those convicted had been up to some badness, just not
necessarily that badness. Well, fuck that.

'Good girl,' said Cumming, stroking her cheek.

Kay had expected Cumming to come up with some help. Standard procedure was that witnesses and the accused should look as conservatively well dressed as they could. It cost a good few quid but paid dividends with juries. Cumming knew Kay had just been barely surviving and never managed to replace any of her classy dress suits. He knew but did nothing. So she borrowed a couple of grand, got herself togged out just right and waited for the day. Cumming arrived early in the morning.

'Good,' he said.

'What?'

'You look good, but here,' he fumbled in his pocket, 'ye'll need these.' Cumming handed Kay a small bag containing around thirty blues.

'I've had something,' she declared, telling the truth.

'High stress day, hen, take them. Take them all.' By the time she reached the courthouse Kay had swallowed all the pills. Sitting in the witness box her legs felt weighted down, her voice sounded like a slow-speed distorted record and her head was full of spiders' webs. But she seemed to have done all right, or so the others told her later.

Iain O'Reilly was found not guilty. As soon as the result was announced celebrations broke out. Outside the High Court Bud Cumming grabbed Kay in his arms.

'See, Ah told yese,' he breathed, kissing her on the face. 'The winner takes ALL.' The blues were still kicking in, making Kay's brain sticky, her mouth and speech slow. 'Tell ye whit we should do now,' Cumming went on, still hugging her. 'Ah'm gonnae take ye tae see big Paul.' Kay had craved to visit Paul's grave since the day he had been buried. She needed to go there. Her grief was stuck some place deep in her stomach and wouldn't let loose till something happened. She thought that something was seeing him there, buried in the ground. Kay smiled and nodded at Cumming. 'And you and me,' he continued, 'we are gonnae shag each other oan the grass. Right oan top o the cunt's grave.' Kay couldn't believe what she was hearing. She knew Bud Cumming could be crude and cared little about other people but this was a new all-time low. If she could have found the words she would have told him so in no uncertain terms to his face right there in front of his troops. Instead she just shoved him back and walked away.

'TOLD YE, KAY,' he shouted after her, 'WINNER TAKES ALL.'

Iain O'Reilly had been found not guilty and released in spite of being found with traces of gunpowder on both hands. In retrospect Kay's evidence was useful, but just. The star defence witness was a senior medic from one of Scotland's largest hospitals. A middle-aged woman, grey-haired, dressed in a dark sombre suit, who saved lives day after day. She was a witness that juries would believe. She told the court how on the day of the murder she saw the shooting and another car of a slightly different colour but entirely different make had driven away at speed. Compared to the rough-spoken, inarticulate lollipop lady there was no competition. Pity the jury hadn't heard Bud Cumming's boasts that the medic's son had a heroin problem and his debts to the dealers had just been written off as well as a threat to phone the tabloids now removed. Pity that.

There had been one disappointing witness, however.

JAS O'REILLY

When Paul was killed Jas O'Reilly had looked Kay in the face and burst into tears. He had been the only one. It was a moment that could be interpreted any way. People weep with relief or happiness or because of stress. Kay knew Jas was weeping with grief and guilt. He hadn't been coping well since.

The last time Kay saw Jas was in the corridors of Glasgow High Court when his brother, Iain O'Reilly, was declared not guilty of Paul Sim's murder. In the sea of happy celebratory faces he was a man set adrift. The last time his wife Aggie saw Jas was on the street outside their home getting into a taxi to go to a meeting with Bud Cumming and his team.

Months later, when Jas had not returned home, Aggie received a visit from George Lennon and Vinnie Mallon. They told her he had betrayed them and his brother. That he was in danger of betraying her so they would all end up in jail. He had to be punished — they had no choice. They told her he was killed and dumped in the nearby marsh.

Aggie O'Reilly searches the marsh during all daylight hours. She sleeps at night with a large kitchen knife under her bed, convinced they will come to her to stop her finding her man. She tells her young children that their father has gone away to work and he'll be back soon. Then the next morning she drops them off at school and sets off for the marsh again.

Every day Aggie O'Reilly walks that marsh, Bud Cumming and his team share a private joke. On the day that they shot Jas through the head they wrapped him in a blanket and drove him to a refuse dump. One of George Lennon's covers is that he is still officially employed by the local council, not that he works. For a regular weekly fee equivalent to half his wages, the gaffers clock him on and off. George Lennon knows his history. He knows that more gangsters have been brought down for non-payment of tax than for the murders they have committed. The Inland Revenue are not interested in Lennon — he is well covered.

Another side benefit of Lennon's faux job is

ARMED CANDY

access. Easy and legal access to his council premises, including a furnace. Aggie O'Reilly is searching for a body where there is none. At best Jas O'Reilly may be the finest falling of ashes all washed into the earth by the first light rain.

The trial and Jas going missing cast Kay into a downward spiral. When she heard that Shuggie Patterson had stripped his clothes off and walked naked through the scheme talking of reincarnation, hellfire and damnation she became so sad her insides felt broken.

SHUGGIE PATTERSON
Shuggie was met first by neighbours and secondly by police. They ensured he was sent packing to the local psychiatric hospital where he was promptly committed and diagnosed as schizophrenic. To this day he sits in the hospital ward describing terrible events. In a loud voice he describes dying women, rape, knives cutting through flesh, bodies burning, skulls exploding. No one listens anymore. The rantings of a madman are of no value to anyone. A loony bin is not the best place to be, that's for sure. But if on the day of the naked walk Cumming's team and not the police had been summoned, Shuggie Patterson would not be in the care of the National Health Service but in some marshy shallow grave or ashes blowing in the wind.

MALKY MACKIE
Malky Mackie was given Paul's territory and his customers. Overnight he went from street bully to power merchant. Trouble was he thought he was impregnable and licensed. A young girl who refused

260

his advances was slashed through the mouth, shredding her cheeks down to the jaw bone. A taxi driver who asked for his fare was stabbed in the neck. A junky who was short on the deal was set on fire. Mackie had a reputation now, a reputation of the gutter. People on the streets began to wish for Paul Sim back.

VINNIE MALLON

Vinnie Mallon didn't say a word. He couldn't say that life had become worse since Paul had been killed. How could he when he had been one of the first to shoot Paul Sim in the head? But life had got worse. The team were all eyeing each other up with suspicion. They had killed big Paul, Jas O'Reilly, Danny James, Angie Baby and others. They were all loyal people. He realised that too late. Now all the bit-part street players thought they stood a chance of promotion in Cumming's outfit. Vinnie Mallon felt out of place and scared for his life. He didn't say anything at all. Just threw some things in the boot of his car and drove north. When he found the right spot – the place his old man used to take him for picnics when he was a child – Vinnie threw the rope over the tree and hung himself.

KAY

Now it was Kay's turn. Stoned out of her head as usual, Amabel introduced her to two new people, a couple, man and woman. He was a junky but they were good fun and had a hefty stash of dope. Kay went along to their place for the laughs. At some point in the night she woke up lying on the floor. As her eyes slowly focused she realised that the man was sitting by her side, rolling up her sleeve, tapping her veins. The first flush of heroin rushed through her arteries, buzzing and running, heading for home, and she sat up with a start, thumping the guy on the side of the head. Most junkies are not strong and this one was no exception. The man crumbled over, dropping the hypo, leaving it sticking in Kay's arm. She hit him again as hard as she could. Then stood up and booted him once, twice, again and again. The effort killed her legs. They were buckling, barely keeping her upright. Kay pulled the syringe from her arm and headed for the door.

One taxi ride later she arrived at the door of the casualty department of the Southern General Hospital. The driver helped her into the building where she was grabbed by nurses and rushed straight to treatment. Before she passed out Kay lifted her fist still clutching the syringe of heroin.

Two days later when she was fully awake they told her straight that she almost died. The syringe contained three times the amount and twice the purity that a smackhead of twenty years' experience could cope with. The syringe was a death sentence as sure as a bullet from a gun.

For three days Kay lay in the hospital bed and thought things through. For the first time in a long, long while her head was clear. Too much had happened. Too many people had gone. For a year she had been trying to kill herself and now they were doing it for her. She had no doubt who had ordered the little surprise. Bud Cumming for sure. It was his style, she knew all of that. But what had made her waken and grab that junky? The same energy that made her mind up that day. Kay decided she was going to cease to exist. Be a person no more. It was the only way she was going to live and live she would.

Time Out

Kay knew how to disappear. To make it effective you have to tell no one. No one at all, not even those you believe you can trust. It's the main consideration for most people – leaving behind friends and loved ones and often the weakness in their plans – a pet dog taken along, a mother who talks in her sleep, a return trip to visit a seriously ill relative. You have to give them all up. That was the easiest part for Kay at that time in her life. She had no one to trust, no one to love, no one to miss.

The second trick is to be thorough. Bank accounts, car records, phone rentals, council tax, rent books, book clubs, credit cards, the works. Easy for someone like Kay because she wasn't known to any of those institutions of normal day-to-day life for most of us. When you are a working girl or a street player you try to stay hidden. She was halfway there already.

Then there's the name. It's not just a case of changing it to something that doesn't resemble your own name at all, you also have to get used to it, own it, respond to it as smoothly as if you had been called by that handle from birth. The name has to be ordinary, unremarkable. Kay chose Susan White for no particular reason.

Then there's your appearance. Unless you take it to extremes and go for plastic surgery – the stuff of Hollywood – there's a limit to what you can do. Kay had always been known for her lovely hair. Long, auburn, thick and shiny. She had had it shorn on the day of Paul's funeral and kept it short since. Now she dyed it blonde and let it grow.

Kay moved to Greenock. It was about twenty miles from

Glasgow down the River Clyde towards the estuary. In miles it seems close but people from Glasgow just don't go there unless they really have to and Kay had no intention of going to Glasgow. Greenock had been a centre for shipbuilding. Now that the industry was in terminal decline so was the town. What it did have was a vast amount of tenements empty and available in large unruly schemes as wild as any to be found in any city. Some might have worried about a small woman, on her own, moving into that neighbourhood but Kay had seen it all and made the video. Besides, she was going to have as little as possible to do with Greenock as she could. Keep herself to herself, make no friends, be polite but never too open.

Money was a problem. When you want to disappear you can hardly sign on for welfare benefits. Apart from that the civil servants would want to know where Kay had been all her adult life. In spite of her heavy consumption of drugs Kay had kept to a disciplined regime of physiotherapy and exercise over the previous few months. As a result her physical health was almost perfect, she could see, her face muscles had relaxed and, most important, as far as money was concerned, she was in great shape. There was only one thing for it – she would have to be a working girl again.

Kay travelled to Edinburgh one night. At least there she wouldn't be known. Glasgow and Edinburgh suffer from a myth of deep animosity – all nonsense. But what was true was that johns liked their pleasures locally and she was sure she would go undetected. She cruised the streets, found a sauna and waltzed straight in. Ten minutes later she was employed. At least, Susan White was employed. Susie they called her. But Susie had no reputation in the capital city. In Glasgow Kay would have been offered higher rates, overnighters and special clients but as Susie she had to prove herself from scratch. The money was less, but enough – a small price to pay for anonymity. Well worth it to stay alive.

Kay was quite happy just to be another working girl in a sauna. One pretty face among many. She showed no ambition, just competence, didn't grumble or complain and got on with her work. As the months passed she grew in confidence, feeling stronger.

One night she was chosen by an unusual-looking punter. The guy seemed younger than most and dressed like a radical, maybe a cool academic, a club kid. Tall and rangy, he had a round head, close-cropped hair and pleasant, chubby cheeks. Kay didn't think too much about it. Why should she? She had seen everything and was ready for anything. Once in the room she asked the guy what he wanted.

'This'll do fine,' he said and she could smell beer on his breath.

'What?' she looked at him carefully to see if there was something she had missed. Maybe a roll of barbed wire around his waist under his shirt? Pain and the company of a beautiful woman equalled orgasm for some masochists. But there was no hidden agenda. Just a good-looking young guy who wanted to talk. 'What do you want to speak about?' she asked.

'It's just I pass here most days and see the women going to and fro sometimes and I wonder how they got here?'

'That old question,' replied Kay. 'I've lost count of the number of times guys have asked what a good-looking woman like me is doing working at this lark.'

'That's not what I'm saying,' he went on. 'It seems to me that people tend to think of you as a label . . .'

'Aye, whore, prostitute, slag, cum bag . . . take your pick.'

'That's what I mean and maybe I'm as guilty as most.' Kay arched her eyebrows, anticipating an outburst. Maybe the young guy was one of those talk-dirty freaks. Well, she wasn't sure she was going to put up with that. 'Just want to reach beyond my own blocks cause I know that the labels are fucking crap.'

She didn't know why or how but that night Kay spoke about

herself for the first time in a long while. Slithers of her life, just tasters, but it felt good, cleansing and healing. She was so busy chatting that she ran over the guy's time limit, a cardinal sin unless the punter is willing to pay more money. She panicked and he laughed, coming with up the cash immediately. Kay was amazed that such a scruffy-looking guy had just dished out over one hundred quid to listen to her speak. Mind you, he was beginning to look familiar. She couldn't place him but was convinced she had seen him before. Probably he had come in as a punter another time and the sketch of his face had remained inscribed as just a vague memory among all the faces of all those other punters.

'Listen,' he said finally, when he really had to leave, 'I've enjoyed this so much. I didn't like to say but I'm a writer and I'd like to turn your story into a short story or maybe a script.' Kay had enjoyed the young guy's company but was he taking the piss?

'No way,' she blushed, opening the door and signalling for him to get out. 'I'm sorry, I just couldn't.' He tried to convince her some more before promising to come back another night and finally leaving.

It had been the first time Kay had tried to make some sense of her life out loud to another person. The first time ever and she had been paid for it. The words and memories she had shared with the young guy lay heavily on her mind as she drove home to Greenock. Then it came to her where she had seen him. His photograph had been in all the Sunday colour supplements, the music magazines and more. He'd written a bestselling book. The guy wasn't lying, he was a writer and a bloody good one.

Arriving back home Kay was still tickled at the famous writer's interest in her life and she hadn't even started to tell him half the truth. He was a nice guy, she liked him and was looking forward to his next visit – if he came back. Too many punters said they would and never did. He maybe only wanted to listen, but the writer was still a paying john. Just another punter. Then her mobile phone rang. 'Can I speak to Kay Petrie,' said the gruff male voice.

'Who? Sorry, you must have the wrong number.' Kay panicked. The phone had been bought since her move to Greenock. Paid for in cash. Pay as you go with no need to give a name for rental or line agreement. Yet someone had tracked her down.

'Kay, I know it's you. I've a message . . .'

'You've got a wrong number . . .'

'. . . keep your trap shut or else.'

'I don't know what you're speaking abo . . .'

'Or else, Kay.' He hung up.

All night she fretted. Every now and then she went to the window, scanning up and down the street for cars full of men. If they had found her number then what else had they found out about her? Everything? How could they trace that phone? She gave the number to no one, only using it for calling out. Always she withheld her own number.

Kay reviewed her precautions in keeping her identity secret. No matter how she looked at it she had been disciplined and consistent. Then she had an idea. Picking up her mobile phone she pressed last number redial. It came up. The idiot hadn't withheld his number. Either he was stupid or he didn't care if she found out who he was. She hadn't recognised the voice. But so what? She carefully wrote down the phone number then switched her phone off. Switching it back on again she dialled 141 followed by the man's number. It rang out. The fear ached in her gut, taking her breath away. A man's voice answered. A different voice with a polite, efficient approach. The man had just said that it was one of the major police stations in Glasgow. A police station?

'Somebody has just called me from that number and asked me to phone back. But I've forgotten his name,' Kay said, surprised at how quickly the ruse came to her. She was getting back on form.

'Who's calling, please?' the man asked. Shit, quick.

'Sandra McIlroy,' said Kay, plucking the name out of nowhere.

'I'm sorry Mrs McIlroy but there's no one else here – I just answered the phone in passing.'

'He said it was urgent I call back. Could you not . . .'

'No, I'm sorry. The phone is in an interview room and any one of the blokes could have come in here to call out.'

'It's just . . .'

'Look, I'll put the word around the station. Sandra, did you say?'

'Aye, Sandra McIlroy.'

'Could you leave me a number to phone if I . . .' Kay hung up.

The police station named was slap bang in the middle of Bud Cumming's territory. What Kay didn't know was that it was also a station used by The Licensee to trade in guns for charges to be dropped. If The Licensee had allies there then so did Bud Cumming.

Kay didn't sleep a wink that night. Between pacing the floor and checking the street she smoked and thought. By daybreak she had made a decision.

'Hello?' the man's voice was tired, distracted.

'Bud, it's Kay.' Silence. 'Can you talk?'

'Eh . . . aye, aye. How are you?' asked Cumming, recovering his cool.

'Never mind that – I want a meeting.'

'Aye, come oan . . .'

'I'll be at your house in an hour.'

'NO . . . eh, naw. Ah'm, eh, going oot.'

'Where then?'

'Make it The Dovecote in, say, four hours.'

'Fine – now be there, eh?'

'Aye, sure Ah'll be . . .' Kay hung up on Bud Cumming. She was going to spend the time getting ready. Kay was back on form and was going to look a million dollars.

When Kay walked into The Dovecote she was beyond fear. She had grown tired of hiding and running. All she wanted was to ask Bud Cumming a straight question. One question with a one-word answer. It should take two minutes and could change her life forever. Then she saw them. Sitting at a table at the far end with his back against a wall was Bud Cumming. Near him were the familiar faces of George Lennon and Iain O'Reilly. Around them were about a dozen men. Big men, hard-faced, staring at her with cold eyes. Every one a stranger. Kay stood at the end of the table facing Bud Cumming.

'Sit doon, hen, pull up a pew,' he said. Kay ignored Cumming and looked around the group of men. She heard one whisper something to another in an Irish accent. Carefully she worked round the semicircle with her eyes. At least half were carrying pistols from what she had been able to work out. Outsiders definitely – most Glaswegians carried their guns in the back of their trouser waistbands, not inside their jackets. It was a standard protection set up when the meeting couldn't be avoided but trouble was expected. She should know, she'd been there herself. What did Cumming think – that she was setting him up? Right there in that room Kay realised that Bud Cumming was more terrified than she was.

'I have one question, Bud,' she said, still standing. 'And I want a straight answer.' Cumming looked pale-faced, ill-slept and nervous. He nodded. 'If I move back into Glasgow will I be left alone?' He took his time in replying. Did he think that she was wired up for the police? Was he watching the door?

'Of course you will,' he said, trying to sound reassuring but failing.

'I have your word?' Kay demanded.

'Of course you do. I wouldn't hurt a hair oan yer heid.'

'Right,' said Kay, 'I'll be seeing you about then.' She turned and walked to the door, a smile crossing her face at what all the new muscle thought of Bud Cumming's precautions for a two-minute meeting with a woman who stood five feet one inch tall in her heels.

Driving back to Greenock for the last time, Kay felt freer than she had for many years. She didn't know what would happen next, who ever does? She only knew she was free again. Free of fear at last.

THE BEGINNING

Even when the threats came in Kay continued to trust me.

For over a year we had met, mainly in my room, the curtains pulled, cigarettes lit, coffee going cold in the mugs. Kay had spoken and I had listened, interrupting now and then to poke a question or direct her back to a topic. Not once did she hesitate or refuse. Sometimes, late at night, the phone would go and it would be Kay, remembering some event lost in the mists of her journey.

'Is that important?' she would ask about the details of such horror they would never be forgotten by anyone with an average life. I'd sigh and draw on the cigarette that was helping me stay awake.

'Yes it is, wee pal,' I'd reply. 'Thank you.'

'Wee pal! Love it when you call me that,' she would laugh.

When I carried out my own investigations and found relevant information, I would choose carefully when to tell her, in order to be sure that she was in the right frame of mind to hear. You can't live Kay's life and escape the burden of extra baggage. But when she heard, her eyes would open wide, she would think for a second and say, 'That must be why . . .' and we were off again.

Sometimes she would phone anxious and worried. Someone had been at her door, the police had been seen in her street, the telephone had rung and no one was there. In a second she would work out possible implications, overreacting to the mundane as unresolved wounds and fears came to the fore. Afterwards she would feel stupid, embarrassed.

'Don't blame yourself,' I'd chide. 'Most people who had lived your life would be dead, cracked up, have lost it entirely. The remarkable thing is you survived.'

'Yeah,' she would mutter, letting the thought slip home. 'You think so?'

'There's no doubt — you are remarkable, wee pal.' And she is.

I asked her numerous times why she had told me her story. Kay revealed that at first she didn't want to talk to me. We were introduced by a mutual friend, an ex-player who trusted me. Kay had resolved to meet me once and tell me politely to go away. Three hours later I knew I had met someone with an important tale to tell and she had talked and talked. We never looked back. Maybe it was timing. Maybe it was because I didn't judge and she needed to talk . . . at last she needed to talk. Who knows? Even when the threats came in she went quiet for two weeks and then started again, happy with my plan to change all the key names, all the places, obscure the dates.

'This isn't about blame,' she said. 'Why should we blame anyone when the same type of thing is happening now all over the world.'

'No,' I agreed, 'it's not our job to blame anyone.'

'That's for the police,' she said.

'And the public,' I added.

'And some will judge me badly,' she offered.

'Yeah, and some will understand better. Understand how it really is.'

'Yeah, that's important. So folk know how life is for many people.'

'It's what this is all about, wee pal. Telling it how it is.'

'Let's go for it then,' she decided.

'You certain?'

'Absolutely.'

Now she had read the finished manuscript. I looked across my room at the woman I call Kay. Tiny, yet beautiful. Thick auburn hair with hints of red that flash in the light. A figure that turns heads. Large expressive eyes that can change her face from glee to sadness in an instant. Beautiful, yes, and courageous and tough, but vulnerable too. So vulnerable that at times I just wanted to cradle her in my arms, to protect and comfort her. This was the same woman who had marched into Bud Cumming's den and stood in front of his massive armed bodyguards and confronted him. She had just finished reading that chapter and said,

'It was a stupid thing to do.'

'It was brave.'

'Standing in front of those guys, I could've been killed.'

'But how did it make you feel when you walked out?'

'Free. Free like I've never felt before.'

'Did you wait long to move?'

'One week later I had this house in Glasgow.'

'Lovely place, but did you deliberately choose somewhere slap bang in the middle of their territory?'

'Yeah, oh yeah, I wasn't going to hide anymore. I'm through with hiding.'

'Do you see any of them around the city?'

'Almost every week. Just driving or going about my life. They always look. Always clock me. But I don't bother with them. Don't need to bother with them.'

'And they . . . do they bother with you?'

'That's another story.'

'Some say you're taking a huge risk to tell your story. What do you think?'

'I don't know – maybe. All I know is that it has to be told.'

'You know I haven't been able to get all the events in, all the details.'

'I know but we have to end it somewhere.'

'So, do you think this is the end?'

'The end? No, this is just the beginning . . .'